Archipelago of Justice

Archipelago of Justice

Law in France's Early Modern Empire

Laurie M. Wood

Yale

UNIVERSITY PRESS

New Haven & London

Published with assistance from the foundation established in memory of William McKean Brown and from the Annie Burr Lewis Fund.

Yale University Press books may be purchased in quantity for educational, business, or promotional use. For information, please e-mail sales.press@yale.edu (U.S. office) or sales@yaleup.co.uk (U.K. office).

Set in Bulmer type by IDS Infotech Ltd.
Printed in the United States of America.

Library of Congress Control Number: 2019949070
ISBN 978-0-300-24400-7 (hardcover : alk. paper)

A catalogue record for this book is available from the British Library.

This paper meets the requirements of ANSI/NISO Z39.48-1992 (Permanence of Paper).

10 9 8 7 6 5 4 3 2 1

For my parents

Contents

Acknowledgments ix

A Note on Sources and Translations xiii

Maps and Tables xv

Introduction 1

ONE

The Human Ecology of Justice 22

TWO

Justice Between Plantation and Port 60

THREE

Between "Île Deserte" and "Île de France" 93

FOUR

Entrepôts in a Changing Empire 131

Conclusion 170

Glossary 183

Notes 187

Bibliography 229

Index 253

Acknowledgments

THIS BOOK, LIKE many of its characters, weathered many voyages: among them, two hurricanes, a marriage, and a birth. I am delighted to thank so many fellow travelers. Three public institutions supported this project from its inception to completion: the University of Texas at Austin, the University of Wisconsin–Madison, and Florida State University. At the University of Texas, the College of Liberal Arts and History Department underwrote research and conference travel to France and in the United States. To thank Julie Hardwick properly for more than a decade of cheerful, persistent advice requires a volume unto itself. This book would not exist without her unflinching critical eye and her relentless encouragement to keep going. She is the rare mentor who tells unvarnished truths about academia while maintaining a buoyant optimism about its core enterprise, learning. My committee members, Bob Olwell, John Garrigus, Neil Kamil, and Susan Deans-Smith, also offered indispensable support and advice.

A year-long Law and Society Postdoctoral Fellowship in the Wisconsin Law School's Institute for Legal Studies challenged me to reach scholars beyond history: in law, sociology, anthropology, and geography. I thank especially Mitra Sharafi for her mentorship and enthusiasm, which continues to the present, and Howie Erlanger, who invited me to Madison. Beth Mertz and Stewart Macaulay modeled interdisciplinarity by welcoming me to their Sociology of Law class.

At Florida State, I was fortunate to receive early and ongoing advice from senior faculty across campus. The FSU Council on Research and Creativity financed follow-up research with a Planning Grant. The Florida State College of Arts and Sciences granted a subvention for the maps and illustrations. At FSU, I would not have survived the first couple of years as a tenure-track professor without Courtney Preston's endless hospitality and Katherine Mooney's solidarity. Suzy Sinke's collegial mentorship proved essential, as did the support of Rafe Blaufarb, Cathy McClive, Will Hanley, Fritz Davis, Andrew Frank, Jen Koslow, Tarez Graban, and Ed Gray.

External fellowships from domestic research libraries sponsored the revision of my manuscript as I incorporated new evidence from their collections. I thank especially the archivists and librarians who guided me toward overlooked resources at the Huntington Library, the Newberry Library, the John Carter Brown Library, and the UCLA William Andrew Clark Memorial Library. A travel grant from the Society for French Historical Studies and the Western Society for French History financed research in Paris and Aix. I thank, too, the librarians and staff of the Archives nationales, section d'outre-mer, the Bibliothèque nationale de France, the Bibliothèque Mazarine, the Beinecke Lesser Antilles Collection at Hamilton College, the Benson Latin American Collection at the University of Texas at Austin, and the Florida State University Libraries. I am indebted to Marianne Hansen, Curator and Academic Liaison for Rare Books and Manuscripts at Bryn Mawr College Library, for her speedy help in obtaining the cover image.

I received ongoing advice and encouragement from Rafe Blaufarb, Susan Deans-Smith, John Garrigus, Dirk Hartog, Neil Kamil, Bob Olwell, Jennifer Palmer, Sue Peabody, Rebecca Schloss, Kerry Ward, and Sophie White. John Garrigus graciously shared Saint-Dominguan notarial records from his research, catalyzing this project in the form of an early graduate seminar paper. This project depended upon the model scholarship and generosity of Richard Allen, Ned Alpers, Guillaume Aubert, David Bell, Vincent Brown, Gwyn Campbell, Alta Charo, Paul Cheney, Matt Childs, Nancy Christie, Adam Clulow, Nina Dayton, Kate Desbarats, Suzanne Desan, François Furstenburg, Matthew Gerber, Malick Ghachem, Sally Gordon, Frank Guridy, Sarah Hanley, Steve Hindle, Chris Hodson, Heinz Klug, Elizabeth Kolsky, Michael Kwass, Mindie Lazarus-Black, Sida Liu, Kenneth Loiselle, Renisa Mawani, Darrell Meadows, Philip Morgan, Robert Paquette, Bianca Premo, Bhavani Raman, Kate Ramsey, Pernille Røge, Lou Roper, Brett Rushforth, Jim Sidbury, Cristobal Silva, Philip Stern, and

Natalie Zemon Davis. While I was a Davis Center Fellow at Princeton University, Angela N. H. Creager helped me navigate the completion of this first book and simultaneously launch my second project.

Fellow scholars and historians-turned-friends whose advice permeates these pages—and to whom I offer deepest thanks—include Danna Agmon, Juandrea Bates, Debjani Bhattacharyya, Kristen Block, Ben Breen, Mikki Brock, Will A. S. Brown, Randy Browne, Melissa Byrnes, Claire Cage, Jim Coons, Manuel Covo, Matthew Crawford, Jesse Cromwell, Elizabeth Cross, Christian Ayne Crouch, Rohit De, Helen Dewar, Claire Edington, Yvie Fabella, Casey Faucon, Sarah Ghabrial, Julia Gossard, Kit Heintzman, Rachel Herrmann, Jane Hooper, Hadi Hosainy, Marie Houllemare, Katie Jarvis, Eddie Kolla, Ada Kuskowski, Andrew Lipman, María José Afanador Llach, Jessica Luther, Nathan Marvin, Katherine Mooney, Tessa Murphy, Jeannine Murray-Román, Libby Nutting, Aaron Alejandro Olivas, Lindsay O'Neill, Rachel Ozanne, James Palmer, Kalyani Ramnath, Meghan Roberts, Gabriel Rocha, Jessica Choppin Roney, Michael Schoeppner, Lisa Scott, Danielle Skeehan, Blake Smith, Cameron Strang, Rob Taber, Jerusha Westbury, and Nurfadzilah Yahaya. I am grateful to be a part of so many lively scholarly communities. All flaws remaining in this book are my own.

My family possess an array of graces and talents I could never deserve, but they have lavished them all on me as I have labored on this project. I dedicate this book to my parents.

THE URLS FOR digitized archival and printed sources are listed in the bibliography. These include Marine personnel records (ANOM Série E) and books available on Gallica, the digital portal for the Bibliothèque nationale de France. All URLs current as of 31 August 2018.

All translations are my own, unless otherwise noted.

Maps and Tables

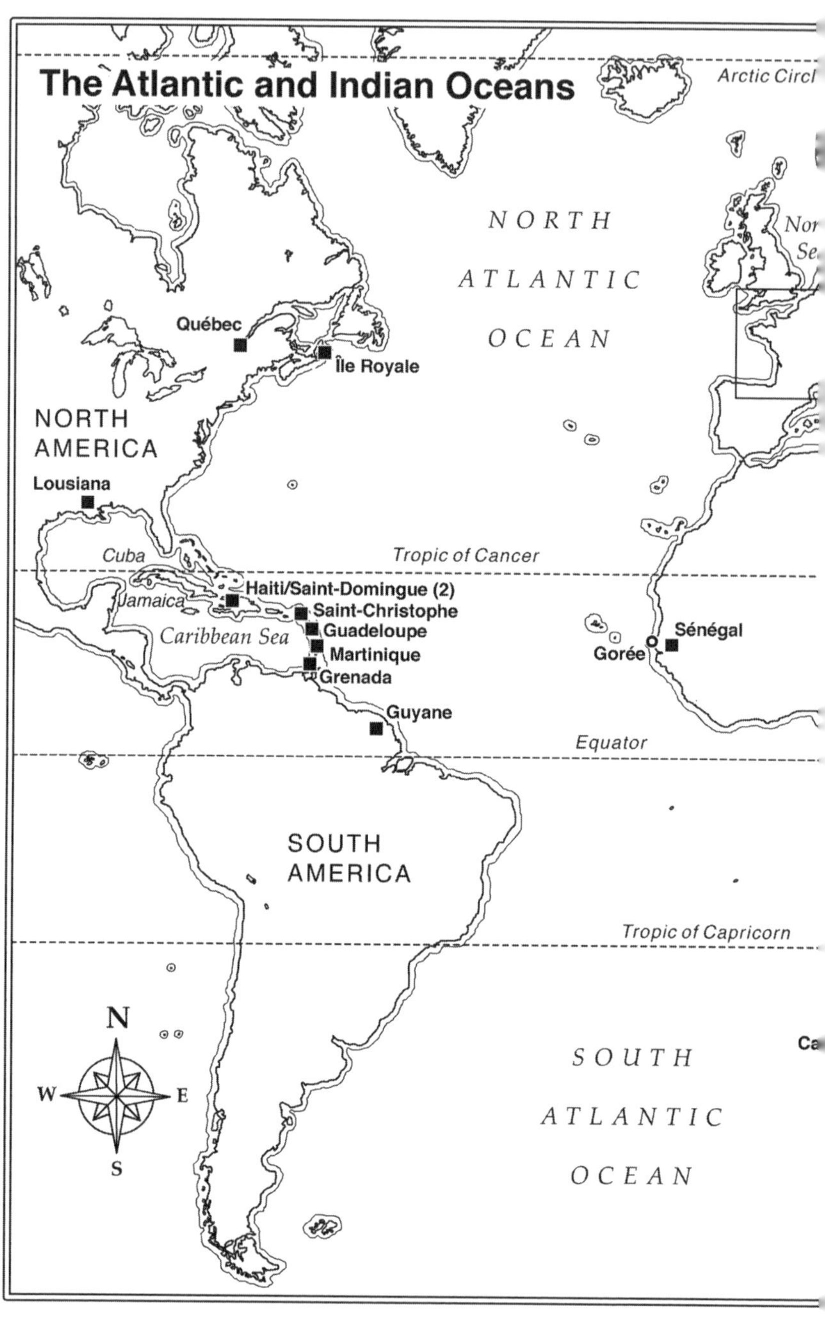

Map 1. *The Archipelago of Justice in the Atlantic and Indian Oceans* (Tom Willcockson, Mapcraft)

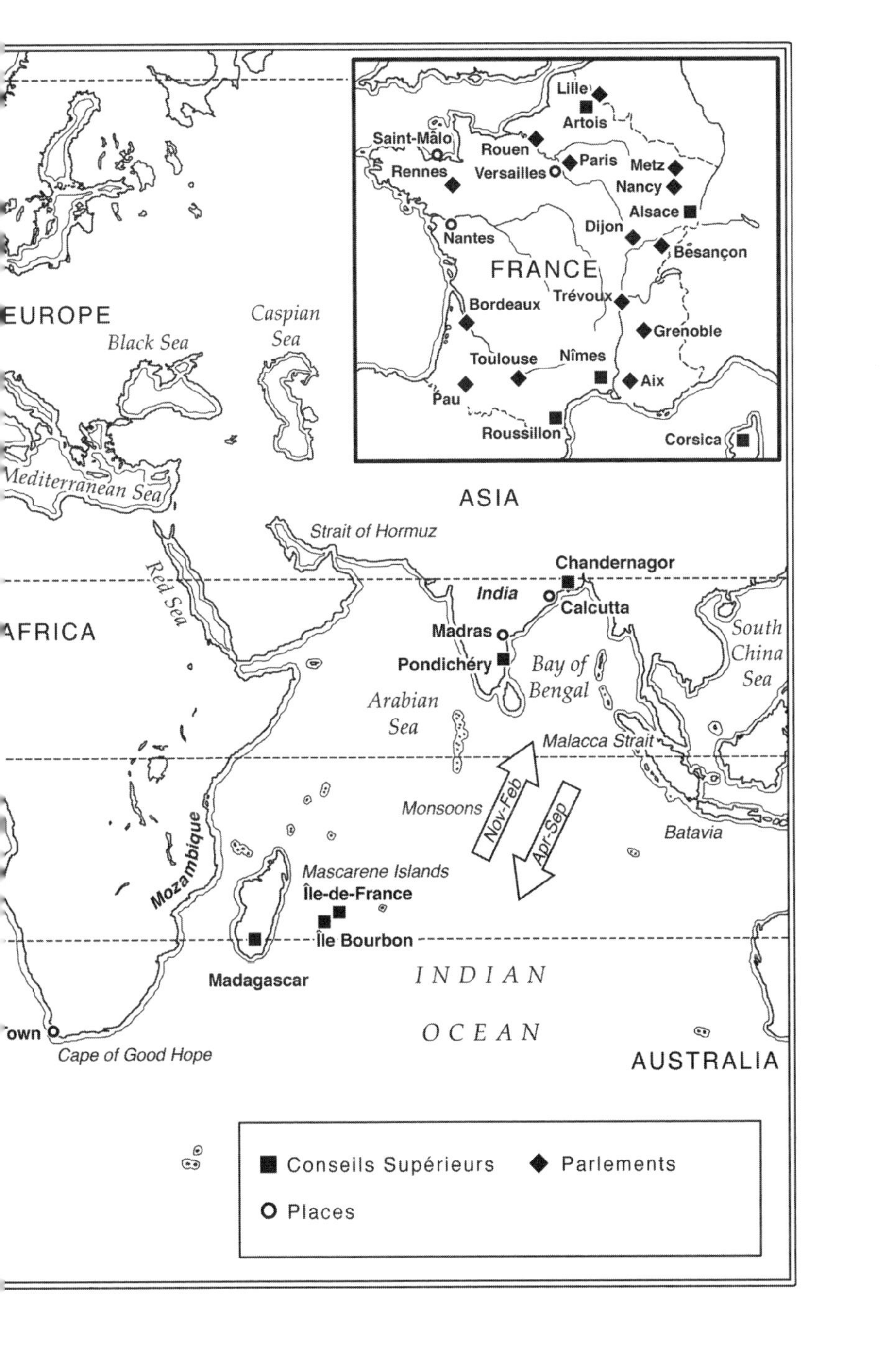
EUROPE
Black Sea
Caspian Sea
Mediterranean Sea
AFRICA
Red Sea
Mozambique
Madagascar
Cape of Good Hope
own
Saint-Malo
Rennes
Rouen
Versailles
Nantes
Lille
Artois
Paris
Metz
Nancy
Alsace
Dijon
Bésançon
FRANCE
Bordeaux
Trévoux
Grenoble
Toulouse
Nîmes
Aix
Pau
Roussillon
Corsica
ASIA
Strait of Hormuz
Chandernagor
India
Calcutta
Madras
Pondichéry
Bay of Bengal
Arabian Sea
Malacca Strait
South China Sea
Monsoons
Nov-Feb
Apr-Sep
Batavia
Mascarene Islands
Île-de-France
Île Bourbon
INDIAN
OCEAN
AUSTRALIA
Conseils Supérieurs
Parlements
Places

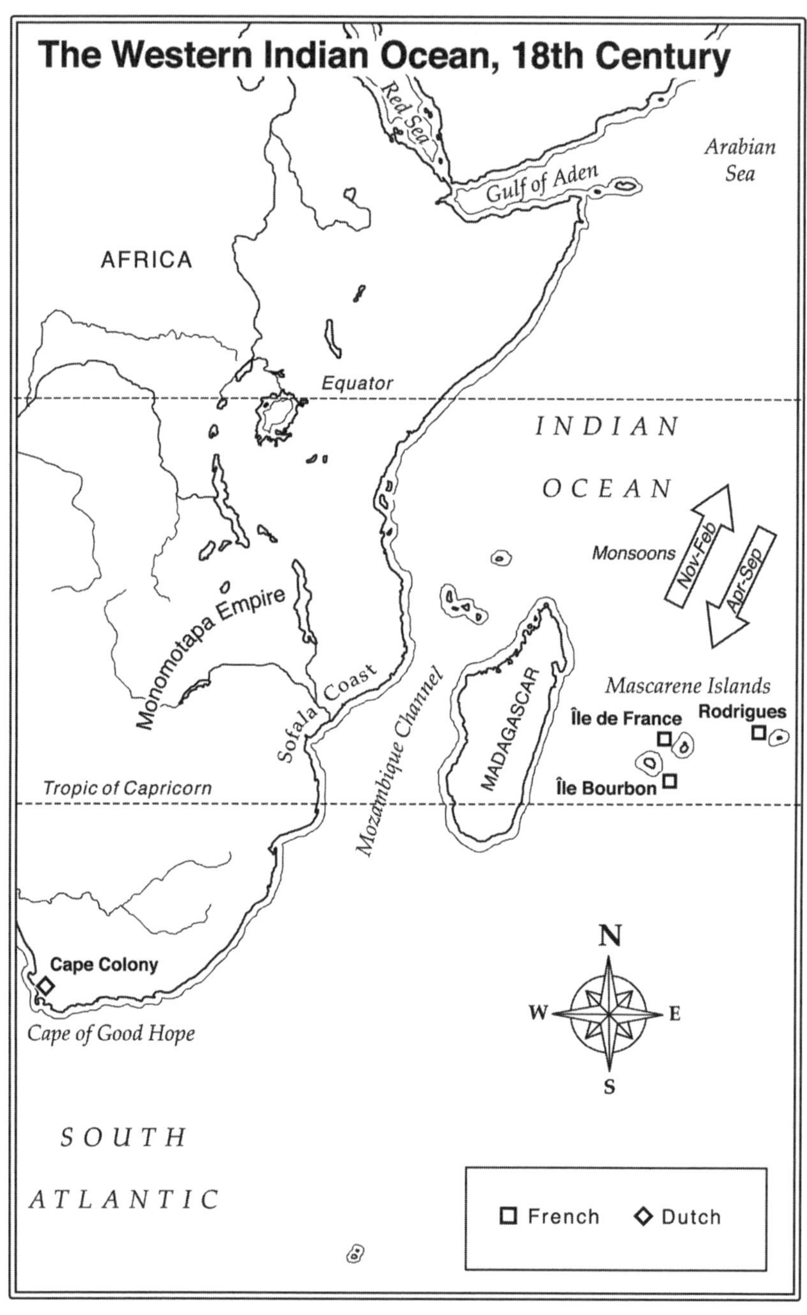

Map 2. *The Western Indian Ocean, 18th Century* (Tom Willcockson, Mapcraft)

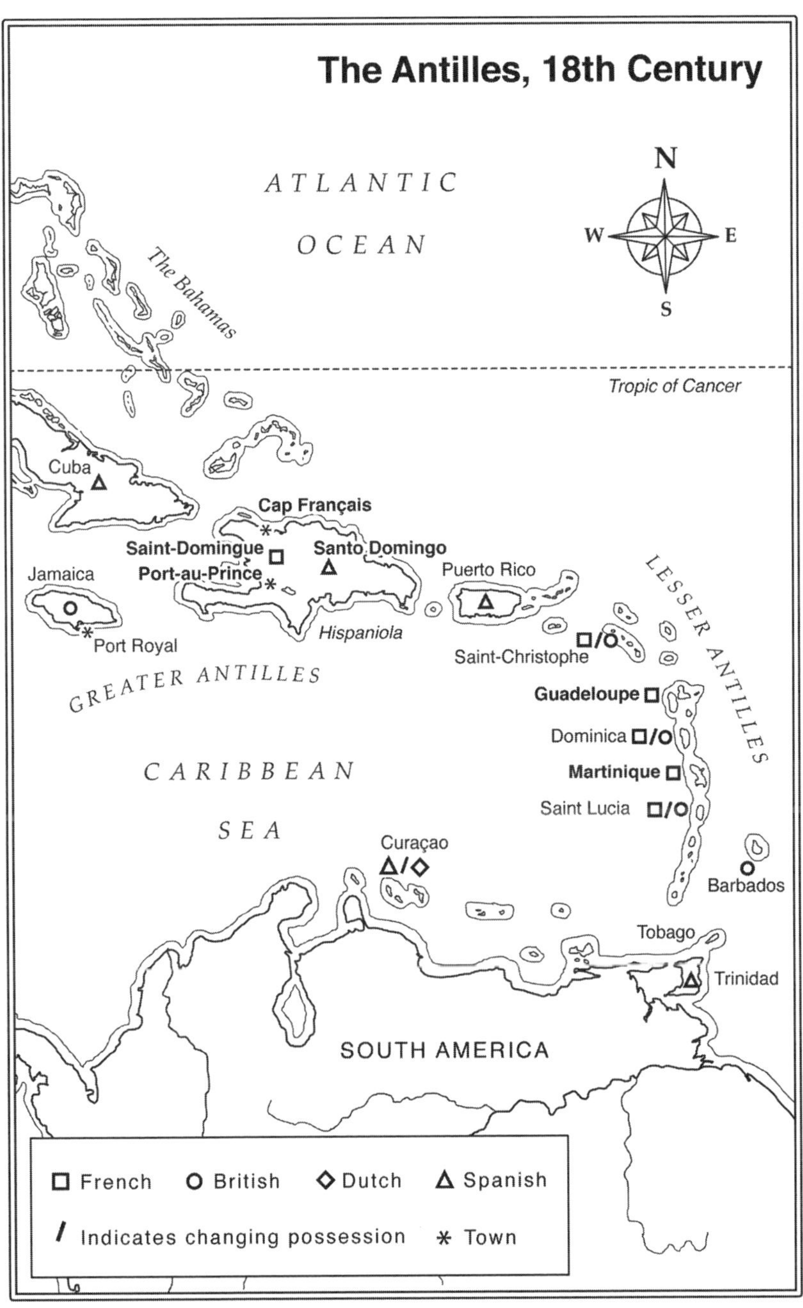

Map 3. *The Antilles, 18th Century* (Tom Willcockson, Mapcraft)

Table 1. The conseils provincials and supérieurs, by date established[a]

Province/colony *(Capital)*	Date est.
Saint-Christophe *(Basse-Terre)*	Pre-1682
Artois *(Arras)*[b]	1640
Roussillon *(Perpignan)*[c]	1660
Québec, aka Canada or New France *(Montreal)*	1663
Martinique *(Saint-Pierre, then Fort Royal)*	1664
Guadeloupe *(Basse-Terre)*	1664
Alsace *(Colmar)*[c]	1667
Madagascar *(Fort-Dauphin)*	1669
Pondichéry *(est. at Surate, then moved to Pondichéry)*	1671/1701
Saint-Domingue 1 *(est. at Petit Goave, then moved to Léogane, then to Port-au-Prince)*	1685
Saint-Domingue 2 *(Cap-Français)*	1701
Guyane *(Cayenne)*	1701
Chandernagor *(Chandernagor)*	1703
Île Bourbon *(Saint-Denis)*	1711
Île Royale *(Louisbourg)*	1717
Île de France *(Port Louis)*	1723
Louisiana *(Nouvelle-Orléans)*	1723
Senegal *(Gorée)*	1735
Mahé[b]	Pre-1766
Corsica *(Bastia)*[c]	1768
Nîmes *(Nîmes)*	1771
Grenada	1779

[a] Some were established as conseils provincials or conseils souverains, then promoted to conseils supérieurs a few years later. The dates listed indicate the initial founding of the courts, whether as conseils provincials, souverains, or supérieurs.

[b] Established as a conseil provincial.

[c] Established as a conseil souverain.

Sources (where not corroborated in at least two archival sources cited in manuscript): Saint-Christophe—ANOM COL E 95, de Courpon, and ANOM COL A 24 f. 29, 3 August 1682, *Extrait de la lettre du marquis de Seignelay à Blénac, où il est reproché à Courpon, conseiller du conseil de Saint-Christophe, d'avoir prescrit des ordonnances de son propre chef, et où il est spécifié que toute l'autorité pour l'exécution des arrêts du roi émane des conseils seulement* (no. 26). Madagascar—A royal letter from 1669 ordered the Madagascar conseil souverain to recognize the new governor, but it was followed soon after (in 1670) by a king's council ruling that suppressed the conseil. ANOM COL B 1 F° 189 (4 December 1669), ANOM COL B 3 F° 11 (12 November 1670). French designs on Madagascar would prove as long-standing (and doomed) in the Indian Ocean as similar plans for Guyane in South America throughout the seventeenth and eighteenth centuries. Chandernagor—Thomas, "Le Conseil supérieur de Pondichéry," 43. Sénégal—Régent, *La France et ses esclaves*, 64. Mahé—ANOM COL A 19 F° 255, 14 January 1775, *Arrêt qui annule la sentence de confiscation prononcée par le conseil de Mahé le 11 février 1766 et qui ordonne que Pereyra sera remis en possession des biens qu'il avait en Inde, à moins d'oppositions et de contestations qui seront alors jugées à Mahé et Pondichéry (n° 46)*. Mahé conseil cited without dates of existence in Mole, "Mahé and the Politics of Empire," and Piat, *Mauritius on the Spice Route*, 52.

Table 2. The parlements, by date established

Province (*Capital*)	Date est.
Île-de-France (*Paris*)	1260
Languedoc (*Toulouse*)	1443
Dauphiné (*Grenoble*)	1453
Guyenne (*Bordeaux*)	1462
Bourgogne (*Dijon*)	1477
Normandy (*Rouen*)	1499/1515
Provence (*Aix-en-Provence*)	1501
Dombes (*Trévoux*)	1523
Bretagne (*Rennes*)	1553
Béarn (*Pau*)	1620
Trois-Évêchés (*Metz*)	1633
Flanders (*Lille*)[a]	1686
Franche-Comté (*Besançon*)[b]	1767
Lorraine (*Nancy*)	1776

[a] Parlement first at Tournai, then at Douai from 1686.

[b] At Dole from 1422 to 1676.

Introduction

He's "traveled throughout the world."
—Louise Aubert, twenty-eight, resident of Île Bourbon, describing the sailor
Pitre Paul, about forty, whom she had seen in Paris and Île Bourbon
on separate occasions, 18 July 1725[1]

The prison doors will be open to him, if he is ever returned
there for any other reason.
—Definitive sentence by the Rennes (Bretagne) Parlement acquitting
Pitre Paul of polygamy charges, January 1727[2]

IN 1725, A ship worker named Pitre Paul was brought on charges of polygamy before the *conseil supérieur*, or high court, in France's overseas colony of Île Bourbon (now La Réunion) in the Indian Ocean. According to witness testimony, Pitre Paul (there is some confusion as to which was his first name) had three wives: one in Île Bourbon, another in France, and a third in France's Atlantic colony of Martinique. He had married a woman named Fontaine in Île Bourbon in 1721, but French court records indicated an earlier marriage to a different woman in France in 1712. Witnesses pointed to a third woman in Martinique, alleging that he had fathered an illegitimate son with her. As his career in ship construction took him to various parts of France's ancien régime empire, Paul left a trail of coworkers, mistresses, and progeny.[3] As state authorities began to question his activities in each location, however, he was drawn into the legal circuits that connected France and its colonies via the conseil law courts and their equivalents in France. As Pitre Paul's case traveled through courts in metropolitan France, Martinique, and Île Bourbon, it generated performances of justice in each courtroom and revealed empire-wide networks of legal personnel and subjects.[4]

Historians have often treated Atlantic and Indian Ocean routes separately. But Pitre Paul, and many others like him, navigated the Atlantic and Indian Oceans seamlessly. No source visualizes this point more explicitly than Jacques Nicolas Bellin's 1755 world map. In stark red ink, he delineated major maritime travel routes from France to important colonies and trading entrepôts in the Atlantic and Indian Oceans (Figure 1). This indicates a bi-oceanic understanding of France's early modern empire: tellingly, the Pacific is excluded from this map save for a red line that indicates the route into the Strait of Malacca, but no farther. This map was drawn at the height of France's early modern territorial reach (before, for example, the loss of Canada). But the scattered dots of territorial empire are not colored in pink like the famous later maps of Britain's empire. Instead the *pathways* between them are electrified in crimson.

Pitre Paul traversed France's early modern empire as a marginal figure. He was born in Flanders and never spoke French very well. Sailors in Bordeaux had taught him to read but not to write. He was known to have worked from time to time for pirates. One witness testified that Pitre Paul's son in Martinique had embarked upon a pirate ship (*vaisseau forbans*) and later taken a Dutch prize in Île Bourbon. But the son had been killed in Madagascar, at the approximate age of eighteen. A second rumored child born in Martinique had since moved to France. (Asked about his pirate son, Paul replied that the boy only called him "Dad" because they shared the same name.) In a series of depositions taken by the Île Bourbon conseil, witnesses pinpointed his whereabouts variously at Paris, Saint-Mâlo, and Mocha (along the Red Sea). Interrogated himself, Pitre Paul mentioned the Cape of Good Hope and China among his ports of call. Louise Aubert spoke for them all when she summed up that Pitre Paul had "traveled throughout the world"—a statement that in its subtext judged Paul's romantic travels with the three women, too. Eventually, the conseil officials gave up their investigation. Having retrieved records from across France's early modern empire, they couldn't confirm the charges against Pitre Paul. They acquitted him of all charges, warning him in the boilerplate legal language of the day that "the prison doors" remained open to him if he were to return to court on different charges.[5]

The legal and physical pathways marked out by Pitre Paul, Bellin, and others are the subject of this book. Their distinct but interwoven trajectories reveal how mobile subjects navigated France's early modern empire.[6] In France, parish priests testified to Pitre Paul's original marriage to a woman named Julienne Datin. Sailors averred that they, too, had known Pitre Paul and Datin in the port town of Saint-Mâlo (see Map 1 inset and Figure 1). In Île Bourbon, Marianne Fontaine used her testimony to argue for the legitimacy of her marriage to Pitre Paul, claiming that the previous women had only been his "concubines." Pitre Paul himself tried to craft a narrative that would justify his unconventional relationships and satisfy the conseil magistrates. In his interrogation, he told a meandering story about his transient past, from a childhood spent in shipyards in Norway, Spain, and Guinea to his adult life, traveling between France, Martinique, and Île Bourbon. He never denied the charge of polygamy outright but rather sought to connect the places he had visited into a linear (if not exactly logical) explanation of his string of relationships.[7]

Intervention

Evaluated together, the trajectories of mobile subjects reveal—like Bellin's crimson lines—three crucial, but previously unrecognized, features that bound this first French global empire together. First, regional law courts known as conseils formed a global network of legal entrepôts, sites for legal services, that allowed subjects around the world to access French law and judicial processes. Conseils were found in frontier regions within France, such as Alsace and Roussillon, in Caribbean and Indian Ocean sugar islands, such as Saint-Domingue and Île de France, and in other colonies, from Pondichéry in South Asia to Québec in North America. This hitherto uninvestigated network interfaced with the older and well-known metropolitan system of regional *parlements*, or law courts, law-making bodies that also exercised judicial and administrative functions.[8] In all, twenty-one conseils provincials or conseils supérieurs were established in France's

Figure 1. Detail, *Carte réduite des parties connues du globe terrestre . . .* (Bellin), 1755, Gallica, Bibliothèque nationale de France

POLOGNE
Warsovie
VOLHINIE
Bielogorod
Vienne
HONGRIE
Presbourg
Belgrade
TURQUIE
D'EUROPE
Mer Noire
Constantinople
TURQUIE
D'ASIE
Candie
Chipre
MEDITERRANEE
Sicile
MOSCOVIE
Kazan
Uia
ASTRACHAN
Wolga R.
Gurien
Petite Tartarie
Airachan
Circassie
Georgie
Armenie
Erivan
Karasm
Mer Caspienne
Mer d'Aral
Karakalpak
Omskaja
Irkuck
Calmuks Eluts
Kalk
Gete
PAYS
TARTARIE
Desert
TARTA
Mo
Bucarie
Turkhend
Pays de Tibet
Budian
PERSE
Khorasan
Esterabad
Ispahan
Bagdad
Balk
Syrie
Jerusalem
Damas
Basra
Bender
Kerman
G. Persique
Hormus
Mekran
Sindi
R. d'Asham
Bengale
R. d'Ava
Yunnan
EGYPTE
Mer Rouge
Medine
ARABIE
Oman
INDES
Bramas
Surat
Gomron
G. de Cambaye
Decan
Orixa
Carnate
Coromandel
Golfe
de
Bengale
Pegu
Cochinchine
G. de Siam
ARABIE
Arabie Heureuse
Yemen
Detroit de Babelmandel
I. Socotera
les trois Freres
Laquedives
Canal des Maldives
Malabar
Cochin
Ceilan
I. Nicbar
Sumatra
ABISSINIE
Adel
Zendero
Machidas
Mujaco
MER DES INDES
Maldives
Loango
Nimeamay
Ruengas
Mabe
I. de l'Amirante
Route
C. des Bassas
Jean de Nove
Savia di Malha
I. Rodrigue
OCEAN
les Trieles
I. des Cocos
Congo
Angola
Masesi
Lac Aquilunda
Lac de Maravi
Benguela
Pais Inconnu
Cimbebas
Mozambique
Madagascar
Canal de Mozambique
St. Marie
I. de France
I. Bourbon
Tropique du Capricorne
ORIENTAL
Pays des
Hotentots
Rio de Infante
Cap des Aiguilles
l'Inde
Retour
I. d'Amsterdam
I. S. Paul

peripheral territories, within and beyond Europe (see Map 1 and Table 1), though they did not all exist simultaneously.[9] These supplemented the fourteen parlements in France (see Map 1 inset and Table 2).[10] They were built during a period of imperial growth that began in the 1680s and lasted into the decade that preceded the French and Haitian Revolutions, the 1780s.[11]

Conseils, like parlements, became legal entrepôts for French subjects but catered to those subjects who colonized new territories and sought new trading opportunities beyond Europe. The term "entrepôt" usually identifies trading hubs, such as Singapore and Saint Eustatius, that occupy (or have occupied) strategic locales along trade routes.[12] Here the term usefully draws attention to the ways that conseils attracted judicial participants from within and around the empire as hubs for legal services. Though imperial administrators, based at Versailles, initiated the construction of this global network of conseils, each conseil developed unique traits that elucidate the social and legal texture of France's early modern empire. "Entrepôt" highlights the concentration of law in certain areas without denying its presence elsewhere. Entrepôts formed key spaces in which emerging empires imposed legal, not just economic, infrastructures to serve passing subjects such as Pitre Paul.[13]

Second, these legal entrepôts became, by the mid-eighteenth century, staffed by members of a global themistocracy: a class of mobile legal experts whose careers shaped and, ultimately, braided Atlantic and Indian Ocean legal cultures together. For Parisian legal elites, Richard Mowery Andrews has described a "themistocracy" that comprised "a blend, or hybrid, of disparate, even contradictory social elements within Old Regime civilization. The majority [of themistocrats] were middling (*bourgeois*) in social origin. By the nature of their judicial offices, they were a technically savant, vocational, and even modernistic governing class."[14] Evidence from the Antillean and Mascarene conseils, read alongside Andrews's assessment of Parisian personnel, strongly suggests that this metropolitan pattern extended to overseas colonies.

As in France with regional administration, imperial administrators essentially outsourced a portion of colonial governance to local elite families, which governed the colonies in dynastic fashion through membership in the conseils. The emergence of a themistocracy with such global reach created a source of social stability by the late seventeenth century for the Antilles and the mid-eighteenth century for the Mascarenes. Over time, these families increasingly sent their sons to train in metropolitan law schools. By the end of the eighteenth century, a noticeable and growing proportion of colonial magistrates had admittance to the Paris Parlement.

Additional strategic imperatives strengthened the cohesion of a global themistocracy. Separated from metropolitan France by great oceans, Antillean and Mascarene conseil officials recognized that they needed vigorous institutions like the conseils to advocate for their interests to French imperial administrators. Conseil personnel, including magistrates and lawyers, began to promote conseil governance through published legal codes and treatises. These publications testified to the conseils' concentration of local political and legal power over the course of the long eighteenth century. Conseil officials also advocated for local and regional interests to imperial administrators. To counter royal oversight embodied by intendants sent to colonial outposts, themistocrats often aimed to concentrate local and regional power in the conseils. The conseil institution enabled them to frame these claims as equal constituents within France's global state.

Finally, these global ties were reinforced by interjudicial correspondence among themistocrats, court users, and imperial personnel. Interjudicial correspondence consisted of letters sent among members of and participants in France's early modern legal system. Interjudicial correspondence enabled conseil officials, such as magistrates and governors, and court participants, such as plaintiffs and their relatives, to initiate and sustain relationships within and across the ancien régime empire. This correspondence allowed subjects to bypass and supplement formal avenues of legal action by appealing directly to administrators, patrons, and well-connected kin.[15] Thus this book reconfigures assessments of how formal legal institutions functioned in France's empire by clarifying how they worked in tandem with informal and extra-institutional systems of authority and power. For ancien régime France, legal historians have discussed the negotiation of criminal matters outside formal legal channels as "infrajustice."[16]

Following this recognition that informal and formal mechanisms worked in parallel and together in ancien régime legal forums, the conseils enabled and supported correspondence along pathways between legal entrepôts. Interjudicial correspondence networks thus formed webs of relationships between and among participants in legal entrepôts. Interjudicial correspondence networks were thickest between imperial institutions, especially between the Ministry of the Marine and the conseils.

A Global and Comparative Framework

France's ancien régime empire was wholeheartedly global, not just Atlantic. This book assesses the Antilles and Mascarenes, as well as their Atlantic and Indian Ocean contexts, together in each chapter so that comparisons can be made at a more local and specific level. It sets up Île de France and Île Bourbon in the Indian Ocean as peers of Martinique and Guadeloupe in the Atlantic Ocean. This strategy initiates comparisons among colonies at points throughout this book, highlighting their simultaneous and overlapping development. It contrasts with singular case studies in which the metropole becomes, explicitly or tacitly, the recurring comparison. This approach also emphasizes regional affinities and local adaptations by colonial residents, rather than positing a linear transformation from "model" to "fully developed" colonies.[17] Antillean and Mascarene legal cultures sat along common pathways within a global French legal regime. Travelers, and with them information, moved between and among these sites.[18]

Martinique in the Antilles and Île Bourbon (now Réunion) and Île de France (now Mauritius) in the Mascarenes influenced the development and endurance of an early modern global legal order despite their small size. Each island sat at the center of an important early modern oceanic trading system, and each became a tropical slave society. By the 1780s, all four islands (Martinique, Guadeloupe, Île de France, and Île Bourbon) discussed in this study were home to enslaved majorities of at least 80 percent.[19] Each colony reported to an imperial headquarters in France: the Ministry of the Marine (navy) at Versailles, which managed colonial affairs from 1710 onward.[20] During this time, French colonial government was organized under the navy, or Ministry of the Marine, even though courts like the conseils supérieurs were analogous to the parlements, which had civil and criminal jurisdiction and were not military courts. The colonial office was created within the Marine Ministry (navy) in 1710, and in 1715 a Navy Council was created to manage all overseas and naval affairs. Ample colonial documentation from before 1710 exists in Navy Council archives.

Archipelago of Justice demonstrates the interconnectedness of the Atlantic and Indian Ocean worlds, reworking the prevailing Atlantic paradigm to show how it intersects with the recently revitalized Indian Ocean field.[21] It thus models a comparative case-study approach for global history.[22] The book treats French Antillean and Mascarene colonies as part of the same early modern matrix of state building and legal regime creation.[23] Within this rubric, it focuses on case studies from Martinique and Île de France (now Mauritius), while referencing other French colonies such as Saint-Domingue (now Haiti) and Pondichéry (now part of Puducherry in India) where relevant. The legal services and employment offered by the Martinique and Île de France conseils appealed to French subjects precisely because they sat strategically at the center of the two largest and most dynamic oceanic zones of trade and imperialism during the early modern era.[24]

By framing law courts across France's ancien régime empire synthetically, rather than as separate colonial and metropolitan spheres, this book accomplishes three goals. It first recasts in a global framework scholarship on social collaboration and judicial negotiation within emerging European states, which took place through the parallel creation and development of courts and legal tools in Europe and in overseas colonies. The now-classic debate about these patterns, initiated by William Beik, has continued to inspire new research, but this debate has remained centered on the parlements and France's Continental nation-state enterprise. This book, by contrast, demonstrates the simultaneous emergence of state institutions, the conseils, in overseas territories.[25] Maintained by the growing participation of subjects such as Pitre Paul and the legal experts who staffed these law courts, the conseils became an enduring network of legal venues, replicated in every major new territory of the ancien régime.

Second, this project charts some of the imperial agendas, physical trajectories, and feedback loops that ricocheted among both new and old territories. Such a global approach breaks down conventional narratives of metropole and colony, nation and empire. Shannon Lee Dawdy has emphasized the locally dictated norms, or "creole legalism," articulated by Louisiana magistrates and lawyers, while Julie Hardwick has explored the domestic issues spurred by women and artisans in seventeenth-century Lyonnais courts. A global framework, however, has yet to be attempted. Malick Ghachem and Sue Peabody have evaluated negotiations over the distinguishing colonial issue of slavery in Saint-Domingue and in France, while John Garrigus has elucidated the racial aspects of this debate, but this was by no means the only legal matter to concern both colonial and metropolitan conseils. Rather, even the most classic and ubiquitous jurisprudential concerns—like murder—prompted a wide range of French subjects to press into a global network of local tribunals and thereby leave their imprint.[26]

Third, these imprints become more legible via early modern conceptions of space and mobility, made clearer by the application of insights from scholarship on legal geography. Though many legal historians favor questions about doctrine—that is, the ideas of law—this book focuses on what David Delaney has called the "nomosphere," or the "placeness," of law.[27] This latter approach insists that legal actions take *place*, and therefore that notions of legality (what is acceptable or not as "law" in a given context) depend upon the social matrix (defined by boundaries and presence) in which they occur. The conseils became concentrated nodes of imperial power and legal resources for French subjects who passed through these places, even in sites that later became spaces for alienation and exile, such as French Guiana in the era of the French Revolution.[28] The physical form of the *palais de justice* housed the magistrates and clerks who composed the conseils supérieurs.[29] These structures thereby manifested French law as it was imposed upon overseas territories, whether insular (as with Île de France) or borderland (as with Pondichéry and Louisiana). As the editors of a recent volume have emphasized, "law is always 'worlded' in some way . . . social spaces, lived places, and landscapes are inscribed with legal significance."[30] Attention to law and space together, in the words of three other legal scholars, thereby draws "our attention to the way distinctive localized cultures are expressed in legal norms . . . [and defines] the social processes through which the place of law is created and maintained, exploring new places or spaces within which legal authority might be deployed."[31]

Comparative research has only begun to incorporate the Indian Ocean islands into analyses of the better-documented Atlantic colonies, most often on the topic of slavery, but has rarely explored the common judicial culture that united French territories around the globe. Scholars who have focused on the Indian Ocean, like Hubert Gerbeau and Richard Allen, have often felt the need to argue forcefully against the influence of the dominant Atlantic model of transoceanic and colonial interaction.[32] As Gerbeau, Allen, and others have shown, however, Indian Ocean colonies had remarkable similarities to the Atlantic ones in terms of agricultural products, labor systems, and patterns of slave trading. Megan Vaughan has investigated a classic Atlantic theme—creolization in a slave society—in the newer field of Indian Ocean studies.[33] These studies have usefully brought Atlantic and Indian Ocean cases into dialogue. French scholarship has more often employed an analytic lens that synthesizes Atlantic and Indian Ocean examples, in large part because Martinique, Guadeloupe, and Réunion (Île Bourbon) constitute overseas departments of France today.[34]

This book advances these preliminary Atlantic and Indian Ocean dialogues by comparing evidence from both places to account for the similarities in imperial political construction of these colonies. It demonstrates how Antilleans and Mascarene residents relied upon the same metropolitan center in Paris as an access point for legal recourse, especially via interjudicial correspondence and global careers of court personnel. Additional sources from the conseils and related archives reveal direct links between the Antilles and the Mascarenes. Maritime travelers visited both colonial outposts, often one after another, to reprovision along transoceanic journeys between the Americas, Europe, Africa, and Asia. Correspondence among imperial, especially conseil, personnel stationed in the Antilles and Mascarenes reinforced these ties and, over time, established knowledge networks that sometimes bypassed the metropole.

An Ancien Régime Empire

The conseils exercised legislative, judicial, and executive functions. They represented mainstream justice in the empire. When Montesquieu conceptualized his famous principle of separating different kinds of political power, he was looking at a legal landscape made up of law courts that included the conseils. These law courts administered justice through jurisprudence (for example, of criminal and civil matters), executive orders, and bureaucratic administration.[35] Sometimes, conseil magistrates sat as admiralty courts to decide maritime matters, such as prize cases.[36] This comprehensive power contrasted with large metropolitan courts like the parlements, which adjudicated matters such as criminal cases in separate chambers, like the Bordeaux Tournelle. In the parlements, magistrates served in rotation in these chambers, but in the conseils the same magistrates would decide all sorts of cases in succession.[37]

Conseils supérieurs formed one of the primary instruments of early modern state building and empire building, establishing the institutional beachheads from which new territories were woven into the political, and especially legal, patchwork of France. Conseils were created in new territories during the seventeenth and eighteenth centuries but especially during the era of reforms under Louis XIV and his finance minister Jean-Baptiste Colbert toward the end of the seventeenth century (see Table 1). In the 1640s and 1650s, new territories on the European borders of France, such as Artois and Alsace, were given courts, initially called provincial councils (conseils provincials), which were gradually upgraded to the status of conseils supérieurs. Once promoted to "supérieur" status, these courts gained full capacity to hear cases on appeal and as a last resort, with final appeal possible only to the king and his personal council of advisers.[38]

These territorial acquisitions in Europe coincided with France's piqued interest in an overseas empire, and so conseil installations proceeded apace in all of these areas. This pattern invalidates assumptions that an embryonic early modern French empire only matured once the nation-state had been realized.[39] Rather, these institutional beachheads were a key component for incorporating new territories into an emergent state as soon

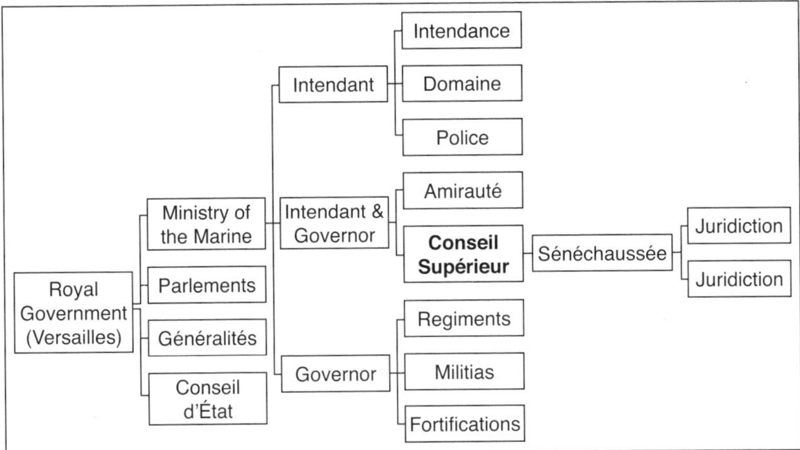

Figure 2. Conseils in context: the French court system

as they were acquired. The southwestern region of Roussillon was annexed to France in 1659, its conseil founded in 1660. Québec's conseil was founded in 1663, only three years later. The next year, 1664, Martinique's was formed in 1664.[40] More than a century later, this strategy was still in place: the Corsica conseil emerged in 1768, in the immediate wake of the island's takeover by France.

The conseils were key objects within an early modern Continental legal consciousness (Figure 2), despite their occlusion in scholarship on state building and social collaboration, which has privileged the parlements and other metropolitan institutions.[41] Legal handbooks, such as *L'État de la France*, acknowledged new courts in France and its colonies during the ancien régime. In the mid-1700s, the *Encyclopédie* gave detailed information about the Martinican conseil as well as those in Roussillon and Alsace. In the 1770s, Le Moyne des Essarts compiled information about the composition of conseils in the Indian Ocean and the Atlantic compared with metropolitan courts in his judicial handbook. Martinique's conseil, in particular, caught the attention of Continental observers, meriting full descriptions in the former publications as well as in the 1749 judicial handbook *L'État de la France*, alongside much briefer mentions of the Québec and Saint-Domingue conseils.[42]

An ancien régime French empire, and a complementary legal order, was thus built concurrently with a new bureaucracy-driven monarchy developed primarily by Jean-Baptiste Colbert from the end of the seventeenth century. Historians have amply dissected the European dimensions of Colbert's nascent "information state," but its global magnitude, which centered on the conseils, has been little explored in a systematic way.[43] Metropolitan historians have noted that "due to a broadening dissemination of French legal culture, popular access to law and state power increased over the course of the eighteenth century."[44] Historians of early modern France have frequently turned to legal institutions, such as courts, to explain the emergence of a modern nation-state, but they have yet to incorporate colonial courts, especially the conseils as the chief metropolitan equivalent, into this analytic.[45] Though scholars such as Roland Mousnier have described ancien régime governing structures and personnel in metropolitan France in detail, no equivalent guide exists for the overseas colonies, which has made it difficult for scholars to build adequate comparative studies.[46]

Early modern observers, however, recognized a common purpose and structure shared by the conseils and the parlements. Like the parlements, the conseils were courts of last resort. Like the parlements, the conseils were entrusted with the task of registering new laws and ruling on a wide variety of civil and criminal cases. The conseils could also negotiate with the king over royal legislation, a process known as remonstration.[47] Colonial conseils were granted similar privileges: not as an afterthought to the European conseils but as part of the same process of territorial and jurisdictional integration that remains a classic theme of early modern historiography.

Colonial subjects had fewer choices of legal forums from which to choose, however, and so more legal matters were channelled through the conseils. Overseas colonies and new Continental territories (such as Alsace) had fewer courts overall, with no merchant or ecclesiastical courts, in contrast to the core regions of Continental France, where myriad specialized courts supplemented and supported the parlements and royal councils.[48] Colonial courts in areas of intensive agricultural production and trade, such as Saint-Domingue, Martinique, and the Mascarenes, flour-

ished, while in smaller continental enclaves, such as Pondichéry and Louisiana, law courts tended to be limited to just the conseils. Paris and the
metropolitan Île de France region had at least twenty-two courts, some of
which were highly specialized. By contrast, only ten courts existed in Martinique and only five in Île de France (now Mauritius), but each of these
sites received cases from throughout the Atlantic and Indian Ocean regions,
often from lower courts in other locales, such as Saint Lucia and Pondichéry. These included lower courts (called *juridictions* or *sièges*), mid-level
courts (called *sénéchaussées*), admiralty courts, and the conseils, court forms
also common within Continental France.[49] Sitting at the intersection between these most localized forums and institutions with empire-wide jurisdictions (such as the Marine and the king's councils), the conseils became
spaces in which imperial and national legal standards collided with local
legal concerns.

The Archives of the Conseils

A holistic examination of archival collections related to France's ancien régime empire reveals a wide range of imperial subjects who rarely thought in
terms of Atlantic or Indian Ocean, or even European, categories. Rather,
these subjects saw themselves as participants in a global empire. Well-
documented administrators, such as Pierre Poivre in Île de France and
Pierre Dessalles in Martinique, appear in these collections, as do hitherto
unknown subjects such as Madame Blot, an innkeeper.

Surviving conseil records have provided rich evidence for colonial historians to explore such topics as the practices of slavery. Council records in
the form of court registers (*greffes*) appear scattered throughout administrative and personal correspondence as well as law codes, customs, and commentaries.[50] The Cap-Français conseil supérieur adjudicated the famous
trial and execution of the Saint-Domingue slave revolt leader, Macandal.[51]
Enlightenment codifiers, such as Médéric Louis Élie Moreau de Saint-Méry,
published conseil decisions and correspondence in multivolume editions,
such as his widely subscribed six-volume *Loix et constitutions*, which publicized conseil decisions and colonial laws for Saint-Domingue. These sources

have usefully undergirded studies that explore the ambivalent development of tropical slave societies. They have testified to the lives of a wide range of colonial actors. These sources came from the registers of Saint-Domingue's two conseils, which included legal decisions issued both locally and from Versailles. The *Loix et constitutions*, by preserving such decisions on an encyclopedic range of topics, constitute one of the best and most widely consulted sources for prerevolutionary Saint-Domingue.[52]

The present book, however, recontexualizes colonial court documentation by interrogating their creation in the shadows of the conseils supérieurs. It thus follows through on Kathryn Burns's call to "look *at* our archives, not just through them."[53] Close reading of these sources delineates the processes by which judicial actions and imperial correspondence were collected and codified, exposing how legal practices evolved over time. It also begins to reveal patterns of participation by judges, witnesses, and other actors.[54]

The lives of previously anonymous colonial participants—such as sailors and colonial clerks—emerge from a database built from an extensive collection of more than nineteen thousand colonial personnel records in the Archives nationales d'outre-mer in Aix-en-Provence.[55] This collection includes records from all of France's ancien régime colonies, with ample representation for the Atlantic and Indian Ocean colonies that form the core of this book. By mining this archive for conseil participants, the book partially reconstructs the individual lives of imperial subjects who converged in conseil courtrooms.

The collection also permits the cross-referencing of individual conseil participants as they appear in other archival sources, such as military fortification records (for example, building plans and maps) and contemporary travel accounts (by such writers as Jean-Baptiste Du Tertre for the Antilles and Jacques-Henri Bernardin de Saint-Pierre for the Mascarenes). Such close reading of archival sources against each other reveals networks of conseil staff and imperial administrators. Together, they reveal that Martinique's conseil was centered very much on a local body of elites within the Caribbean, while Île de France's conseil tended to be much more connected to metropolitan centers and ventures throughout the Indian Ocean.

This archive's construction as part of the Marine (Navy) records also underscores the military nature of French overseas rule, despite its integration with civil-oriented metropolitan institutions, such as law courts.[56]

Change over Time

Archipelago of Justice shows how conseil practices changed over time, documenting the distinct but interwoven trajectories of Atlantic and Indian Ocean legal cultures. The legal transformations that took place in this era have been overshadowed by the bookends of early modern debates about state building (in European scholarship) and eighteenth-century discussions of the French and Haitian Revolutions (in European and colonial/Atlantic historiography). Reframing this chronology highlights France's ancien régime empire as a work in progress, not a doomed project, and emphasizes the contingency of the entire enterprise rather than its weakness at a few critical moments, such as in the revolutionary era. This strategy also foregrounds the formation of an ancien régime empire via colonial legal institutions that were embedded with better-known metropolitan counterparts.[57]

This book elucidates three historical phenomena within the period from roughly 1680 to 1780. First, across this period it documents the gradual formation and integration of France's first global empire, which enabled connections (and sometimes careers) that spanned the Antilles, in the Atlantic, and the Mascarenes, in the Indian Ocean. Direct royal rule supplanted company administration in the Antilles in 1674, while the Mascarenes were governed by companies until 1767, much later. Conseil rule, however, preceded these developments in both areas.

Second, the book highlights the transformative effects on legal practices that were brought by the Seven Years' War (1754–1763) through British occupation of the French Antilles and a transition from company to royal rule in the Mascarenes. During this global imperial conflict, the Antillean and Mascarene colonies became critical objects of contestation for their sugar cash crops. These islands also served as strategic bases for military operations in the Atlantic and Indian Oceans. As military regiments circulated between European bases at Rochefort and sites of confrontation in the Carnatic and along the Coromandel coast, they stopped over at insular stations like Île de France and coastal entrepôts like Pondichéry.

Finally, the conseils were at the center of debates that emerged between 1750 and 1780 about how to reconfigure France's empire in response to the fiscal and territorial losses precipitated by the Seven Years' War. Conseil administrators, such as Jean-Baptiste Thibault de Chanvalon in the Antilles and Pierre Poivre in the Mascarenes, supervised new initiatives to develop plantation economies in these now-precious territories (following the cession of substantial Canadian and South Asian possessions). Antillean *themistocrats* and court users sought new political influence in the metropole via the *conseils*. Their Mascarene counterparts pressed for stronger ties between longstanding Indian Ocean trading networks and newer metropolitan administrators.

A Note on Terminology

This book highlights the interactions of French subjects in Atlantic and Indian Ocean contexts, drawing attention to patterns of similarity and overlap while foregrounding important regional and local patterns. It uses the terms "Antilles" and "Mascarenes" to emphasize that these places are islands, thus, for example, distinguishing Martinique from the circum-Caribbean mainland, which stretches from modern Mexico to the Guianas along the Caribbean's western and southern edges. I use "Antilles" throughout as the most precise general term for the Caribbean insular region, rather than "West Indies," which tends to be an Anglophone preference and thus often connotes Jamaica and Barbados only, or "Caribbean," which refers most precisely to the Caribbean Sea but can also indicate the entire region from Central America to Florida. "Mascarenes" is the universally recognized collective noun for Île de France, Île Bourbon, and (uninhabited) Rodrigues.

Throughout the text, I also avoid using the descriptive term "creole." Commonly used during the long eighteenth century, and since by scholars, it has developed multiple overlapping, but often contradictory, meanings applicable in both Antillean and Mascarene contexts. Besides the common use of "creole" in French texts from the period, historians often use the term to distinguish between "metropolitan" and "colonial" (as "creole") points of view, but—as this book makes clear—these categories did not always divide so neatly in the minds of people at the time.[58] Michelle Warren has helpfully disambiguated the three most prevalent usages, which can be difficult to tease out without an explicit explanation each time the term arises:

> Within the broader scope of European colonial history, *créole* encompasses three mutually exclusive definitions, often in use simultaneously and with different historical developments in different places. From a Eurocentric perspective, *créole* designates white Europeans born in the colonies, who avoided intermarriage with other immigrants; this definition still appears in French dictionaries. *Créole* also can refer to anyone or anything of insular origin, regardless of their respective relations to Europe. Finally *créole* can signify the mixing of races, cultures, and languages that takes place when groups of disparate origins live in close proximity. *Créole* thus encompasses a range of incompatible meanings: colonial Eurocentrism, overseas inhabitants of any race, the syncretic effects of colonial society.[59]

In addition, the broad geographical applicability of "creole" obscures important regional and local idiosyncrasies that changed over time. Its emphasis on colonial variations suppresses hybridities within France (and the "metropole" writ large).[60] Racial mixing, for example, in the Antilles involved African enslaved people of origins different from those in the Mascarenes. Slave traders to the Antilles favored West African sources for captives, while their Mascarene counterparts favored East African, Malagasy, and (eventually) South Asian human cargo. Demographic and cultural patterns even within the Francophone Caribbean varied. Louisiana's famous Creole culture, such as its food and architecture, emerged out of out of a unique Mississippian context, strongly characterized by its many indigenous inhabitants in dialogue with Caribbean, African, and European influences.[61]

Chapter Outline

Archipelago of Justice lays out these claims in four chapters. Chapter 1, "The Human Ecology of Justice," explores the local configuration and context of the conseils. It demonstrates how the physical setting of justice was critical to the creation and negotiation of legal knowledge as subjects circulated into and out of courtrooms from urban markets, overseas expeditions, and plantations. The situation of the conseils in colonial capitals, combined with architectural clues from conseil buildings, guided the physical movement and behavior of court participants, such as magistrates, bailiffs, and onlookers. This strategy draws out the ways in which a colonial human ecology, or a configuration of conseil participants both in relation to each other and to the conseils as institutions, fit into a wider logic of French legality. This chapter makes clear the distinctions of the Atlantic and Indian Ocean tropical legal entrepôts. Where the Antillean conseils relied much more on their proximity to each other and a regional identity, the Mascarene conseils prioritized ties all the way back to France in an expression of vulnerability.

Chapter 2, "Justice Between Plantation and Port," explores how negotiations between court participants and magistrates through conseil proceedings, as in some sedition cases, untangled the concentric circles of authority that emanated from the innermost chambers of the conseils (especially the registrar's chamber, where legal documentation was kept) out past insular coastlines into the haziest maritime jurisdictions. This chapter delves into the public and private aspects of court proceedings, as court participants gave oral testimony in front of magistrates and onlookers and as magistrates chose to punish convicted defendants, sometimes secretly in court chambers and at other times in public processions and executions. It tracks court participants as they moved among French legal entrepôts through both formal and informal legal channels, such as judicial appeals, interjudicial correspondence, and traveling from one court to another.

Chapter 3, "Between 'Île Deserte' and 'Île de France,' " turns to the problem of dislocation. What happened when French subjects could not reach a legal entrepôt? What kinds of informal and formal legal recourse did they reach for, and in what situations did they obtain aid? Cases like the banishment to a deserted island of Jean André de Ribes, an Île de France conseil prosecutor, demonstrate that crimes against authority like blasphemy and insolence—perceived or undeniable—could leave conseil participants quite literally stranded. These cases raise questions about how imperial structures, especially courts, could fail subjects marooned outside French jurisdiction. It focuses on two types of contention, local revolts and imperial court suppressions, to understand how judicial crises affected colonial legal regimes. Local and imperial pressures converged on the conseils supérieurs, which became key sites for debates about legal and political power and thus attracted a range of actors who sought to manipulate these contentions to their own ends. Sometimes participants—even conseil members—were displaced from these forums, however, compelling them to seek alternatives.

Chapter 4, "Entrepôts in a Changing Empire," explores the regional situations of Atlantic and Indian Ocean conseils, respectively. Within these lively and increasingly interconnected oceanic systems, the Antilles initially gained prominence for their sugar production, and the Mascarenes formed what one traveler called "the arsenal of our forces and the entrepôt of our commerce."[62] These transformations, however, prompted the migration of court users, from sailors to traders, to legal entrepôts that linked continental entry points like Pondichéry in South Asia with insular way stations like Île Bourbon in the Indian Ocean. The conseils supérieurs gained strength over the course of the long eighteenth century through a combination of colonial vulnerability, which generated a need for local institutions, and professional opportunities, which enabled aspirant legal and military officials to advance their careers through the conseils. A unique convergence of colonial expertise, especially regarding cash-crop production and trade, and military skills, regarding colonial defense and imperial objectives, enabled the conseils to remain, and grow, as entrepôts at the center of a global ancien régime empire.

The Human Ecology of Justice

Monsieur the General de Poincy, and Monsieur du Parquet, when their health permitted it, were always found at the weekly hearing [*audience*], the first under the great fig tree at the Basse-Terre in Saint Christophe, and the second at Martinique under his gourd tree [*calbacier*] at Fort St. Pierre, where they accommodated all the disputes [*differents*], and never sent the parties back without having made agreement, nor without embracing one another.

—Jean-Baptiste Du Tertre, *Histoire générale des
Antilles habitées par les François*, 1667[1]

AS EARLY AS 1667, an Antillean observer described public hearings overseen by colonial magistrates: in Martinique they were held under a gourd tree; in Guadeloupe, under a fig tree. These hearings recalled the medieval king Louis IX's iconic rendering of justice under the Oak of Vincennes. Well-known trees at the center of emerging towns shaded outdoor courtrooms for gatherings of colonial subjects: townspeople and slaves, administrators and magistrates. In regional (here, colonial) capitals, the rituals of French justice played out in familiar ways for centuries, though the landscape grew more formalized and permanent with the construction of wood, then stone, courthouses.

This changing landscape was animated. Court days often coincided with seasonal markets (Figure 3), enlivening regional capitals that often lay quiet in between the busy arrivals and departures of ships, which exchanged supplies for cash crops, such as sugar. Market women—free and enslaved, of European, African, and local (sometimes called "creole") descent—set

Figure 3. *A Linen Market with a Linen-Stall and Vegetable Seller in the West Indies* (Brunias), ca. 1780, Yale Center for British Art, Paul Mellon Collection

up stalls to hawk produce.[2] Planters and overseers took care of business in town. Courts often hired local tavern keepers to cater long days of back-to-back hearings and deliberations, only later tallied into administrative, civil, and criminal categories. Pierre Monnet, for example, reserved a room in his tavern for Martinique's conseil meetings in the 1670s, before the conseil had a designated building. He also catered the meetings in exchange for a tax break.[3]

Antillean and Mascarene conseils were embedded in empire-wide rhythms of judicial process. In both Atlantic and Indian Ocean contexts as well as in metropolitan France, court meetings created a local routine of judicial activity that brought in magistrates and litigants from rural areas, especially plantations in the colonies, into regional capitals for hearings every month.[4] Conseils were specific and important sites for legal negotiation by colonial subjects because they were places where many different groups met in person in the colonies to discuss matters that pertained to both local politics and France's first colonial empire as a whole.

Most conseils, such as the one in Martinique, met nonstop from the first day of each month until they had finished deciding open cases, which usually took about a week. Conseils worked continuously to clear their backlog of cases, while the cabaret owners catered food and drink.[5] Sometimes sessions began early in the morning to avoid the tropical heat.[6] This monthly meeting cycle created a regular and predictable pattern of judicial processes. This implies steady, but by no means continuous, caseloads for the conseils. By comparison, two of the busiest courts in France, the Châtelet and the Parlement of Paris, met for a "relentless" average of 250 days a year.[7] Caseloads were big enough that monthly, and sometimes bimonthly, sessions were standard across the overseas empire.[8] Even judges appointed to serve in conseils during the early development of overseas colonies, such as Île Bourbon in the 1730s, were told to work with "all regularity."[9] As conseil members and French subjects became more and more accustomed to these processes, they contributed to a growing sense of local governance that was not always dependent upon metropolitan assistance.

Though a binary logic of master-slave relations permeated Antillean and Mascarene plantation societies, court days permitted reconfigurations of these relationships within and around the courtroom, not just in the marketplace.[10] In French Saint-Domingue, Malick Ghachem has traced the trajectory of enslaved petitions against master cruelty from the plantation to the courtroom.[11] In his 1986 *Worlds Apart*, Jean-Christophe Agnew explored how the market and the theater gradually ritualized social relationships to reconfigure social patterns in the eighteenth-century British Atlantic.[12] The present chapter proposes a corollary: that as court personnel such as bailiffs and lawyers crossed the threshold between courtrooms and colonial capitals, they transmitted legal knowledge throughout France's ancien régime global empire.

The conseils thus contributed to the vitality of port towns by overseeing the legal activities of French subjects oriented outward, toward the urban and maritime world of the Atlantic and Indian Ocean (and ultimately global) trading networks, and inward, toward the rural interior, where enslaved Africans and European planters grew the cash crops that fueled these economies. First, they drew in court users from outside the towns.

Planters litigated land disputes with their neighbors. Slaves sometimes entered complaints against masters, citing the Code Noir's restrictions on excessive cruelty. Conseils also became the terminus for maritime matters, like the Salavy shipboard duel/murder case (described in chapter 2), and were staffed to act as admiralty courts when warranted. As court users awaited their turn to appear in front of the magistrates, they shopped in the market and drank in the taverns.

Second, conseil employees moved outward toward colonial residents, into the streets and their homes. Conseil personnel gathered evidence from crime scenes and took depositions from crime victims and witnesses. These officers also visited the homes of the deceased to gather succession documents. The conseil's attorney general was responsible for signing off on estates once they had been cleared successfully. An estate might consist of the meager belongings of a sailor, no more than could fit into a trunk. Or it might reveal complex assets of wealthy planters and merchants: slaves, real estate, annuities. It would almost certainly contain substantial debts, too.

This chapter explores Atlantic and Indian Ocean conseils as courtrooms in colonies with specific local characteristics. It assesses the physical landscape of Antillean and Mascarene port towns, where courtrooms occupied town squares. It begins with a survey of the conseils and their settings in the sugar colonies of the Antilles and Mascarene Islands. This section characterizes the conseils as physical places of meeting in colonial towns where conseil members gathered to hear cases, issue sentences, and administer laws. The geographical configuration of colonial towns—especially as they relate to ports and navigational routes connecting them to the metropole—is an important clue to how colonial residents and administrators understood the colonial and imperial worlds they were creating.

Second, this chapter grapples with the relationship between two facets of legal practice, expertise and physicality, that stand out within this lens. Lower-level employees, such as the court bailiffs (*huissiers*), deployed their expertise by policing court hearings. They also circulated within colonial capitals to spread news of court decisions. Trained professionals, such as the lawyers (*avocats*), brought specialized knowledge to court proceedings that synthesized local custom and metropolitan law (including, but not limited to, the Custom of Paris, which applied in the colonies to all family- and civil-law matters). Many lawyers were new to the colonies, however, having sought overseas appointment primarily as a means to financial advancement. Local elites who made up the overwhelming majority of magistrates (*conseillers*) represented the planter (and in the Mascarenes also the merchant) class, expressing their power both in the courtroom and on the plantation.

Courtrooms in Colonies

French subjects could expect to encounter this common array of court employees and the common configuration of courtrooms as palais de justice across French territories, in and beyond Europe. Prospective conseil employees relied upon this similarity to negotiate new employment in both the colonies and the metropole. Royal administrators drew upon this common pool of personnel even as French territorial claims changed drastically over the course of the eighteenth century. Local elites increasingly used the common training of conseil officials to advocate for their interests in language that could be understood by royal and colonial audiences alike.

The development of legal entrepôts in each of France's territories made it possible for a global legal culture to develop in the eighteenth century that connected each of these disparate sites.[13] Justice was concentrated in the conseils, which preserved legal knowledge physically in the form of court registers. Magistrates worked at the very center of the court complex, between the partially open public courtyard that conveyed court users from the city streets to the courtrooms and a walled (and likely somewhat fortified) backyard for prisoners bordered by jail cells. The magistrates collected new laws issued in France by the king and his ministers in the palais de justice, and from the palais they distributed these laws to colonial subjects, alongside their own court rulings. Court administrators conveyed legal knowledge performatively through court hearings, which then circulated into the community via participants and onlookers.

Court spaces such as the Martinican palais were carefully constructed to guide French subjects, such as prisoners and magistrates, through legal activities like deliberations and hearings. In early 1683, one of the first colonial intendants, Jean-Baptiste Patoulet, wrote to the colonial office at Versailles from his station on the Caribbean island of Martinique. He included proposed architectural plans for the renovation of Martinique's palais de justice (law court building), which housed the island's chief court, the conseil supérieur, and its prison.[14] The existing palais consisted of a large rectangular *salle du conseil* (courtroom) for hearings and a smaller *chambre du conseil* (court chamber) for deliberations among conseil members. In the basement, a single prison cell and solitary confinement chamber (*cachot*) could hold criminal defendants—often slaves—while behind the conseil chambers lay a larger walled prison courtyard, with a small house for the jailer in the back corner. Patoulet suggested expanding this complex to add another large walled courtyard to the front of the palais de justice for court visitors. This more public courtyard would open onto the streets of Martinique's capital, Fort Royal, from a single central gateway set off by a porter's room and a common room, presumably so that guards could monitor the arrival and departure of court users and personnel.[15]

Patoulet's plans articulated a vision for colonial judicial proceedings that resembled court structures in France and other colonies, but they went unrealized for many years. By the 1710s, the "palais du Conseil," or palais de justice, had moved into a house that had been rented from a Sieur Gros on the Place d'Armes, or central square, in Fort Royal.[16] The building had a large main room for court proceedings that was divided by a railing, on one side of which was a raised floor for the large table (decorated in fleur-de-lis) at which the conseil members sat en banc. To each side of this main room, there was a room for the conseil members and the greffe, respectively. On the floor above this main chamber were eight rooms that could be rented out by council members who were visiting for the monthly meetings. These rooms were very expensive, however, so the conseil members appear to have continued to stay in local inns or cabarets. The house was large enough that it also had a central courtyard. Along two sides of this courtyard were the rooms of the jail, including cells, a covered exercise area (*préau*), and the jailer's rooms.[17]

Courtrooms were also gateways for colonial subjects who sought conseil audiences as a means of accessing metropolitan authorities via judicial

Figure 4. *The Sign Poster* (Tubières), 1742, Metropolitan Museum of Art

appeal or interjudicial correspondence, negotiating conceptions about legality (legal practices, as opposed to legal doctrine) both locally and imperially.[18] French subjects who had witnessed court proceedings shared legal
knowledge as they gathered in public spaces, such as taverns. Town criers
publicized court rulings orally and by posting printed broadsides (Figure
4). Likewise, subjects brought expectations about justice collected from
these public sources with them as they took their cases to the conseils.

Within the social field of the courthouse and the courtroom itself,
courthouses occupied central sites in port towns and colonial capitals.
They lay at the intersection of diverging paths carved out by court officials
and participants and by transient sailors and market women. Sometimes the
crimes prosecuted within the walls of the conseils happened just outside
their doors. In 1728, a substitute king's attorney (*procureur du roi*) named
Charles Haudoyer was murdered right in front of the palais de justice, or

main court building, on the main road of Fort Royal, Martinique, quite literally in the shadow of justice.[19]

The conseils were considered supreme on the islands and many cases
originated in the conseils. Court cases also arrived on conseil dockets via
little-known local courts of first instance (primarily juridictions and sièges)
and intermediary courts known as sénéchaussées (which existed only in
some of the bigger territories).[20] They could judge all cases that were
brought to them directly and rule on appeals to decisions made by royal
judges and their lieutenants. Conseils served as clearinghouses for legal
matters, whether they had local or empire-wide significance, and so they
became arbiters in determining which legal proceedings deserved attention
at the highest level of appeal in the king's royal councils at Versailles and
which lower court decisions sufficed.

Local Expertise: Bailiffs (Huissiers) and Town Criers

Bailiffs, known as huissiers, were located within the legal space of the conseils but made excursions beyond it to the wider colonial community. They
interacted with the public by spreading legal information and managing the
flow of litigants, witnesses, and other people in and out of courtrooms.
Their connection to the judicial (and thus imperial) institution of the conseils meant that bailiffs carried a bit more authority than the police, however. They were responsible for executing judicial orders and managing the
various parties who came to the conseils for dispute resolution, and so they
performed an essential role as go-betweens among conseil members, other
court participants, and the general public. The *Encyclopédie*'s definition
emphasized the bailiff's role outside the courtroom as well as in it, including enforcing judgments and publicizing laws throughout the community.
Archival sources also often mention *huissiers-audienciers*, bailiffs who presided over official proceedings within the courtroom (*l'audience*), rather
than enforcing judgments, publicizing laws, and other activities within the
wider community.[21] All bailiffs helped govern the order of conseil proceedings and communicated legal decisions and the provisions of specific laws
to French subjects living within each conseil's jurisdiction (*ressort*).

Colonial residents would have recognized bailiffs as the everyday faces of the courts, but because they provided no documentation of their own they have left a much fainter record than other court employees. By a count of their appearance in personnel records, bailiffs (as huissiers) are about as well documented as lawyers (avocats): representing 160 and 148 of more than nineteen thousand records, respectively. Most of the bailiff files comprise requests for employment or estate cases, in contrast to the many detailed reports and correspondence that survive for lawyers. The position of bailiff also had a lower status than writing-intensive jobs such as clerk (*greffier*), which many lawyers sought as a temporary position as they awaited slots to open in the conseils as lawyers or magistrates. Bailiffs thus appear in passing in many court records, but these ephemeral clues in fact demonstrate their importance as transmitters, if not creators, of legal knowledge.

Though bailiffs were busy in the courtroom on court days, they spent most of their time outside the conseil offices, traveling throughout each conseil's jurisdiction to collect information relevant to court business. These day-to-day activities sometimes resembled policing as they circulated through towns and along colonial roads, transferring information. As in metropolitan France, bailiffs acted as process servers, delivering new suits issued by the attorney general (and other litigants) to people, whether on their plantations or in the colonial towns.[22] In succession cases, bailiffs sometimes joined *procureurs* (similar to solicitors) and notaries as the people who went out to inventory what goods the deceased left behind—especially for cases (quite common in the tropical colonies) where people died intestate. In 1769, a bailiff and royal sergeant named Jean-Antoine Guichard accompanied a notary and clerk for vacant estates to the home of Ursule, a recently deceased free woman of color in Saint Lucia (a Martinique dependency) to help with the sale of her belongings. The succession noted that Guichard and the other officials had made it widely known about the sale, making it a matter of public record both in print and in spoken form.[23]

Bailiffs, sometimes with the help of slaves, also communicated legal decisions. Often they posted as broadsides rulings deemed important enough for public dissemination, such as those concerning notable crimes and punishments.[24] When Ribes, an attorney general in Île de France, complained that he did not have enough help to file cases and conduct investigations, he specifically mentioned the local police but not the bailiffs. Laws requiring the public notification of important conseil rulings included high-profile criminal cases. Broadsides posted in the colonies frequently described the punishments of runaway slaves and other criminal offenders.[25]

The role of bailiffs as knowledge sharers was especially crucial in far-flung colonies that depended heavily upon the conseils as information clearinghouses. Where reliable information about the law could not be found, rumors abounded. In colonial and imperial society as a whole, fact was often difficult to discern from fiction. Numerous official letters as well as court decisions complained about this problem, most frequently employing the term "bruit" (literally, "noise"), which referred to rumor or gossip and news obtained through word of mouth. For example, court officials talked about the news (bruit) that they received concerning events that happened on colonial frontiers as they deliberated about new rulings. The Pondichéry conseil, for instance, considered reports of varying reliability in its efforts to discern how many South Asians were killed by the French military in a skirmish, presumably with the intent of reallocating military units and prosecuting French civilian deaths.[26] Rumor and misinformation likewise circulated between metropole and colony. Word reached the Marine (navy/colonial) offices in 1715 that the governor of the colony of Saint-Domingue (now Haiti) had died, but it turned out that the report had confused the governor with his brother who had died.[27]

As public informants, bailiffs were best situated to bring public information about unprosecuted crimes to the court because they, more than other court officials, circulated among the local population. In courtroom settings, rumors supplemented written law and official statements by court participants. Lacking reliable witness testimony, courts could home in on criminal suspects thanks to public rumor (*bruit public*). The perpetrator of a 1770 murder in Martinique, for example, was "accused by the public voice" rather than individual witnesses.[28] In Île de France, a mysterious death was surrounded by rumor, but court officials had a difficult time determining the facts of the case.[29] Here, rumor did not necessarily signify inaccurate information but rather pointed to generally accepted knowledge that could, in the aggregate, have the weight of more direct sources such as eyewitness testimony. The fourth (1762) and fifth (1798) editions of the *Dictionnaire de l'Académie française* associated publicity with crime as a factor that rendered crimes more deserving of punishment, implying that to the extent a community witnessed a crime, it had the power to sanction it.[30]

Lawyers and magistrates around the empire applied the Criminal Ordinance of 1670 to colonial criminal matters, much as they did the Custom of Paris for family and property law. Its Title II, Article IV, ordered criminal justice officials (including a type of bailiff) to arrest "criminals caught in the act or due to public outcry" (*clameur publique*). In contrast to "outcry," the Criminal Ordinance stated its intent to ensure public order (*repos public*).[31] In wider usage in Europe, the "public" evoked an imagined "supreme tribunal" as well as a theater.[32] A similar understanding of publicity played into Mascarene jurisprudence, as society as a whole rendered justice informally by circulating public opinion through the vehicle of public rumor (*bruit public*).

While some document collections were no doubt destroyed during the French Revolution, Île de France's town criers noticed an increase in printing at the outset of the Revolution. The amount of legislation and official proclamations increased rapidly during this period. An explosion of pamphlets, broadsides, and other materials that has now been catalogued in French archives testifies to this development, especially in contrast to the paucity of material available from the ancien régime. Auguste Toussaint has noted copies of broadsides such as those posted by two Île de France town criers named Gosset and Fournier and deposited with the greffes. These have deteriorated due to poor conservation, however.[33]

The role of public intermediary required such intensive labor that it could bifurcate into two positions: one for the towns and another for rural regions. By the 1770s, for example, Île de France had one or two designated town criers (*crieurs publics*), who would go throughout the streets of Port Louis (but not beyond) to post broadsides with new laws or rulings. They worked for the royal siège (or court of first instance) in Port Louis but reported back to the conseil supérieur greffe when they had finished.[34] Town criers became familiar heralds of legal news but limited their role to the space demarcated by the town's boundaries. A town crier named Bourgeois was so popular that "as early as 1790, his name was given to a bridge in the rue Moka, in the Western suburb of Port Louis, which is known to this day as pont Bourgeois," at the boundary of the town crier's area of coverage.[35]

Their circuits through colonial towns and the countryside took town criers along paths traversed by local police. In September 1792, the Île de France town criers Gosset and Fournier appealed to the local commune for extra payment, as their workload had drastically increased since the start of the French Revolution. Having formerly done the job themselves, they now required the help of two slaves to distribute and post all the new publications. Worse, the colonial assembly had not paid them for this labor. The communal government agreed with their request and awarded them six hundred livres in back payment as well as a salary of five hundred livres a year.

While the town criers (with bailiffs) focused on urban areas, local officials known as *syndics* covered the much larger rural areas. Usually of lower to middling backgrounds, like small planters, low-level military officers, and cabaret owners, *syndics* managed municipal and neighborhood tasks like censuses and militias, especially those that hunted runaway slaves (maroons). They were also charged to publicize legal knowledge, as in a 1762 Île de France regulation issued by the conseil supérieur. *Syndic*s would articulate the island's new laws, police regulations, and some transactions like the sale of property. They could also stand in for court clerks to oversee the death of a person, including consultation with a surgeon about the cause of death, the removal of the body, and the beginning of estate proceedings.[36]

Despite the proliferation of printed broadsides, oral forms of knowledge endured as a key component of Mascarene and Antillean legal culture. Court and local employees read legal documentation aloud as they copied and posted manuscripts and printed notices. Town criers and bailiffs employed by local courts were responsible for posting legal broadsides around colonial towns (Figure 4). Town criers also deposited copies of broadsides into the court registers (conseil greffes). Nearly all these legal decisions, in France and its colonies, ended with a boilerplate phrase attesting that they "had been duly read and posted up in the customary places."[37]

Within the courtroom—and in stark contrast to the "noise" attributed to the cabarets and public rumors—legal matters were discussed methodically with a "deliberative voice" (*voix délibérative*). This concept referred to the measured and rational register of speaking that magistrates used as they conferred with each other to decide cases. Deliberative voice was particularly linked with the right of magistrates to participate in court meetings (*séances*), especially the private adjudication of cases by several magistrates in the courtroom. These meetings were conducted in enclosed spaces, such as the court's chamber. Magistrates used their deliberative voices to make private decisions that only became public once they were shared beyond the courtroom through printed rulings and the other practices of publicizing verdicts discussed above.

Legal publicity acted as a countervailing force against rampant rumors by enforcing standardized articulations. Colonial jurists, especially those with reformist and political aspirations, applauded the "publicity" of written and circulated local laws as "written reason" in an era of Enlightenment valorization of rational thinking and writing.[38] Written and publicized laws were designed to drive away these unreliable "noises" (a literal translation of the word "bruits") and replace them with clear articulations of legal fact and official correspondence. Sometimes the Île de France conseil would issue rulings (*arrêts*) to publicize other decisions. In April 1780, the Île de France conseil ordered the publication of a ruling from the previous December that set the fees for various court clerks.[39]

Many scholars have explored how legal scripts could become tools for subaltern groups to negotiate and resist imperial laws in the early modern era.[40] This present examination of legal publicity, however, demonstrates how colonial subjects learned about these legal scripts in the first place. Conseil-sanctioned publicity set legal narratives and valorized rational and reliable jurisprudence, thereby setting a model of how legal knowledge should be articulated. This component of legal publicity reveals the surprising importance of apparently useless boilerplate legal language: repetition molded public understandings of law.

As conseils sought to educate the public about their activities, even lower-ranking court employees who tended to stay out of sight behind mounds of court registers (registrars were sometimes called pen pushers, or *plumitifs*) began to supplement and reinforce the urban circuits of the bailiffs by acting as town criers. In 1753, Sieur Giraudet was commissioned simultaneously as greffier and notary in the royal jurisdiction of the small town of Petit-Goave on the southern peninsula of Saint-Domingue. His commission stated that he would reside in the nearby smaller town of Grand Anse. It also assigned him joint employment in a local jurisdiction there.[41] In small jurisdictions, and in cases where conseils were short-staffed, greffiers and notaries almost certainly played similar roles in Martinique and Île de France.

Imperial Expertise: Lawyers (Avocats)

While local officials such as bailiffs relied upon oral knowledge and printed broadsides as sources for generating a *nomosphere* within and around the conseil, other personnel increasingly prized formal legal training in the French metropole. Lawyers were one such group. For roughly the first half of the long eighteenth century, conseillers and court advocates tended to read and apply the law as they saw fit based primarily on their experience as administrators, military officers, and wealthy landowners. But by the mid-eighteenth century, these conseil personnel stressed expertise in French law as a crucial supplement to local knowledge. Originally trained informally through apprenticeships, by the mid-eighteenth century many magistrates and court advocates were lawyers educated in French law schools and admitted to the bar of specific courts, usually the parlements in France. In the Paris Parlement, two lawyers (*avocats généraux*) and one attorney general (*procureur général*) represented the king and were referred to as a group as "the king's men" (*les gens du roi*).[42] Certification as a lawyer thus conferred much prestige and implied specialized legal training and practice, and so prospective employees of the conseils and other courts often made sure to mention these credentials in their letters to the Ministry of the Marine. Magistrates and other court personnel were often recommended based on their legal expertise, but this did not imply formal legal training until the middle of the eighteenth century.

Lawyers across France's colonial empire, especially in the sugar colonies of the Atlantic and Indian Oceans, formed an important part of each island's judicial elite and were engrained in key networks of familial, royal, and commercial power. Perhaps the most famous white Antillean activist of the eighteenth century, Moreau de Saint-Méry, was a lawyer in the conseil supérieur of Cap-Français in Saint-Domingue. He was also the scion of a prominent family of Martinican planters and magistrates.[43]

In both the Antilles and the Mascarenes, the legal professions remained strictly off-limits to people of mixed race, as the white planter class emphatically, and increasingly, policed racial boundaries. This pattern contrasted with such professions as planting (*habitant*) and trading (*négociant*), in which by the mid-eighteenth century a free colored elite had emerged in the Caribbean. Mixed-race counterparts also existed in the Mascarenes. The practice of law was also strictly limited to white men, though some were born in the colonies and others in France.[44]

Conseils welcomed lawyers for their expertise, but in both the Antilles and the Mascarenes conseil magistrates and administrators sought to control any undue influence by defining the power of lawyers within their jurisdiction. In overseas colonies, lawyers were less common, but their numbers and influence increased over time. The Martinique conseil ruled in July 1769 that lawyers could be integrated into the conseil (and other courts), but only once they had proven that they had been admitted to the bar and had practiced law in the metropole for at least three years.[45] This ruling reflected a desire to limit the number of people who could be added to the colonial courts, but it also showed an increasing desire to include legal experts (as well as military officers and planters) in the colonial judiciary. A similar ruling appeared in Île de France, but not until 1781. This law allowed lawyers to practice their profession freely (though under advisement from the conseil) in the conseil's jurisdiction.[46]

Lawyers in strategically located insular colonies such as the Antilles and the Mascarenes were well situated to help court users navigate France's ancien régime by using the conseils as legal entrepôts. These lawyers were often embedded in Indian and Atlantic Oceans family and trading networks. Colonial lawyers—especially by the second half of the eighteenth century—had frequently gained preliminary admission to the Paris bar. This eliminated the need for a specific colonial bar and created tight connections between networks of legal experts in the Antilles, the Mascarenes, and the Parisian metropole.

A metropolitan constitutional order, based on the Custom of Paris, prevailed in overseas colonies, where it was interpreted as integral to, and fully incorporated into, the local constitutional order. With the imposition of royal direct rule in most colonies by the end of the seventeenth century (though not until 1767 in the Mascarenes), colonies came under the jurisdiction of Parisian customary law for family and civil matters. The Custom of Paris became so familiar to colonial lawyers that a Martinican jurist omitted it from a compilation of Martinican laws, citing it as the "municipal" law of French colonies.[47]

The prevalence of lawyers across France's ancien régime empire counters a common narrative, based in North American sources, that overseas colonies lacked legal experts, especially lawyers. Bans on lawyers in Louisiana, for example, reveal instead that administrators aimed to prevent access to the colonies by the groups most inclined to challenge royal authority and to limit what they perceived as excessive litigation.[48] Louisiana lawyers developed a particular reputation for corruption and litigiousness, which led to an outright ban on lawyers that coincided with the establishment of the colony's conseil and the implementation of the Code Noir. Such North American colonies, however, often lacked metropolitan oversight of all kinds. Limited administrative resources, channeled through the Marine, tended to be focused on Antillean and Mascarene territories, which had smaller populations but higher strategic and economic value.

Lawyers appear throughout Antillean and Mascarene archival documentation. Legal personnel recognized the strategic value of these colonies for their own benefit, too. In 1789 Julien François Guérin requested a letter of recommendation from a Marine official for employment as a lawyer (avocat) and clerk (greffier) in Île de France and Île Bourbon.[49] Guérin had worked as a lawyer in Paris for most of his career, but he wanted to move to the Mascarenes to contribute to his family's interests in the East Indies, though through a legal rather than a commercial career. The Mascarene intendant Poivre had sent one of his relatives to Ceylon (now Sri Lanka) to search for spices. The responding marine official chose not to sign or approve Guérin's letter but rather jotted a note in messy handwriting: "To write a vague letter of recommendation."[50]

Throughout the long eighteenth century, legal professionals like Guérin sought employment in the colonial conseils supérieurs even though many of them had started their careers in metropolitan courts, such as the Parlement of Paris. Family ties, like Guérin's uncle (a high-ranking military officer in Île de France), and interjudicial correspondence, such as Guérin's letter to the Marine, supported the efforts of judicial personnel to make careers in metropolitan France, the Mascarenes, and the Antilles in the eighteenth century, from the first creation of these courts under Louis XIV to the dissolution of the ancien régime in late 1789, shortly after Guérin wrote his letter.[51] Court employees like Guérin crafted the legal infrastructure of France's ancien régime empire as they helped adjudicated cases in each conseil. As they worked in each of these legal entrepôts—from Paris to the Île de France—they contributed to the creation of a common legal culture that stretched from metropolitan France to overseas territories, including the Mascarenes and the Antilles.[52]

Early conseil membership tended to be made up of local elites, usually planters and military officers, who would step in as lawyers when needed. Lawyers participated in the exchange and spread of French legal knowledge throughout the ancien régime's global imperial network in person, moving from colony to metropole and back (for colonial lawyers) and from the Paris to the colonies (for metropolitan lawyers). For families with origins in both the metropole and the colonies, status as a lawyer was a common prerequisite to employment in the colonial conseils, as lawyers as well as magistrates and clerks. Admission to the Paris bar added an appealing mark of distinction. Requirements for admission varied drastically across both the geographic regions and the time periods covered in this book. James Pritchard asserts that only the attorney general in each conseil was required to be admitted to the Paris bar, but individual edicts testify to a range of educational requirements (Figure 5). A 1778 regulation in Île de France required lawyers and other personnel (*praticiens*, presumably those

Figure 5. *The Gallery of the Palace of Justice* (Bosse), ca. 1638, Wikimedia Commons, Metropolitan Museum of Art

who would present matters before the magistrates) to produce evidence of their legal training within fifteen days, on pain of losing their licensure.[53]

By the mid-eighteenth century, an accelerating flow of legal professionals between colonies and metropole strengthened connections among French judicial personnel throughout the empire. Some lawyers, such as Jean Périnelle-Dumay, started out as metropolitan lawyers only to move to the colonies and begin a new career in the conseils. Périnelle-Dumay first served in the Paris Parlement for several years, then in 1719 began an appointment as conseiller in Martinique, and finally became the Martinique conseil's attorney general. As with many Antillean families who created dynasties of conseil members, Périnelle-Dumay's son likewise served as a Paris lawyer and later a Martinican conseiller in the 1750s–1770s. In addition, the first Périnelle-Dumay's grandson and great-grandson became Paris lawyers, then Martinican conseillers, extending the family's influence well into the nineteenth century.[54]

Finally, by the 1760s to 1780s, a new class of legal experts began to agitate for colonial reforms from the board of magistrates that composed the conseils supérieurs. A new wave of colonial and metropolitan lawyers came to the colonies beginning in the 1760s, having been educated in French law schools. These men synthesized their metropolitan educations with their experiences growing up and serving as conseillers in the colonies to shape new arguments for colonial legal reform.

Political reforms in the metropole also catalyzed desire for colonial legal posts. As the king's judicial enforcer in chief, Chancellor Maupeou had sought to reform France's inefficient (and venal) tax-farming system but ran into opposition from the powerful Paris Parlement, whose magistrates often depended upon profits from the tax farms. In January 1771, Maupeou dissolved the parlement and demanded the resignations of its conseillers, a move he repeated in later months with other parlements. Lawyers (avocats) who had been terminated in the dissolutions of the Maupeou coup (as it became known) applied in droves to become conseillers in the colonies, especially Saint-Domingue.

Many legal practitioners in France actively sought conseil employment as a useful stepping-stone to lucrative legal and political careers that spanned the ancien régime empire. For ambitious legal practitioners, conseil careers opened the door to investment opportunities in tropical sugar plantations and overseas trading interests, such as Asian textiles. Whether from personal trading interests overseas or perhaps a desire to initiate overseas investments, many magistrates and lawyers in hexagonal France requested employment in the conseils. William Doyle has highlighted a concentration of family networks in the Bordeaux Parlement that was created primarily through the placement of eldest sons in the *magistrature*, but parlement magistrates in port cities such as Bordeaux often looked far beyond the boundaries of parlement networks for employment opportunities. Even the Paris Parlement, the most important parlement in terms of both geographical jurisdiction and prestige, contained many legal professionals who sought employment overseas through requests they submitted to the Marine.

By the mid- to late eighteenth century, many metropolitan parlement members—even in the prestigious Paris Parlement—sought positions in the colonial conseils supérieurs, particularly in Saint-Domingue, where a government job could also open doors to investment in the riches of the sugar and coffee trades. During the Maupeou crisis of 1771 to 1774, metropolitan parlements were suspended, and so even more lawyers and judges sought new employment in the colonies.[55]

A metropolitan expertise but a local outlook characterized the opinions of Antillean lawyers in the second half of the eighteenth century.[56] Philippe Cornette de Cely of Martinique gained a reputation as a staunch defender of Antillean interests against the royal and metropolitan commitments of the governor and the intendant. He got into trouble in 1751 for trying to block the appointment of Moreau (Moreau de Saint-Méry's father) as conseiller. Later, he provoked controversy with the intendant Pierre-Paul Le Mercier de la Rivière over a conseil decision quashed by the intendant.[57] This pattern created a cycle of exchange in which an increasingly metropolitan-educated colonial elite became more strongly tied to colonial interests but also more involved with political arguments in metropolitan France.

Metropolitan residents, especially in Paris, had the Antillean colonies on their mind more than the Mascarenes, a pattern that intensified as Antillean elites increasingly sent their sons to populate many of France's law schools. There, aspirant lawyers rubbed shoulders with wealthy planters and learned about the colonies as they also learned about the intricacies of French law. Indian Ocean elites, by contrast, tended to move more in commercial circles so their networks were anchored in smaller metropolitan trading ports like Saint-Mâlo. They also seem to have had less stake in maintaining a force of opposition on the conseil like the Antillean lobbying tradition epitomized by Cornette de Cely, Dessalles, and others. Ribes and other Mascarene magistrates emphasized their compliance with metropolitan norms more than their objections to them. The link between a mobile class of lawyers, part of the global themistocracy, and colonial conseils can be tracked to both the Atlantic and the Indian Ocean contexts, but it varied in intensity and motivation.

French lawyers were mindful of Atlantic and Indian Ocean legal entrepôts, and many requested employment in the Mascarene and Antilles law courts. Though both the Mascarenes and the Antilles had economies based on cash crops like sugar and coffee, legal experts in the Mascarenes tended to come more from the area of commerce, especially spice trading, than from the pan-Caribbean and Atlantic networks of military and planter families that characterized legal experts in the Antilles. Metropolitan lawyers saw opportunities for financial gain and status in both regions, but the patronage ties and other connections required to obtain colonial positions depended upon regional distinctives.

Lawyers sought work in the colonial conseils for a variety of reasons. Entrance into Martinique and Guadeloupe's well-established plantocracy was more difficult, but it could guarantee good connections and possibly economic success, at least by introduction to a Mascarene heiress if not access to plantations themselves. As in Martinique and Guadeloupe, the attempt by Guérin to work in the Indian Ocean hinged less upon his legal expertise and more upon whether he could convince Marine employees that he had a reason to go there—especially to follow in his uncle's footsteps. Similarly, Desgranges de Richeteau sought employment based upon a family connection in the Mascarenes and hoped that his brother's recommendation was sufficient to help him escape from his father and other disapproving relatives.

Parlement lawyers (avocats), originally based in the metropole, appear frequently in the Marine personnel records, pointing to a substantial group of legal personnel who held posts across France's ancien régime empire. Most of these records include requests for employment in the conseils. Surprisingly, several of these people asked for lower-level jobs as greffiers pending the availability of conseiller openings, indicating that legal employment was more important than the particular station of magistrate and that many applicants anticipated working their way up through the ranks of the conseil.[58] The vast majority of these lawyers requested employment in Saint-Domingue, the largest and wealthiest French colony during the eighteenth century.

These patterns imply that conseil applicants wanted to participate in plantation investment or the sugar and coffee trades as a more lucrative business than the practice of law in France, while also recognizing the prestige and practical political power that came with conseil membership.[59] Lawyers worked in all of the Antilles and Mascarenes, however, taking their metropolitan legal expertise to the conseils supérieurs and applying it in these local colonial contexts.

Some Antillean lawyers, such as Cornette de Cely of Martinique, studied law in France as preparation for dual careers managing plantations while serving on the conseils. He was admitted to the bar as a lawyer in the Paris Parlement, but he became a substitute magistrate (*assesseur*) in Martinique in 1736, with promotion to full-fledged magistrate (conseiller) the following year. This career trajectory increasingly became a tradition as other prosperous Antilleans (particularly in Martinique and Guadeloupe) sent their sons to be educated in French law schools with the hope of them returning to the colonies to represent local interests, counter metropolitan influence of governors and intendants on the conseils, and run family plantations.[60]

This pattern also appears in the Mascarenes, which lacked a strong local, homegrown judicial elite, so a much higher percentage of metropolitan lawyers served on the conseils. Guérin had served as a lawyer in Paris until 1773, at which point he first requested employment in India. By 1775, he had arrived in Île de France; in that year his father wrote a letter to Marine officials asking them to send him back to France on a royal ship. He was the nephew of Poivre's commissaire de la Marine in Île de France, Prévost, who had procured important spices "for France" at "the risk of his life and to the detriment of his fortune."[61] The request by Guérin emphasized his previous familial connections—a pattern that matched the reliance on patronage common to the Antilles and the French metropole as well at the time.

The nature of his connections differed, however: Guérin's relative had been involved in the spice trade, not a legal profession. Furthermore, the political connection the relative did have, as second to Poivre, depended upon the commercial nature of the spice trade and Poivre's support of it rather than Poivre's function as an important imperial officer.[62] We recall that the responding Marine official chose not to sign or approve Guérin's letter but simply jotted a note "to write a vague letter of recommendation." By

February, the Ministry of the Marine had decided against Guérin and wrote to him that it was sorry to reject his request for free passage but could give that only to official employees of the French kingdom.[63] Guérin's unfruitful efforts to find legal employment in the Mascarenes illustrate a lack of administrative support for sending legal experts to this region (especially as no record seems to show a replacement for Guérin) as well as enthusiasm on the part of Guérin. While Marine officials declined to send him in his uncle's footsteps, his request shows that Parisian lawyers (at least) were quite aware of the judicial apparatus that lay beyond France's European borders.

Though some lawyers were drawn to the trading world of the Indian Ocean through family ties, others sought to escape their families in France. Like Guérin (and most Antillean lawyers), Guillaume Desgranges de Richeteau had been admitted as a lawyer to the Paris bar in the mid-eighteenth century. In Île de France, Desgranges de Richeteau worked as both a police inspector and la awyer for the island's conseil during the 1770s. He had practiced in the Paris Parlement for more than ten years (roughly 1747 to 1757), having obtained a doctorate in law and followed his father into a career that was both lucrative and prestigious.[64] He had, however, made a bad marriage, to the dismay of his family, who had become "irritated with [him]," and so he had decided to leave France for the colonies in search of a new career.[65]

Desgranges de Richeteau looked to only one place, Île de France, to start over. His brother, Jacques Guillaume Desgranges de Richeteau, had served in Île de France as a lieutenant in the military since the mid-eighteenth century and could offer Guillaume the recommendation necessary to obtain a judicial appointment there.[66] Guillaume did receive the necessary recommendation, because he had arrived in Île de France by 1757 and began work as a clerk for a M. Du Petlival, with the ambition of working his way into the conseil.[67] After several years, he gained the attention of the governor, René Magon, who gave him a job under the attorney general, Jean François Anthoine de Bacourt.[68] By the 1760s, the new governor, Antoine Marie Desforges-Boucher, appreciated Desgranges de Richeteau's work enough to give him the additional job of police chief, which included more compensation and also allowed him more direct legal influence over the island through enforcing the laws created and maintained by the conseil. By the 1770s, he was working as a lawyer in the Île de France conseil, a job that more directly matched his previous experience at the Paris Parlement. Through family connections and legal expertise, he translated his prosperous Parisian career into a similarly lucrative life in the Mascarenes.

Blended Expertise: Magistrates (Conseillers)

The Antillean and Mascarene plantocracy, not the parlements, supplied magistrates (known as conseillers) for the conseils. With property and agricultural interests in the colonies, conseillers tended to have long careers in their home conseils. This dedication to single law courts, whose jurisdiction usually covered the magistrates' land and relations, contrasted with the peripatetic careers of lawyers across metropolitan and colonial, Atlantic and Indian Ocean law courts. Conseiller appointments depended less upon legal training than one's status as a local *notable*, an informal but significant status that could often be attributed to long-standing residence and property ownership. Conseillers ranked among militia captains, responsible for defending islands from foreign invasion and internal slave revolt. Above all, their role as masters in slave societies granted them a particular and local power that became amplified in the conseil courtroom, in which slave masters became adjudicators of empire-wide principles of justice.

A three-step pattern of change over time becomes apparent from an assessment of the legal cultures of the Antilles and the Mascarenes in light of key geopolitical transformations. In the initial stages of colonization, conseil members were most often part of the military or trading elite that had helped found new colonies, especially in the late seventeenth and early eighteenth centuries. They became supplanted in the second generation by colony-born elites (often called *créoles*), usually referred to as "notables" to designate their status as untitled aristocrats. Their interests were most fully entrenched in local colonial politics, so they were the most likely to rebel against metropolitan instructions with which they did not agree.[69]

A third and final generation of conseil elites emerged after the collapse of French imperial interests in South Asia and North America at the end of the Seven Years' War, as the monarchy and the Ministry of the Marine sought to consolidate their now small, but still lucrative, overseas holdings. These legal experts, including conseil members in this period from roughly 1763 to 1780, claimed local legitimacy and gained permission from Versailles to govern based on their ability to run the colonies efficiently, especially in terms of finance.[70] Conseil members, such as the Mascarene merchant Rheims Rose, who understood metropolitan politics and who could make sure the empire profited off colonial products were thus in the best position to stay in power or even to advance to higher offices. Together, these experts composed the emerging global themistocracy.

In both Atlantic and Indian Ocean colonies, a pattern of familial island-hopping bound family networks together into larger regional groupings. Families such as the Huraults and the Valminières moved to Martinique and Guadeloupe from Saint-Christophe after it became crowded with English and French settlers. Settlers in Martinique migrated to the island of Grenada to the south and to the colony of Saint-Domingue on Hispaniola to the north as early as the 1650s. Military service also often led families to be stretched across several colonies (or between France and the colonies). Some military officials, for instance, worked in both Caribbean and Indian Ocean islands during the eighteenth century: François Millon served first as attorney general (procureur général) in Île Bourbon's conseil and later as a *sénéchal* and judge in Saint-Marc, Saint-Domingue.[71] Politically aspirational individuals such as Médéric Louis Élie Moreau de Saint-Méry, the creole lobbyist and codifier, grew up in Martinique, served in the Paris Parlement, and then became a judge in Saint-Domingue, marking a back-and-forth pattern between colonies and metropole that characterized the lives of many Antillean and Mascarene magistrates. Local expertise developed in colonial courts was thus transferred across colonies and back to the metropole through the movement of magistrates and military officers.

These patterns, established early in the colonial history of France's first empire, continued throughout the eighteenth century and appeared in stronger forms by the 1780s. By then, these family networks included military officers and scions of ruling families who often chose to move to neighboring colonies in order to escape the shadow of their parents and develop their own plantations or branches of the family's trading business. This process meant, however, that children of local elites often took their legal knowledge and experiences with them, too, creating networks of elites who argued for the continuance of their dominance based on their experience in administrative units like the conseils supérieurs. They thus set a precedent for a local oligarchy of military and judicial families that would gradually shift to having a more commercial character, while maintaining a heritage of military service through honorary titles.

Throughout the eighteenth century, conseillers tended to be promoted from within the judicial ranks, whether from inside the conseils or by requesting colonial posts after serving in metropolitan parlements. Charles Toussaint Jocet became a magistrate in the Île de France conseil in 1775 after having been an advisory member of the conseil (assesseur) for several years. His promotion came with a recommendation that he had been instructed in law and adjudication, presumably in France, though where was unspecified.[72]

Martinique's conseil depended upon old, local families more than any other conseil. Out of 109 Martinican magistrates documented by Émile Hayot over the course of the ancien régime, fifty came from only twenty families (even fewer if one accounts for high levels of intermarriage among these conseil families). Within the same pool of magistrates twenty had been born in the islands, two more were born of local mothers, and thirty-seven were born in the metropole—*but* twenty-four of the metropolitan magistrates married local women.[73] Well over a plurality of magistrates had deep ties to Martinique. And nearly two-thirds of those with metropolitan backgrounds married into Antillean families.[74] Martinican magistrates insisted throughout the early modern era that this long judicial and administrative tenure had uniquely suited them to local rule.[75]

Local elites (often called *notables* in French) increasingly sought to outweigh the influence of royal administrators through the conseils supérieurs, where they could amass power against both the intendant and the governor. This pattern built on a tradition from the seventeenth century in metropolitan France in which local elites in the provinces used regional law courts and assemblies, like the parlements and estates, to counter royal initiatives, like new taxes, that were implemented by the intendants. In the middle of the seventeenth century, for example, the estates of Guyenne (the region surrounding Bordeaux) had fought with intendants and other royal officials over supremacy, as had the parlements, both before and after the Fronde of the 1640s and 1650s.[76] This tradition culminated in the colonies with rebellions like the Gaoulé in Martinique in 1717 and the Dumas affair in Île de France in 1767, when conseils supported by local groups of *notables* converged against intendants and governors.

Deeply invested in the local colonial economy and society, conseil magistrates acted as a counterbalance to the governors and intendants who reported directly to Marine officials in Versailles. Though the governor and intendant represented a team of royal military and fiscal power, the conseillers who formed the majority of the conseil's tribunal embodied a convergence of the other elite professions that controlled colonial society and economy. Council members primarily included planters, traders (négociants), and military officers: the three groups of elites who were often referred to collectively as the *notables* of the islands.[77] Such *notables* could also circulate on and off local courts, including the conseils, in cases where sufficient certified magistrates could not be found.[78]

Like conseil lawyers, the officials who made up the colonial judiciary of the conseils supérieurs often had legal experience in metropolitan courts that they drew upon when deciding cases. Many were themselves invested in colonial agriculture and commerce, owning plantations and ships, so they likewise relied upon their own financial expertise to decide how the colonies should be managed. The freedom to participate in trade contrasted with metropolitan magistrates, such as those in the Bordeaux Parlement, who were forbidden commercial activity.[79] These interests created a mixture of local interest and metropolitan thinking among the members of each conseil, who worked together—though sometimes acrimoniously—to decide cases. Upon marrying the daughter of a Guadeloupean militia major, the Bordeaux Parlement conseiller Jean François Cazaux Du Breuil moved to Guadeloupe and joined the Guadeloupe conseil, with full rights to "rank, hearing, and deliberative voice" granted by a royal order.

Conseils sometimes contested even this assertion of royal authority over their organization, however. The appointment of Cazaux Du Breuil was met with resistance by the Guadeloupe conseil, which expressed concern that he did not spend enough time on the island to serve in the conseil (presumably as an absentee planter).[80] Though Cazaux Du Breuil brought the requisite qualities of legal expertise and local investment backed by royal approval to the Guadeloupe conseil, conseils like it insisted on vetting their members themselves. Family members often held seats for many generations across several colonies in different colonial councils, and so councils can reveal intercolonial commercial, social, and informal legal relationships.

The magistrates' power was engrained in family commercial and landed interests, but these interests also depended upon the specific privileges attached to the office of conseiller, which matched metropolitan magistrates' privileges in several critical ways. This consistency supported a global French legal culture in which officials could expect to have similar rights and responsibilities whether they adjudicated cases in Île de France, Martinique, or metropolitan France.

The power vested in conseillers depended upon two defined rights known as *séance*, which was the right to sit in on conseil deliberations, and voix délibérative, which conferred the right to contribute an opinion to deliberations. Acting council magistrates were known as *conseillers titulaires* and adjudicated cases according to the written law in sessions convened by the corporate body of conseillers.[81]

The legal basis for adjudication matched analogous rights that were granted to conseillers in metropolitan courts that extended from a formal grant of the right to enter the courts in the first place. For the Paris Parlement, like magistrates for the conseils, the archbishop of Paris, the chief abbot of the Cluny order, the governor of Paris, and high nobles such as the princes of the blood (from age fifteen) and the peers of France (from age twenty-five) enjoyed rights to *séance* and voix délibérative. Entrance (*entrée*) was counted as a key privilege for the metropolitan parlements. These rights, however, were not always granted together. In France and in the colonies these rights could be tied to admittance to specific different sections of courts in France.[82] Magistrates who were born in the colonies and obtained metropolitan posts found the procedures in parlement very similar to conseil practices, and vice versa.

Conseil magistrates tended to stay on for life, usually following an active career with several years in a semiretired position known as *conseiller honoraire*, when illness or age forced them to cut back on time spent in the conseil. This practice contrasted with the careers of magistrates in metropolitan law courts, such as the Bordeaux Parlement, where they usually served short terms of less than ten years.[83] Conseil magistrates were appointed in one of two ways. For councils under company rule, as in the Mascarenes before 1767, conseillers were nominated by the company's board of directors.[84] Under royal rule, conseillers were nominated by the conseil or the Ministry of the Marine and confirmed by the intendant and the governor.[85]

In addition to the laws they received from royal ministers and customary law, conseil members were authorized to make decisions about every aspect of colonial life. They could make police rules, enforce restrictions on the activities of slaves, and oversee duels. They regulated professions (like notaries, surgeons, and so on) and watched over commerce to make sure that it was legal and properly conducted. They also dealt with international crises like skirmishes with neighboring nations (such as Malagasy tribes and Caribs) and decided how to punish smugglers, thieves, and murderers.

Other privileges emphasized the conseillers' command of colonial spaces outside the palais de justice and reinforced imperial and local hierarchies through visual clues like the space at the front (not the back) of a church. In the late seventeenth and early eighteenth centuries, the role of Martinican conseiller came with several privileges as well as formal legal rights, including a front-row pew in church and exemption from the head tax (*capitation*) on twelve of their slaves. Conseillers also had the right to be saluted by canon if they walked through town as a group ("se déplaçaient en corps"), and could march in front of militia officers in official cortèges.[86] Walking in front of militia officers, for instance, illustrated a precedence of imperial power through judicial means (personified by conseil officials) over the brute force represented by militia officials. Military force, however, also backed up conseil authority symbolically in these processions and in reality, as militias acted as police forces to ensure the colonial social order outlined in colonial laws administered by the conseil.

Once conseillers had served for many years (usually at least twenty), they could become semiretired conseillers honoraires, who still had influence in the outcome of cases and the courts' judicial policies.[87] This office dated back at least to the early seventeenth century and existed in metropolitan as well as colonial France.[88] Conseillers honoraires retained the right to sit in on both civil and criminal conseil proceedings and to exercise the voix délibérative, which allowed them to participate in the decision-making process and ceremonial processions outside the conseil. They did, however, lose access to tax exemptions and other benefits. They were also limited in seniority by the oldest regular conseillers, who retained all their privileges. This allowed experienced magistrates to keep an interest in court proceedings and politics and created a long-term continuity among the conseil's membership, as magistrates could serve for many decades even after they had officially retired.

The lack of monetary rewards for service on the conseil further created opportunities for local elites to emphasize colonial justice over allegedly corrupt metropolitan justice, even though judicial services were in practice affordable to a very limited proportion of colonial subjects. Martinican magistrates were forbidden to take any payments for their offices ("toute rétribution de leur charge"). Instead, the king gave them an expense account of five hundred to six hundred livres each year to cover the cost of attending conseil meetings.[89]

This contrasted starkly with metropolitan France, where fees (*épices*) regularly funded the judicial process. In the Alsace conseil, the amount for a case (*procès*) varied according to the amount of work it would incur for the court staff; cases tended to cost an average of between ninety and 120 livres. This was still a large amount of money. Unskilled laborers in Paris, for example, only made an average of 230 to 320 livres a year in the eighteenth century. The rates for Alsatian courts were low compared to those for other regional courts in France, such as the Breton Parlement at Rennes. In 1771, épices were abolished in the conseils supérieurs as well as elsewhere. As a trade-off, metropolitan magistrates, at least in Paris, were not allowed to participate in commerce, especially following a 1701 edict.[90]

In the same section where he outlined the division of government work among military and civil officials in Martinique, Chanvalon explained that the conseils were meant to provide legal services—justice, in his words—to colonial residents, which would (he implied) encourage the creation of an orderly civil society: "Justice in the conseils supérieurs of our colonies is freely given to those who claim it. The officers of these conseils restrain neither place nor their work, neither gifts [*épices*], nor wages, nor recompense [*émolumens*]. However, there as elsewhere, the procedures incur considerable expenses."[91] This was not just Chanvalon's assertion: a report on the 1716 composition of the Martinican conseil and its subsidiary courts (for example, in Marie-Galante and Grenada) had made a similar statement about Antillean court costs—in contrast to Canada, which evidently charged épices found in most metropolitan courts.[92] Building on this history of free justice, Chanvalon's defense of the conseillers articulated a distinct Antillean ideology that equated magistracy with moral virtue—a counterargument to prevailing stereotypes about the degeneracy of colonial life.[93] Chanvalon contextualized the conseil's judicial duties within colonial (and especially American) society as one feature out of many political features of colonial governance, though one with moral superiority, based on its connection to the preservation of justice. Like the order for colonial processions, Chanvalon emphasized the role of law and order (including public safety) as a complement to military power as expressed by local troops. The conseil's magnanimous dispersal of justice without any expectation for payment did, however, form a superior kind of charity and public service. Furthermore, the conseil magistrates offered their services for the common good of the community, though it was limited to those who would claim legal assistance. Those who participated in judicial arbitration via the conseils, then, counted as part of an orderly and legal community that chose discussion over arms.

In the Indian Ocean territories, conseillers similarly defended themselves as guardians of justice in contrast to ostensible metropolitan malpractice in their writings to Marine officials. In 1768, one conseiller wrote to the minister of the Marine to confirm that members of the Île de France conseil would likewise "administer [justice] freely" without any fees (épices) and that the courts would not incur more expenses than absolutely necessary.[94] Like Chanvalon, Ribes highlighted the ideal of an impartial judiciary, freed from the constraints of venality. Mascarene conseils did not, however, exhibit the same kind of sustained local advocacy that Chanvalon epitomized in his longer argument. Though commentators like Ribes emphasized the ability of colonial jurists to follow French (and perhaps even universal) standards of impartiality and justice, they did so with a stronger emphasis on a metropolitan *audience* and their own experience in metropolitan courts, like the Paris Parlement, and administration. Both Antillean and Mascarene writers criticized metropolitan jurisprudence, but in a manner that supported, rather than undermined, a concept of a common legal culture by claiming that colonial jurists understood the principles of French jurisprudence even better than jurists in France.

Mascarene conseillers made arguments different from those of Antillean conseillers to achieve the same ends, a pattern that emerged from contrasts in the background and experience of Mascarene conseil members. Mascarene conseillers were most often named from the merchant elite rather than from the planter class that dominated Antillean conseils. Didier de Saint-Martin became the director of commerce on Île de France in 1737, and nearly all his sons went to work for the French East India Company. His daughter married a company director. He also served on the Île Bourbon conseil, starting in 1742 as one of the first council members and the island's munitions guard, and then became governor of the island in 1746.

Saint-Martin excelled at managing colonial trade and had experience in the conseil by the time he became governor. In contrast to the ample military background common among the Antillean elite, he apparently lacked military experience. He finally returned to France in 1749, where he became a royal secretary working on finance and eventually a *syndic* (manager) for the Compagnie des Indes orientales.[95] He and Rheims Rose were both intensely involved in colonial trade throughout the Indian Ocean, but they also took time to administer justice in the local settings of the Île Bourbon conseil. Their expertise in the region and in French commerce illustrate the dominance of a colonial merchant elite in dominating conseil membership in the Indian Ocean. Like Chanvalon and other Antillean conseillers, however, Mascarene magistrates emphasized their local expertise when writing to metropolitan audiences, citing their judicial careers and involvement in colonial enterprise to recommend reforms and offer advice to the Marine.

In the Mascarenes, having personal connections to the islands made a big difference for metropolitan residents like Guérin who sought employment abroad. Conseils were similarly composed of a tightly interlocked elite, but commercial expertise tended to be valued over connections to prominent creole families, who were much less numerous. Rheims Rose's career as conseiller and négociant contrasted with the linear career of Pierre Félix Barthélemy David, the Île de France governor, who had transitioned directly from postings in Senegal to Île de France. Instead, Rose's track record marked a more starburst-like pattern of trading interests that fanned out from a central point at Île de France. Rose and David both corresponded extensively with metropolitan authorities, however, especially the Ministry of the Marine, through whose records pieces of their life stories survive.

Magistrates tended to acquire their conseil appointments after establishing themselves as planters or merchants. But clerks more often sought out conseil posts as a means of getting *into* the colonial elite. Though clerks (greffiers) worked part-time, like the conseillers, the position paid well enough to attract substantial interest across France's colonial empire. In Martinique, greffiers lived in "a modest obscurity," but they collected at least ten thousand livres a year—more than double the salary of four thousand livres per year claimed by Claude-Samout Du Tillet, an Île de France greffier (and even then he earned that sum only after he won a judgment by the Île de France conseil).[96] The office of greffier could thus bring a lucrative salary to those who could convince Marine officials to nominate them.

It could also be a prerequisite for more important positions. Jean André de Ribes began his colonial career as the chief greffier in Île de France in 1754, then became a conseiller in 1763 and finally the conseil's attorney general in 1766.[97] Greffiers were also held in high esteem as members of the white colonial elite, as their position included guarding and maintaining the official colonial records (greffes) rather than just creating them, as scribes or secretaries.[98] The office of greffier, perhaps more than any other nonmilitary office, was a position that granted the possibility of upward mobility within the imperial hierarchy for colonial employees who did not have outside connections through legal expertise (like the lawyers) or local economic expertise (like the planter magistrates).

Clerks who did go to the Indian Ocean often negotiated employment directly with the conseils rather than via metropolitan correspondence. In the conseil reorganization of 1767, Du Tillet was given a royal appointment as greffier in chief, while a man named Jean Lousteau was hired to act as his subordinate (*commis greffier*). Du Tillet had previously made his income by organizing the conseil records and creating legal documents (the latter presumably mimicking a notary's profession), for which he charged fees. He objected to the new legal regime, however, as it would require him to share his income with his new assistant, who would be paid entirely out of the overall greffe income.[99]

Rather than the dispute being resolved informally, it became rancorous enough for the Île de France conseil supérieur, in Port Louis, to take it on as an official case.[100] Du Tillet and Lousteau were both very unhappy with this arrangement. Du Tillet complained that there was not enough total income for him to make a living, much less to share it with Lousteau. He also requested that the cost of drawing up sales documents be fixed at a fee of 3 or 4 percent and demanded the right to decide the commis greffier's functions and to receive the primary benefit of the payments. Lousteau responded that of the four thousand livres that were at stake (as the overall income), he had only received a commission of thirty-two livres over the previous two months and had sunk even lower financially after taking an official trip to France.[101] The court ruled in Lousteau's favor in terms of payment but left the management of the office to Du Tillet. Du Tillet could still take the four thousand livres plus two-thirds of the émoluments, while Lousteau received the final third. The conseil supérieur in Port Louis ruled that it was not a significant enough matter to quash the ruling of the conseil and that it would instead write to Jean Guillaume de Steinhauer, the temporary governor, and Poivre to make this judgment happen. Unfortunately, Du Tillet died only two years later and was replaced by Lousteau. Conseil personnel were thus so important to the constitution of local colonial governance that their own matters became part of official conseil business.

French residents did sometimes turn down employment in the colonies as greffiers. When they did, they cited the remoteness of colonies— especially in the Indian Ocean—in contrast to the bustle of Paris, which was where most of the personnel who immigrated to overseas colonies to join the conseils came from. In 1787, a Sieur Ricatte was nominated to fill a vacant position of greffier in the Île de France sénéchaussée (the type of regional law court directly below a conseil), but he declined the offer and cited his wife and three children as the reason he did not want to leave Paris. Instead, he suggested a peer (unnamed) of the same age but single and an experienced lawyer, with family connections and expertise through his father (a secretary of state) and brother (a Paris notary).[102] Ricatte's decision to turn down the possibility of lucrative work in the Indian Ocean out of concern for his family matches Bernardin de Saint-Pierre's observations in 1768 that few families had migrated to the Mascarenes and that the white population consisted mostly of unmarried young men. Conseil employment, like military service, appears to have been favored by young men who saw these opportunities as a way to make their fortunes.[103]

The existence of other courts, including lower jurisdictions, only strengthened this pattern by creating demand for additional personnel. Once admitted to the legal system, such personnel could be assigned to vacant positions in upper courts. While administrators increasingly favored employees with legal training, availability often won out over expertise. Guadeloupean administrators during the era of the Seven Years' War had particular difficulty. An exasperated intendant wrote in 1764, "Here it is not easy to find subjects as needed to fill the vacated places on the Conseil Supérieur. Currently, there are several colonists in France who are studying law. They make me hopeful that they will not delay in returning. I will choose the most capable, and I will have the honor to suggest them to you." The intendant articulated the court's desire for formal metropolitan legal training—a skill increasingly desired by the second half of the eighteenth century—but supported (with some ambivalence) the hands-on experience of legal personnel across ranks. The same correspondence proposed a man named Moustier as magistrate, as he had served the conseil in the capacity of registrar (greffier) since 1756.[104]

Conseils acted as staging grounds for colonial administration as it expanded to accommodate rising caseloads or new subject populations. Personnel who initially worked in small courts of first instance such as sièges royaux or juridictions often switched over to the conseils, bringing their expertise with them. After fifteen years of service on the lower court (juri-

diction) of the small community of Grande-Terre, Guadeloupe, a king's attorney named Lejean was promoted to the Guadeloupe conseil in 1767.
The request by the administrators for approval by the king's council also
noted the need for additional court personnel, as they had recently created
a second admiralty court on the island.[105]

In the Antilles, local experience in several courts and colonies fostered the careers of personnel who could advocate for clients and family at
home and in France. Charles Ponce Vivant Dognon lived in the Guadeloupe dependency of Marie-Galante in 1778 when he wrote to the navy minister, the marquis de Castries, to request financial and legal help for his sick
and paralytic uncle. Dognon had been called upon because his career included positions as a lawyer in Martinique's conseil and sénéchaussée. He
later requested a job as substitute king's attorney in Grenada but noted that
his French legal expertise would apply only once the English laws previously enforced were replaced.[106]

Metropolitan residents of France were surprisingly aware of vacant
offices in the colonies and wrote frequently to the Marine to request com-
missions in the Antilles and Mascarenes. In 1770, François Auguste Ladreyt
requested the job of greffier in chief for a local jurisdiction (siège royal) in
Grand-Terre, Guadeloupe. He wrote to the minister of the marine, the duc
de Praslin, to request the title of greffier in chief as well as the privileges and
wages attached to that title. In addition, he asked for payment for his passage on one of the king's vessels to Guadeloupe.[107] Ladreyt noted that the
office had been vacant for several years and cited the Guadeloupe intendant, the baron de Moissac, and a Sieur De Cassassus Du Mont as his supporters. Ladreyt had previously served as a *conseiller secret greffier* for a
Saint-Prival in Vivaraix, a small region between Lyon and Marseille.[108]

He had not been paid for this job since 1756, however, so he was willing to search for employment as far away as the Antilles.[109] Ladreyt's awareness of this opening, presumably through patronage and kinship networks,
reveals a wide range of information sharing that made it possible to find out
about and benefit from this employment. Ladreyt had both located and se-
cured references in the Antilles, indicating that he had worked on his own
to become a part of transatlantic communication chains.

In 1783, the Paris Parlement lawyer Pierre Barbe Cullet de Pugieu requested employment as a magistrate (conseiller) in any of the "conseils souverains" of India. Metropolitan lawyers also turn up in such far-flung locales as Senegal, where one Sieur Marcel of the Nancy Parlement became a clerk for the colonial government in 1786.[110] Conseil postings were highly sought by newly wealthy plantation owners and merchants who wanted political clout to match their economic status, especially as a means of developing metropolitan ties that could help their sons get into the best Jesuit schools and law schools and set up their daughters to make strategic marriages. Over time, these choices enabled both Continental and creole families to enmesh themselves into a global French legal culture in which they increasingly held political sway as members of the conseil magistrature.

Conclusion

This global circulation of legal experts reinforced institutional commonalities among legal entrepôts with personal networks that included face-to-face interactions as well as written correspondence. Conseil personnel performed very similar roles whether in the Atlantic or the Indian Ocean, but the conseils were anchored very firmly in their local contexts, whether the more politically conscious plantocracy of the Antilles or the more commercially aligned Mascarene personnel. A wide range of elites—both local and metropolitan—came together through their association with the conseils. Though these patterns mark an increasing assertion of autonomy on the part of colonial elites and rifts between self-styled local and metropolitan factions, an investigation of the composition of French colonial courts actually reveals a more complicated network of local elites that stretched down into the nonelite levels of society (including the slaves who helped the bailiffs) as well as up into the highest levels of royal court society at Versailles (through correspondence with Marine ministers).

Kinship, especially local kinship, mattered in both the Atlantic and the Indian Ocean contexts. Conseil members relied on a tight network of creole families who backed their local experience and history on the islands with the legal expertise they developed through metropolitan education.

Many conseil employees had been admitted to the Paris bar and even the Paris Parlement but chose to practice law in the colonial conseils where they could also take part in plantation agriculture and trade. Family networks and patronage created opportunities for employment in the colonies as well as metropolitan France. For Mascarene and Antillean personnel, the metropole acted as a central station for information exchange and a node of political power that connected to their smaller regional networks. In the Antilles, wealthy planters such as Périnelle-Dumay were increasingly influential as their families occupied conseil offices for generations, while personnel careers and connections in the Indian Ocean show slightly different patterns that depended more upon occupation than family ties.

In both regions, legal knowledge (especially that gained in metropolitan courts) was highly valued and conserved by the clerks and lay practitioners who crafted legal documents. Legal knowledge was created in colonial communities through a cyclical pattern in which court participants gathered for monthly sessions and then were dispersed back into daily routines.[111] Court meetings attracted colonial residents to these specific sites, the palais de justice, but upon the completion of court proceedings those residents were dispersed back into the streets of colonial capitals, into rural agricultural regions, and even out into the wider reaches of the French Empire and beyond as they boarded ships to leave the islands. Conversations about legal matters and ideas about law were brought to bear most intensely in court sessions, but the pattern of court meetings meant that litigants as well as magistrates participated in frequent and expected conversations.

Conseils were strategically located within that process to receive cases from people moving in both directions: from the rural plantation areas and from the maritime sources of trade goods, information, and new people. The colonial societies of the Antilles and the Mascarenes were focused on rural agricultural production of cash crops, but the conseils attracted rural residents to colonial capitals to contend with and deliberate on legal matters. Cash crops were pushed toward colonial capitals and port cities and into global markets, but so, too, were ideas about law as colonial residents stopped at local courts to air grievances and give testimony.

Justice Between Plantation and Port

ON THE NIGHT of 7–8 May 1752, a fire burned parts of Saint-Pierre in Martinique. In the week following, conseillers called an extraordinary session of the Martinican court to punish the perpetrators. Magistrates quickly blamed a slave conspiracy for the conflagration. They charged a mixed-race enslaved woman named Nanette as the ringleader, having found her setting fire to the house of a local resident the morning after the blaze. Nanette tried to single out a boat master named Jean Brisson. Brisson, in turn, accused Nanette in such detail that the conseil was quickly convinced of her guilt. The court immediately interrogated her in the middle of the night. Nanette refused to explain why she had allegedly set the fire, so they forced her to endure judicial torture (*la question préalable*). Nevertheless, she persisted in her claim of innocence. Unconvinced, the conseil sentenced her to be burned alive among the charred houses of Saint-Pierre.[1]

On the night of 24 February 1775, a fire scorched the Île de France plantation region of Flacq, directly east of the capital, Port Louis. Investigators identified three soldiers from the Port Louis regiment as the arsonists, naming them "true criminals" ("les vrais criminels"), a phrase that warned of villainous, incorrigible character. In little over a month, the island's administrators announced that they had completed an initial investigation, lower court ruling, and appeal. Ruling together because lower courts could not prescribe the death penalty, the juridiction and conseil prescribed a punishment that was both gruesome and symbolic. The chief criminal identified by the administrators, François Desperron, was burned alive after having been exposed on the rack for an hour on 11 October. His two accomplices, Baron and Abel, were hanged the next day.[2]

As in the Nanette case, speed and symbolism were the defining traits of these criminal proceedings. Criminal proceedings, unlike civil cases, did not always require extensive documentation gathered from interested parties who lived in many different parts of France's empire. Instead, testimony could be gathered from a few witnesses and confessions could be extracted from defendants using judicial torture.[3] Criminal cases hinged on questions about local conditions and security, so administrators felt justified in using extraordinary means of punishment quickly. The governor and the intendant, Charles d'Arsac de Ternay and Jacques Maillart Du Mesle, signed a report after the punishment, explaining: "We regard [it] as very happy" that it was possible to uncover the people who committed such an "abominable" crime and to make a "striking" (*frappant*) example of them.[4] The administrators reported their actions to the Marine, but they did not request approval for them. The volatility of colonial societies, with large numbers of slaves and soldiers, created incentives for magistrates to make clear decisions about what crimes would and would not be tolerated and to punish them memorably. Conseil sessions in Île de France and Martinique following these fires capture conseil administrators in motion as they gathered accused subjects into the palais de justice for summary judgment.

Striking in their similarity, these cases illustrate the multistep rituals of capital punishment that enforced mastery over slaves in Atlantic and Indian Ocean slave societies. Fluid, but similar, notions of public and private space shaped the way subjects understood their position within France's global empire. Legal personnel such as town criers and posters of broadsides were not the only colonial subjects who testified to the law's content. So, too, did convicted criminals, most often through public executions and associated symbolic performances.

In wider usage, the concept of publicity was associated with crime as a factor that rendered crimes more deserving of punishment, and so publicized crimes were understood to deserve publicized punishments.[5] European colonial legal systems frequently required sentences to be read aloud at various points in a prisoner's trek from the jail or courthouse to the gallows or executioner's block. Criminal law in Demerara, a Dutch colony ceded to the British in the early nineteenth century, required that all criminal "sentences shall be pronounced to the prisoner in the first instance, in the presence of the accuser and with open doors, and again at the place of execution, to the end that the cause of the aforesaid execution may be known to every one, and serve as an example to all."[6] This language mirrored the sentencing statement of the Rennes (Bretagne) Parlement acquitting Pitre Paul of all polygamy charges: "The prison doors will be open to him, if he is ever returned there for any other reason."[7]

Between the global array of French territories navigated by subjects and individual judicial entrepôts laid out by administrators, most French subjects traversed a set of concentric circles of authority that were centered on the conseils supérieurs and their parlement counterparts. These nested spaces originated in each conseil's *chambre de greffe*, a designated room for storing the court's registers (greffes), but radiated out into the courtroom spaces for deliberation, then into town streets, and finally to each territory's limits. Adhesion to the conseils supérieurs in terms of membership (as magistrates) and proximity (as witnesses and bystanders) signified access to justice and a symbolic association with it. Mandatory movement away from the conseils, in the form of punishments, could conversely render a subject incrementally alien from the civil society guaranteed by justice as upheld by the conseils. In extreme punishments, such as execution and banishment, subjects could be alienated entirely from a France's ancien régime empire in all its territorial and jurisdictional iterations.

This chapter untangles these concentric circles of authority by examining negotiations between court participants and magistrates through conseil proceedings. It first lays out Antillean and Mascarene legal circuits. It then turns to Antillean entrepôts, where sedition case studies from Martinique provide a lens for exploring how court participants negotiated these nested spaces. This evidence demonstrates that, as in metropolitan France, litigants and magistrates pushed and pulled against symbolic and legal boundaries that were initially defined by the physical configurations of the conseils described above. Cases regarding speech crimes, such as sedition, blasphemy, and slander, were common throughout early modern France and its empire, particularly as reputation often determined a person's economic and community power. Court participants, whether litigants or magistrates, who entered the conseil *audience* (meeting) generally agreed to abide by the court's rules as governed by the magistrates, which embodied French jurisprudence symbolically (through the physical setting and authority of magistrates) and practically (as colonial laws were enforced and created).[8]

Next, it turns to three Mascarene agents—Rheims Rose, Louis Filet, and Marie Elisabeth Sobobobié-Betty—to illuminate predominant circuits among and within Indian Ocean entrepôts. Scholars of early modern France have amply examined patronage at the royal and aristocratic levels to explore how reciprocal exchanges shaped the emergence of a modern nation-state in both its national and its imperial forms.[9] The ups and downs that characterized the high-profile careers of European colonial administrators, such as Dupleix and Hastings in South Asia, have long generated debates about the nature of political power in the greater Indian Ocean.[10] More recently, French Atlanticists have revisited classic examples of political winners and losers to explore how overseas projects refracted, and sometimes devoured, the designs of imperial and national architects, such as Nicolas Fouquet and Jean-Baptiste Colbert.[11] These Indian Ocean cases, however, broaden this extant literature considerably by showing that legal negotiations conducted in imperial institutions encompassed a much wider range of participants, whose actions greatly affected how those institutions functioned.

Atlantic Entrepôts and Circuits

Martinique's conseil loomed the largest among the early modern conseils. It became one of the oldest and busiest courts. It also became the best-documented conseil. Even in the eighteenth century, Martinican magistrates such as Jacques Petit de Viévigne and Pierre Dessalles were writing their own legal history, emphasizing the Martinican conseil as the island's chief legal institution. Some Antillean families, notably the Dessalles, composed successive histories of the island well into the nineteenth century and emphasized their legal expertise as conseil magistrates.[12] By the mid-eighteenth century, metropolitan writers had noticed this development, too.

Diderot and d'Alembert's *Encyclopédie*, originally published from 1751 to 1772, described only Martinique's conseil supérieur among the colonial courts.[13]

Other factors enabled Martinique to stand out among French Antillean colonies. The seventeenth-century travel writer Du Tertre noted Martinique's favorable position among the islands in the Antillean chain, as it avoided most hurricanes, which tended to track northward. Contemporary historian Bernard Moitt has emphasized Martinique's defensive role (having a major fort), economic strength (as the first stop for slave ships), and administrative status (as capital of the Antilles, then the Windward Islands).[14] The Martinican conseil was thus well situated as a key institution for legal matters related to the military and commerce throughout the region.

As *Encyclopédie* readers might learn, the conseil was the sovereign court (*tribunal*) of Martinique, sitting at Fort Royal, which was the military and administrative capital. The conseil, according to this article, contained a typical French law court in miniature, with a uniquely strong representation of military officers. Twelve conseillers, one attorney general (procureur général), and two *lieutenants du roi*, who all had a deliberative voice (voix déliberative) in the court, were accompanied by the governor-general for the French (Caribbean) islands and Martinique's governor. In French colonies, unlike British colonies, governors were Marine officers, not civilians. Early conseil meetings demonstrated the military origins of Caribbean colonization: the governor presided over ten members chosen by the king from among militia officers. By 1713, the Martinique conseil included eleven acting magistrates (conseillers titulaires) and five conseillers honoraires (semi-retired).[15] The court was set up to render justice to all French subjects in the colony, and nomination by the king was meant to counteract venality (or the buying and selling of offices).[16] The conseil was required to meet once a month to render justice freely, a mandate that was meant to enable all colonial residents (except for slaves) to enter complaints rather than just a few elite planters.

The Martinican conseil met in Fort Royal from 1678, and later in Saint-Pierre, in borrowed or rented houses, until the intendant leased a house in 1722 and designated it for conseil meetings. A total of around eight to twelve members, composed of magistrates (conseillers) and royal administrators (gens du roi), traveled in to meet every one or two months, sometimes staying in the meeting house. Guadeloupe's conseil shared this configuration, as did the rest of the conseils.[17]

A consistent configuration made it easy for conseils to trade judicial personnel: from at least 1727, Guadeloupe and Martinique had an agreement to admit each other's conseillers reciprocally as equivalent sovereign courts. The number of conseil members had not been well determined in the mid-seventeenth century, but tended to hover around eight from this period onward.[18] By 1713, the number of conseillers had risen to sixteen, but the configuration remained the same.[19] By 1768, a royal edict established the Martinique conseil with a governor-general and an intendant presiding, four military officers, fourteen conseillers (titulaires), one attorney general (procureur général), four substitute magistrates (assesseurs), and one greffier.[20] Though the composition of conseils changed over time to account for the ebb and flow of conseil business and local idiosyncracies, these examples are typical for conseils throughout France's overseas empire.[21]

Fort Royal's main military garrison jutted out from a rocky outcrop into the island's largest bay, known as Cul-de-Sac. Located on the leeward side of the island (away from the Atlantic, facing the Caribbean), the town occupied a strategic position for observing maritime traffic, of French and other ships, that tended to favor the calmer winds of the Caribbean side of the Antilles. The main garrisons at Fort Royal, Caze Pilote, and Saint-Pierre formed a chain of military bases from south to north on Martinique's western coastline, so word could be passed up from one to another (via cabotage, or short-distance maritime transit, and a main road that connected the towns) in the event of a foreign attack. Only fifty miles to the north of Martinique, Guadeloupe lay within not-too-distant reach along this coastal route. Most ships seem to have arrived in Martinique from the south, so it made sense to fortify Fort Royal the most as protection against the more vulnerable and more valuable trading center of Saint-Pierre to the north.

These defensive concerns factored into where colonial administrators lived, especially the governor (a military office) and, consequently, into the location of the conseils. In all of France's overseas territories, new settlements were often initially built outward from military fortifications, but over time the conseils gained centrality as physical sites that guided the movement of subjects through and within colonial and provincial capitals.[22] Conseils supérieurs were based in these fortified urban settings, meeting most often in designated buildings, known as the *palais de justice*, which housed each colony's registers (greffes) and often a prison.[23] Though Martinique's conseil initially met in a palais de justice in Saint-Pierre, in 1692 it moved approximately twenty miles south to Fort Royal, where the Antilles' governor-general and the seat of military governance had moved in 1678.[24] This previous move of the governor-general and conseil to Fort Royal seems to have been prompted by its favorable position, especially after the successful defense of the area in 1674 against a Dutch fleet commanded by Admiral de Ruyter.[25]

Royal representatives were important and consistent contributors to conseil practices. The core of colonial governance, including the site of courts, depended upon the location of key colonial administrators. These included the governor and the intendant and their panel of conseil magistrates, whose presence was essential to the embodiment, as representatives of the king, and the functioning, through adjudication of cases, in each palais de justice, where court proceedings were held.[26] Intendants frequently oversaw conseil sessions, presiding over the deliberations, while governors participated as the king's representative in the colonies.

A variation in authority stemmed from the continuing negotiation of precedence among conseil members, especially the intendant and the governor. Royal policy also changed over time. The governor-general of the colonies was supposed to preside over the Martinique conseil as the king's representative, which gave a regional as well as local dimension to the proceedings. In the case of his absence the intendant or the most senior magistrate could pronounce sentences after having collected the responses of the other members.[27] Governors managed fortifications, including the buildings that housed the conseils. An administration organized around governors also preceded the implementation of an intendant system. Martinique's founder, Pierre Belain d'Esnambuc, managed the colony as governor from the 1630s, while its first intendant, Jean-Baptiste Patoulet, was only appointed for the Antilles in 1679.[28] In practice, however, intendants had more power by administering justice as part of their direct mandate to enforce laws concerning finance and police (the intendant's other areas of authority).

In Martinique and Île de France, the intendant had the power to call extraordinary conseil meetings (*séances extraordinaires*), most often to judge long or complicated cases—especially for crimes—that could not be dealt with during regular court proceedings. In the early decades of colonization in Martinique, he could do this by himself, but from 1718 to 1766, he needed the cooperation of the governors-general. After that, he could again call conseil meetings himself.

Mascarene Entrepôts and Circuits

In the Indian Ocean, judicial structures (and the colonial economy) developed like those in the Atlantic, but at a slightly later pace. Unlike Martinique and Guadeloupe, which had thriving inns due to the busy influx of sailors, traders, and other visitors, the Mascarenes were more isolated, so they received fewer visitors and thus did not have any inns even as late as 1770. Upon arriving in Île Bourbon in 1770, Bernardin de Saint-Pierre learned that "there was no inn at Saint-Denis, nor anywhere else on the island, and that strangers usually lodged with those inhabitants with whom they were doing business." He was forced to seek refuge in the home of a local military officer (Figure 6).[29]

The administration of the Mascarenes by the Compagnie des Indes orientales until 1767 meant that the government of these islands was outsourced to officials who were under the jurisdiction of the company. This company government was based in Pondichéry, India, until 1789, but was always directly administered by royal appointees.[30] Like the Antillean colonies, the Mascarenes were put directly under French law when they became royal colonies in 1767 after having been managed by the company. All conseils (and all parlements) had a mandate to register new laws in their greffes but were given the ability to delay registration and publication of those laws as long as the governors and intendants consented. They could also create their own laws, to be registered alongside royal ordinances in the court's

Figure 6. *Vue du Grand Chemin des Pamplemousses, Île de France* (Milbert), 1812, Wikimedia Commons, British Library

registers.[31] Unlike Martinique and Guadeloupe, the Mascarenes were subjugated to the conseil supérieur at Pondichéry, where the governor-general presided over all French establishments in the Indian Ocean.[32]

Île Bourbon's history has paralleled Martinique's for nearly four hundred years, from its founding to its current status as the overseas department La Réunion.[33] Situated in the Indian Ocean off the coast of Madagascar and not far from the island of Île de France, Île Bourbon came under French dominion in 1638, only three years after Martinique. Like Martinique, it was transferred to a company in 1664, the Compagnie des Indes orientales, and it developed an economy based on sugar and coffee.[34] Île Bourbon has not, however, been subjected to nearly the amount of historical scrutiny that Martinique has, despite the existence of excellent records from the eighteenth century.[35]

Île Bourbon had a provincial conseil from March 1711 to November 1729, when it was replaced by a conseil supérieur, which met on Île Bourbon at Saint-Paul but had jurisdiction over both of the Mascarene islands until Île de France got its own conseil supérieur in 1734, and the seat of government was moved there soon after. In 1767 (based on an ordinance from 1766), Île Bourbon's conseil became judicial only, losing its previous administrative privileges, though in practice the conseil continued both functions until 1791.[36] During company rule, conseillers and other officials (like governors) were nominated by the company, but in accordance with royal laws.[37] Île Bourbon's conseil included the local governor or commander, six conseillers (of whom one answered directly to the intendant), a prosecutor and substitute, four assesseurs, and a greffier.

Early on, the Île Bourbon conseil was located in Saint-Denis, where the *gouverneur particulier* resided, and met in his house. As in Port Louis, few buildings were built of stone—only the main fortifications and a battery. Behind the town lay a large plain known as the Champ de Lorraine.[38] Conseil registers from this era report on the construction of a defensive palisade and emphasize the obligation of local inhabitants to defend their property from attackers. Such town and property boundaries were crudely policed; extensive discussions survive concerning the need to brand cattle to identify and certify their owners.[39]

By the mid-eighteenth century, however, Île Bourbon's larger land mass had attracted a population that surpassed Île de France's, as more and more people (especially slaves) worked on the slightly larger island to develop the new and growing plantation economy. This pattern makes Île Bourbon more comparable to Guadeloupe, which was similarly more suited to large-scale agriculture than its neighbor Martinique but tended to be more isolated because it was less desirable as a trading entrepôt.[40] Île Bourbon residents sought to overcome their isolation through trading relationships. Residents of Île Bourbon were most often tied to French cities, such as Lyon and Saint-Mâlo, that had long-standing ties to East Indian trade for such commodities as spices and fabric. Pierre Poivre, intendant of Île de France and Île Bourbon from 1767 to 1772, was tied most closely to Lyon, where you can still walk down a street named after him. His correspondence indicates that Île Bourbon's administrators perceived their island as constantly under threat.[41] This was a common worry in Caribbean islands, too.[42]

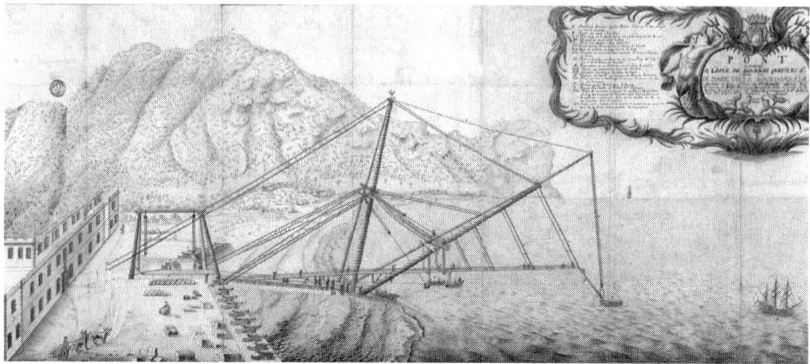

Figure 7. *Saint-Denis, Île Bourbon Bridge,* 1738, Gallica, Bibliothèque nationale de France

Île Bourbon's development has been limited by its large volcano, the Piton de la Fournaise, in the island's southeastern quadrant. In the eighteenth century, the volcano erupted almost every year. Unsurprisingly, the island's two main towns, Saint-Denis and Saint-Paul, hugged the northwestern coastline directly opposite the volcano on an island that is just thirty miles wide.[43] Urban development also proceeded slowly because of Île Bourbon's more rounded coastline, with few inlets and no favorable harbor. With very steep shores, access to Saint-Denis (the largest town) depended upon an eighty-foot-long drawbridge that enabled anchored ships to unload. Everywhere else, arriving passengers had to jump into the water to land (Figure 7).[44]

The Île de France conseil met in Port Louis and included a similar configuration of six conseillers (only slightly smaller than Martinique's typical eight to ten), as well as the intendant, governor, attorney general, substitute prosecutor, four assesseurs and one clerk (greffier). Several military lieutenants also served on the conseil to act on behalf of the governor.[45] According to a 1766 arrêt, at least five conseillers had to be present to render a decision, seven if it was a criminal case.[46] These patterns of conseil personnel match the requirements for the Antilles almost exactly, indicating that the structure of colonial justice was uniform across the Atlantic and Indian Ocean sugar islands.

Île Bourbon's dominance as the center of Mascarene government ended in 1735, when it was subordinated to Île de France upon the arrival of a new governor.[47] Île de France had a good natural harbor on its western edge, where French colonists established the main town of Port Louis. In this respect, it resembled Martinique, whose Cul-de-Sac harbor sheltered the military and (eventually) political capital at Fort Royal. The population of Port Louis developed slowly but was encouraged by its proximity to the island's primary planting region, known as Pamplemousses, just to the northeast.[48] The other major town, Grand Port, on the island's southeastern edge, also had a good port that ships sometimes used. The Dutch had settled at Grand Port as one of the first inhabited places on the island. Prevailing winds to the southeast, however, made it easy to get into but nearly impossible to get out of, so French colonists favored Port Louis.[49]

The Port Louis community was centered around a public square, where people met to gossip several times a day. In 1768, the year after royal governance was established, a visitor noted that Port Louis was known as "the Camp" and that it "has scarcely the appearance of a village." The town was backed by high rocky (volcanic) mountains that were bare of any vegetation, except for a bit of burnt grass that grew for about six months every year. An indifferent stream ran through the town, but its water could not be drunk. More unpleasant, however, was the ground, "bristling with rocks" over which it was "hard not to trip and break your neck." Port Louis's one-story buildings were mostly constructed of wood, with each building surrounded by a palisade along streets set up along a grid pattern. Few fortifications existed besides the main fort at the center and entrance to the town (on the shore side) and a battery across the harbor.[50]

The 1768 visitor, a naturalist and engineer named Jacques-Henri Bernardin de Saint-Pierre, explained that most white Europeans on the island were unmarried. He cited a number of reasons for this phenomenon, including a lack of fortune (on the part of men and women), a desire to make a fortune and then return to France to marry, and above all because the men easily found enslaved concubines. Thus, this young and unattached population found ample time to chat around the public square.[51] Work by architectural historians in the Anglophone Caribbean, building on research done by Virginia historians and archaeologists, has suggested that the immediate goal of cash-crop profits led many Europeans to construct impermanent buildings on purpose. This short-term building agenda was moderated, however—especially in the Caribbean—by the need for hurricane-resistant structures, a severe challenge for Mascarene builders as well.[52]

Antillean Sedition Cases

The setting of conseil deliberations in a specially designated building did not guarantee the tranquillity of court proceedings. Instead, courtrooms could become sites of unscheduled confrontations among colonial residents, breaking up the orderly process of hearings during conseil sessions.[53] In 1718, a Guadeloupean named La Grange was brought before a special criminal hearing by the Martinique conseil supérieur on the accusation that he had made seditious speeches against the king.[54] Though an initial court hearing had charged him a fine of five hundred livres to be paid to the king, he was later interrogated in prison (and likely tortured) and then brought before the special conseil session. While the magistrates interrogated him, La Grange sat on a special seat called a *sellette* for accused persons. In contemporary usage, the sellette was understood as a place in which someone was forced to give up secrets, surrounded by conseillers and onlookers.[55] When the magistrates emphasized that he was "punished according to the ordinances" of French law, they linked the laws specifically to the person of La Grange as mediated through the essential space of the courtroom, confirmed and witnessed by court attendees and magistrates.

La Grange's public punishment was not confined to the Fort Royal palais de justice. Rather, it marked the first in a series of corrections that would acknowledge his misdeeds to an increasingly wide audience of French subjects. He was taken to a public area on the Fort Royal shoreline, where he was equipped with signs to wear on his front and back that said "seditious [person] and disturber of the public peace."[56] The area was known as "le carénage," the part of the port where ships were careened to be cleaned and repaired. Fort Royal was one of the most important French military installations and a regional capital in the Atlantic region, so this part of the town would always have been full of people. Next, La Grange was to be beaten and flayed in public, then ensconced in the pillory for two hours in Fort Royal, then pilloried in the nearby towns of Caze Pilote (where he had originally uttered the seditious words) and Saint-Pierre, before finally being banished in perpetuity from the French islands.

The court relied upon both its own members and the members of subsidiary courts, including local jurisdictions, to accomplish its judgments. The judgment specified that this order would be executed under the auspices (*à la diligence*) of the substitute prosecutors general, each in his local jurisdiction. It also required that the ruling be read, published, and affixed in all the quarters of the island under the management of the conseil's attorney general, an action he would then certify to the court as soon as possible (*au premier jour*).[57] The conseil empowered several of its members to ensure that La Grange was adequately punished by having them travel to the places of punishment and report back to the conseil. Conseil magistrates also engaged the services of lower court officials to personally extend the public's awareness of La Grange's punishment to residents of nearby towns such as Caze Pilote, pushing both personnel from and information about the conseils farther and farther into the small towns and rural areas of Martinique, beyond the urban center of Fort Royal, concentrated at the palais de justice. Because they acted as nexuses between their rural, but agriculturally industrial, hinterlands and the global imperial networks that enabled cash crops to reach European markets, colonial capitals and the conseils that sat in their downtowns occupied a critical mediating space.

Publicity and spectacle were essential components of *all* judicial proceedings, not just executions for criminal cases and extraordinary proceedings, as Foucault emphasized with such examples as Damiens's attempted assassination of Louis XV in 1757. The conseil's response to La Grange's sedition culminated in banishment, not death. The banishment constituted a final step in a procession to a series of public spaces increasingly removed from the center of power at the palais de justice, rather than a concentration of spectators, royal representatives, and convicted criminals at a single spot.[58] This continuum of proximity to the conseils concerned French subjects most intensely at the empire's extremities in places that were paradoxically at the empire's heart economically though physically distant from the political capital of Paris. Colonies, above all Saint-Domingue, generated vast riches for absentee planters safely ensconced in and around Versailles, while smaller but more strategic hubs such as well-established Martinique in the Caribbean and the gateway to the Indies, Île de France, supplied strategic inroads to other areas.[59]

Colonial justice was negotiated on two levels within the palais de justice that defined public and private legal spaces: first in the *audience*, as litigants, onlookers, and magistrates heard and entered case evidence to the court and second in the *séance*, as the conseil members worked together (or in conflict) to deliver judgments and create new legislation. The greffier's report for André Chauton de Bordenave's case used the terms "audience" and "séance" somewhat interchangeably to describe the conseil's sessions in the palais de justice, but each term signified a different kind of deliberation. Here and in other court records the term "audience" tended to connote court proceedings that included everyone in attendance—plaintiffs, bailiffs, and onlookers in addition to the conseillers themselves. *Audiences* meant conseil meetings with an element of publicity as colonial residents, including nonelite whites and possibly even free passersby of color, heard and watched the proceedings. Bordenave's interruption of the conseil *audience* was interpreted as a transgression against the orderly negotiation of justice, which allowed community members to watch and participate in court proceedings, but only as long as they abided by a set of social rules that were set by the conseil magistrates.[60]

Though La Grange's case shows the conseil's desire to illustrate the consequences of public sedition to increasingly wider audiences of French subjects, a slightly later case shows that conseils tied punishments for disruptions within the conseil to the space itself through more private and specific sentences. In 1724, the Martinique conseil supérieur brought criminal proceedings against Bordenave for having disrupted their meetings.[61] According to an extract of the judgment (*sentence criminelle*), Bordenave had "several times disturbed the meeting of the jurisdiction," entering the courtroom uninvited and launching into loud tirades. His rants included several "speeches, derisions, and injurious words" aimed at both the judges and the people who had come to watch the court's proceedings.[62] Bordenave reserved the biggest insults for one member of the conseil, whom he had tried to force out of the meeting.[63] To further alarm the conseil and its attendants, he had also entered the palais de justice armed with a rifle and bayonet after having walked the streets of Fort Royal according to his own testimony (*confession*) preventing the bailiffs (huissiers) from arresting him. Several people in attendance stopped Bordenave, recognizing his "disagreeable character" ("mauvais caractère"), and prevented him from continuing to interrupt the meeting.

Bordenave confirmed his reputation as a disagreeable and meddlesome person by repeating his antics in other conseil meetings. Inside the courtroom, he directly rejected the authority of the conseil and undermined the solemnity of its proceedings, while his threatening behavior both inside and outside the courtroom challenged the colonial social order that the conseil (as a corporate unit of colonial government) represented and maintained through their rulings. The conseil embodied the extension of French law and judicial processes to the colonial setting of Fort Royal, in personnel and in the physical location of the palais de justice. His threats of violence created a challenge to this order within the Fort Royal community that erupted when Bordenave entered the conseil courtroom.

The conseillers tolerated (though by no means affirmed) the actions of Bordenave one or two times, but they responded decisively to his repeated interruptions with punishments that reset the order of conseil proceedings symbolically to reassert their power over him and (by extension) other court participants. In late 1724, the conseil issued a ruling on 6 October that required Bordenave to be "put back" (*reintegré*) into the royal prisons of Fort Royal by the bailiff. There he was forced to wait for more than a month until the first day of a special convocation of the conseil known as an *audience extraordinaire* to determine his fate. This meeting was one of the extraordinary conseil meetings that the intendant or governor could call under extenuating circumstances. Bordenave seems to have limited the number of cases the conseil could clear by throwing off the conseil meetings, so this special session defined the time and attention that he could claim and undermined his insistence on getting the conseil's attention when he wanted it.

The punishment also assured that Bordenave would participate in (and thus submit to) the reassertion of the conseil's authority. By 15 November, the conseil issued a criminal sentence, outlining the punishment that they had devised for him. At the *audience extraordinaire* he would be taken into the *chambre du greffe*, presumably in the palais de justice, in the presence of all of the officers of that jurisdiction, where he would be required to apologize, "unprotected and on his knees" ("découvert et à genoux"), and tell the officers in a loud and intelligible voice that he had "recklessly and inappropriately bothered" ("que temerairement et mal à propos il a troublé") the meeting of the jurisdiction and had neglected to give justice and its judges due respect by the words he had said (as noted in the deposition he gave), and that he repented and requested forgiveness from the siège. He was then required to give a statement (*procès verbal*) recorded in the register (greffe) of the jurisdiction by the greffier, whom the conseil also named as *commissaire* for carrying out this judgment (*arrêt*). Bordenave's punishment would also be entered into the conseil's record.

The conseil sentenced Bordenave to pay three hundred livres as a fine, which would be applied to the prisons of Fort Royal. In case of recidivism, he would be subject to corporal punishment and to pay the expenses for the criminal proceedings thereafter. For white colonial subjects, fines were the most frequent punishment, as they imposed the cost of judgment on the convicted person rather than on the colony. The judgment for more fines in the case of recidivism was meant to be a deterrent, while the addition of physical punishment indicated a higher degree of infraction. For enslaved people (and to a certain extent, free people of color) who did not generate their own income and were legally defined as chattel, fines were an irrelevant punishment, so for them physical retribution became the primary means of correction.[64]

The conseil chose to explain Bordenave's actions as a calculated act of resistance to colonial and imperial authority and a credible threat to law and order—not, as modern readers might expect, as the effects of mental instability or some other illness. The case summary's identification of both "judges" and "justice" as targets of Bordenave's rant indicates that the conseillers saw Bordenave's actions as affronts both to individual state representatives and to the wider colonial judicial system that their *audience* represented. By attacking conseillers in the palais de justice during a session, Bordenave's infraction went beyond the level of personal insult to a near-treasonous level of resistance against the conseil as a part of France's royal body politic.

The requirement for Bordenave to enter the chambre du greffe, a more private room within the palais de justice and the location of the conseil's registers (greffes), indicates the intensity of Bordenave's challenges to the conseil's authority as perceived by the court. Many early modern punishments carried an element of publicity to evoke shame for the punished and to promote good behavior by onlookers. Bordenave, however, was punished only in the presence of the magistrates whom he had insulted, not by a reconstitution of the conseil meeting that he had interrupted. The punishment also contrasted with the very public performance of his scenes in the conseil, undercutting his audacity by refusing to give him more access to a public venue. The conseillers reiterated their supremacy in physical terms by forcing Bordenave to apologize on his knees and uncovered, symbolically claiming their legal authority as the guardians of colonial law enshrined in the conseil greffes, which presumably lay on a table nearby. The court directed Bordenave to speak his confession in a "loud and intelligible voice," filling the space of the chambre de greffe with his guilty admission. This performance compensated for his previous loud and seditious words in the conseil meeting. This created an audience of witnesses to hear of Bordenave's guilt but limited his confession to those conseillers whom he had directly offended. The judgment's provision for corporal punishment in the case of recidivism added an element of increased publicity as a deterrent to future infractions.

Conseil greffes and other records imply that the majority of onlookers would have been other white elites (often referred to as "notables"), such as planters and merchants. It is almost certain, however, that a wider range of nonelites and probably free people of color and enslaved Africans would have been in the vicinity to overhear what transpired, as we know that different racial and economic groups tended to mix in colonial cities much more than in rural areas. Nonelites, including slaves, were also frequently defendants in criminal proceedings and sometimes witnesses. The 1685 Code Noir forbade slaves to participate in civil matters and as civil parties in criminal cases. It allowed witness testimony by enslaved people, however, if judges relied on such testimony solely as an aid to their investigations. Actual court practices tended to be more flexible. The preponderance of enslaved populations in these territories often made it nearly impossible to conduct criminal proceedings without reliance on enslaved testimony.[65] Bordenave's case indicates that conseil meetings tended to have audiences that were bigger than just the plaintiffs, defendants, and witnesses directly involved in litigation.

In contrast, the term "séance" connoted the deliberations of the conseil as it met to deliver a judgment on the cases it received. During their *séances*, the conseil members relied on their own knowledge of colonial law and experience in administering justice to guide their decisions, while in the *audiences*, the admission of evidence, testimony of litigants and witnesses, and informal influence of onlookers created a forum in which local ideas about justice were brought together with the expert professionals of the conseil members and the weight of precedent and legal prescription held by the greffes. Bordenave's punishment in a special conseil *séance* signified the conseil's reassertion of authority as the governing body that held both official authority (embodied in the conseil greffes) to rule on legal matters and informal power over social relationships that Bordenave questioned in his insults of conseil members. Manipulation of the public legal space of the *audience* by Bordenave prompted conseillers to ensure the integrity of the private space of the *séance* through specific punishment limited to an audience consisting of the conseil members (and symbolically to the law books sitting nearby).

Antillean cases sometimes spanned more than just the distance between a conseil and the shoreline. They, like their peripatetic plaintiffs, could travel from one conseil to another, especially within Antillean and Mascarene regions. Magdeleine Françoise, a mixed-race woman calling herself free ("se disant libre") had come to Martinique, accompanied by her two small children. She lodged with the innkeeper Madame Blot while she waited for a boat to take her and her children to Dominica, her home island.

Magdeleine Françoise had stayed for three days at the inn, where her presence was known publicly during this time. Blot repeated this point in her testimony as she sought to prove that Magdeleine Françoise had acted as a free person, not a fugitive slave.[66]

When the ship finally set sail for Dominica on 18 March 1776, Magdeleine Françoise left without any problem, followed by two slave women owned by Blot who had helped carry her children on board. Like many Antilleans, Magdeleine Françoise participated in the busy intercolonial traffic, known as cabotage, that included itinerant traders and other people who operated on the margins of several empires. This was a movement that supplemented the more familiar transatlantic and East Indian routes and often included illicit activity, like smuggling. These activities were frequently concentrated on islands like Dominica and Saint Lucia (to the north and south of Martinique, respectively) that regularly switched hands between empires and had smaller populations than established plantation societies like Martinique and Guadeloupe. Charges that Magdeleine Françoise was a fugitive slave would not have seemed totally out of place, then, as a well-known illicit traffic existed between Dominica and Martinique. Her travel would not have been altogether unprecedented, either, as magistrates were familiar with subjects who had been born on these islands under different rule, giving them citizenship that was sometimes English, sometimes French.

Several days after her departure, a man named Rivière came to Blot to reclaim Magdeleine Françoise. He asserted that he owned her, having bought her from her previous owner (named as Sieur Hellouin). Blot the innkeeper attempted to answer his questions about Magdeleine Françoise's whereabouts, and he left apparently satisfied with her replies. Blot emphasized in her testimony that she had ended the conversation without ascribing anything to Magdeleine Françoise.

Seven months went by without Blot hearing anything more from Rivière. On 7 October 1776, however, he returned with a declaration of *marronage* (running away) that he had registered with the greffe of the local jurisdiction at the small town of Trinité a few months before. Armed with this legal document, he presented the declaration to a judge in Saint-Pierre.

Rivière proceeded to open a suit against Blot for having harbored and hidden Magdeleine Françoise, whom he accused of being a fugitive slave, and for having abetted her flight with her children to the English island of Dominica. He challenged Blot to answer these charges and, if she accepted them, demanded compensation for the value of Magdeleine Françoise and her children. The Saint-Pierre conseil ruled Blot responsible for her escape.

The case was appealed to the metropole. The facts of the case entered the royal council for provincial (including colonial) matters, known as the *conseil des dépêches*, where Blot requested that the king quash a ruling by the Martinican conseil that had held her responsible for the escape of a mulatto woman to Dominica. Blot asserted that the conseil had no proof of the actions imputed to her, and that its judgment had reduced her to a "frightful misery" ("affreuse misère"). Besides, she explained, the mulatto woman had been born free; accordingly, Blot couched her complaint in terms of injustice, emphasizing Rivière's fraud as a breach of public privilege (*droit public*).

Blot made her case on the grounds that she had not concealed any aspect of her activity, thus marking out her steps in a choreography of justice both before and after the point at which the case had entered court proceedings. She specified in her testimony that all of these actions had happened in public, not in secret. Magdeleine Françoise had stayed in the inn "publicly" (*publiquement*), and the two slave women had "openly" (*ouvertement*)—that is, without any attempt to conceal their actions—carried her children onto the boat. Blot maintained that as an innkeeper she had indeed lodged Magdeleine Françoise and her children as free persons, but "in view of everyone" ("à la vue de tout le monde"). She had not procured passage for Magdeleine Françoise, nor had she any direct contact with the ship's captain, rejecting Rivières's claim of her complicity in their escape. She also asserted that she had merely instructed her slave women to help Magdeleine Françoise manage the complicated task of boarding the ship with two small children.

In contrast, Rivière's case depended upon sketchy facts that appeared to rewrite, rather than clarify, the past on the assumption that colonial magistrates would side with a purported slave owner rather than a woman.

Upon further investigation, the court discovered that Magdeleine Françoise had been born free in Dominica on 14 September 1755, while it was under French rule. She was then proven free by evidence that her mother had been freed by her master, Sieur Hellouin, a former inhabitant of Dominica, who had for several years before neglected to cite the mother on his slave census (*dénombrement*). This could have resulted in the confiscation of Magdeleine Françoise's mother, who had later marked her daughter on censuses as of doubtful free status. Rivière had claimed Magdeleine Françoise and her children from a private sale ("sous seing-privé") after their departure for Dominica. He also turned out to be Hellouin's overseer (*économe*), who had gone to Dominica following his initial interview with Blot with a letter from the Martinique administrators to reclaim Magdeleine Françoise and her children.

Antillean courts frequently had to grapple with the uncertain status that imperial territory disputes and warfare created for colonial residents. The court documents noted that Dominica and Martinique, while under British and French rule, respectively, had a reciprocal agreement that allowed them to work together to capture fugitive slaves during periods of peace. At the request of Rivière, Magdeleine Françoise and her children were imprisoned on 22 April 1776, but after judicial proceedings the local court ruled on 2 May 1776 that they were actually free from birth. This explained the seven months of silence that Blot had experienced between the initial complaint by Rivière and his reappearance in October 1776. During this time, Rivière had appealed to the Martinican judges. One would have expected Blot to have cited proof of Magdeleine Françoise's free status from official documents such as intendance or conseil registers as a counterargument to Rivière, but she did not. These documents appear to have been missing due to Magdeleine Françoise's unusual heritage. What would have been a civil case regarding simply a confirmation of status became a more serious criminal case involving a potential crime of aiding fugitive slaves. In this circumstance, Blot's only option was to go straight to the metropolitan government to request a quashing of the conseil ruling.

Evidence appeared to be stacked well in Blot's favor, but different courts could come to different conclusions based on it. At the request of

Rivière, the lower-court judge heard the testimony of two people he suggested, but their answers confirmed Blot's assertions "unanimously and exactly" rather than his. The judge in the local jurisdiction deliberated on the case and dismissed Rivières's charges, but Rivière persisted in his complaint and appealed to the conseil supérieur. The conseil revisited the case without admitting any other evidence but ruled against Blot. The conseil also noted that the original judge had ruled that Blot would pay Rivière the price of Magdeleine Françoise and her children as well as a fine of ten livres a day to account for each day since their escape (noted as a standard penalty for those who aided fugitive slaves). The conseil extended the lower court's implication of her guilt and made it explicit by charging her fines for aiding Magdeleine Françoise as a runaway.

Blot knew that an appeal to the king's council would likely overturn her case, on the basis of the fraudulent transaction, and so she insisted on taking her case to a higher jurisdiction. She begged the king for his protection and a rejection of the Martinican conseil's decision. She also asked that he send the parties to the Guadeloupe conseil, a common method for royal administrators to avoid having to decide colonial court cases. She must have known that this had happened in other cases, so she requested it as a means of getting the king's assistance, while emphasizing her deference to his time and attention to more important matters.

This strategy worked in Blot's favor, but it was helped by the fact that French magistrates tended to rule harshly on charges of fraud. Rivière's apparent conspiracy against Magdeleine Françoise constituted fraud because it was a willful misinterpretation of her free status. It had involved the creation of false legal documents by Rivière, like the declaration of marronage. The royal government did eventually quash the conseil's ruling, on 5 June 1779, two years after the conseil's decision. The metropolitan court also identified the key issue as fraud, especially on the part of Rivière. The decision explained that he had submitted to a decision, after which his requests could only be judged on the evidence in the request. A second issue was that Magdeleine Françoise (always referred to as "la mulatresse") enjoyed a legally justified liberty based on her baptismal record, which predated Rivière's claim by twenty-one years, raising doubts about why Rivière waited so long to pursue her—especially if, as Hellouin's overseer, he would likely have likely known her from a young age.

Though a few irregularities appeared in Hellouin's slave censuses, all other evidence pointed to Hellouin as the originator of Magdeleine Françoise's baptismal record. He was probably her father. Why, the court wondered, would one believe that Hellouin would sell his daughter to his overseer? This conduct suggested to the court a malevolent conspiracy between the seller (Hellouin) and the putative buyer to destroy, if possible, the effect of a liberty given "en fraude" of the law. This seems to have been an established pattern, whereby plantation overseers claimed ownership of slaves on the plantations on which they worked, often through the means of fraudulent or off-the-books transactions (with or without the complicity of the slave owners). Fraudulent commercial activity, then, outranked concerns about race in the understanding of the court.[67] This was an issue that metropolitan and colonial courts fought consistently throughout the eighteenth century, counting fraud (no matter the specific kind) as a crime that seriously threatened the civil order.

Blot won more than her argument against Rivière. In the ruling (arrêt), the royal government required him to pay her restitution for the sums that he had required her to pay him for Magdeleine Françoise. The ruling also referred the two parties to the Guadeloupe conseil for further judgment about the specifics of the case. This outcome reflected a common French judicial strategy whereby the Marine underscored the authority of the conseils to make definitive judgments rather than always outsourcing difficult cases to metropolitan venues, especially the king's personal councils (the highest possible appellate forum). This strategy applied especially in highly contested cases like Blot's. By shifting the case to the Guadeloupe conseil, the Marine acknowledged and acquiesced in the litigants' desire for further legal services but showed definitively that those legal services needed to be obtained in the colonies themselves and through the work of the conseils rather than in the imperial headquarters at Versailles. The conseils supérieurs, not the Marine, were responsible for ensuring Magdeleine Françoise's free status.

This case highlights the tenacity with which free people of color like Blot and Magdeleine Françoise rejected accusations of criminal activity and threats to their free status, respectively. No attorney or proxy was listed in the appeal as working on behalf of Blot, so it appears that she (and Magdeleine Françoise) worked through the various stages of this case on their own. Blot, in particular, displayed an awareness both of how the courts worked and of her rights within them.

Three Mascarene Cases

Though the conseil correspondence defined well-trod (and relatively sturdy) relationships among conseil and company officials, individuals used such thoroughfares to advance their own agendas and thereby worked out unique patterns of interaction in which metropolitan France played only a small role. Three individuals, Rheims Rose, Louis Filet, and Marie Elisabeth Sobobobié-Betty, all accessed the Mascarene conseil supérieurs as a means by which to gain local and royal support for their objectives as merchant and royal lender, slave trader for hire, and Malagasy ruler turned French subject, respectively. Together, their lives outline some of the possible trajectories (and limitations) for agents operating within the Indian Ocean.

Rheims Rose's career demonstrates how Indian Ocean merchants interacted with Mascarene conseil officials in a formal way to supplement a global network of trading contacts with an empire-wide network of political and legal channels that could be accessed via the conseils. A négociant who traded primarily between the Mascarenes and his hometown of Saint-Mâlo, Rose's career spanned more than thirty-five years (roughly 1751 to 1787) and encompassed Asian trading ventures, southeast African slave trading, and investment in local Mascarene plantation agriculture.[68] Early in his career Rose served as a shipping manager (*subrécargue*) for the Compagnie des Indes orientales in 1751, then became the head of Île Bourbon's Bureau of Commerce in 1768 at which point he was elevated to magistrate (conseiller) on Île Bourbon's conseil supérieur. Rose was later called to serve on the Île de France conseil by the intendant of both islands, Jacques Maillart du Mesle, as by 1791 he had been directing nearly all the commerce of the Mascarenes with France, including negotiating to stabilize a currency crisis brought on by specie shortages.[69] Rose boldly stated his own indispensable conduct to the Marine and requested a cordon de Saint-Michel, a royal honor for a distinguished commercial career similar to the Cross of Saint Louis frequently awarded to senior ancien régime military officers.

Disagreements about this qualification illustrated differences between metropolitan and colonial priorities, in which imperial decisions indicated that metropolitan ministers believed that they benefited from, but were not dependent upon, the assistance of colonial traders and magistrates. The marquis de Castries, minister of the Marine, rejected Rose's request for the cordon de Saint-Michel in 1787—the same year Rose sent the request— which seems to indicate a quick decision on the part of Castries, as well as very good mail service between metropole and colony via Rose's trading connections.[70] Rose was undeterred, however. He sent a new request with additional evidence in his favor, including a report showing that he had supplied the Mascarenes with more than four thousand slaves to support their growing plantation economies.

The report enclosed a chart of his ships' voyages around the Indian Ocean littoral that provides a snapshot of the wider commercial world in which the Mascarene islands were enmeshed. Though the chart only covered five years of a thirty-five-year career (from 1772 to 1776 inclusive), Rose's trading consignments for that period included every major commercial center in the Indian Ocean region. Several ships went to Mozambique and Madagascar to buy slaves, while others traveled to China for porcelain. Rose was also savvy about profiting off his ships: when one ship sank in a hurricane, he sold another to a ship outfitter (*armateur*) and a third to the king (presumably, in practice, to the Marine). Most often, his ships went to France laden with coffee and returned to the Mascarenes via Mozambique, where they picked up slaves to work on Île Bourbon and Île de France's coffee plantations. Rose listed nearly all of these shipping voyages as returning to Île de France with full cargoes, emphasizing the efficiency with which he traded by making sure that he had as much merchandise to sell as possible on each leg of the journey. His reports do not indicate any kind of illicit trading activity, though it is quite possible that he participated in contraband trades.[71] This points to a difference in incentives for Antillean and Mascarene traders.

Although his requests for royal honors were rebuffed in 1787, his arguments reveal the kinds of experience and qualifications colonial elites, especially conseil members, thought would appeal most to the struggling monarchy. The emphasis Rose placed on his financial savvy was calculated to capture the attention of ministers who were particularly desirous of running their newly consolidated empire cheaply to make up for the huge debts incurred by a century of imperial warfare against the British. His second argument, highlighting his local political expertise and a ready list of contacts with nearly all of the Mascarene trading elite, signaled his readiness to be what the British called "the man on the spot"—someone who understood colonial dynamics intimately and so could be entrusted to make prudent decisions without too much help from Versailles.

While Rose's career highlights the global scale of trade and the empire-wide connections obtainable through the conseils, the case of Louis Filet (called La Bigorne) demonstrates the ambivalent tensions that could make commercial and political relationships fragile within the western Indian Ocean region (Figure 8).[72] Described by one official as a "dangerous adventurer, having been well known to the Administration of the Company," Filet made his career as an independent agent who offered to supply the Mascarenes with several thousand Malagasy slaves, which he proposed to take by force in a bold expedition. After presenting several plans to the Île de France conseil and company administrators without success, in 1767 he approached the new royally sponsored government under governor Jean Daniel Dumas, intendant Pierre Poivre, and the conseil. Île de France officials disagreed about whether to trust Filet. Some cited his previous unsuccessful proposals to the conseil and his dubious method—essentially a smash-and-grab strategy that continued to damage French relations with "East Malagasy," which had already deteriorated due to broken treaties.[73]

Dumas prevailed in supporting Filet's plan, however, having been won over by Filet's tantalizing offer of slave labor (always in great demand), the lucrative possibility of income from (presumably) reselling the slaves at a higher price to planters, and the priceless local information Filet could gather in Madagascar. Filet was duly sent off in 1768 with official approval, but he quickly double-crossed the Île de France administrators. Hearing

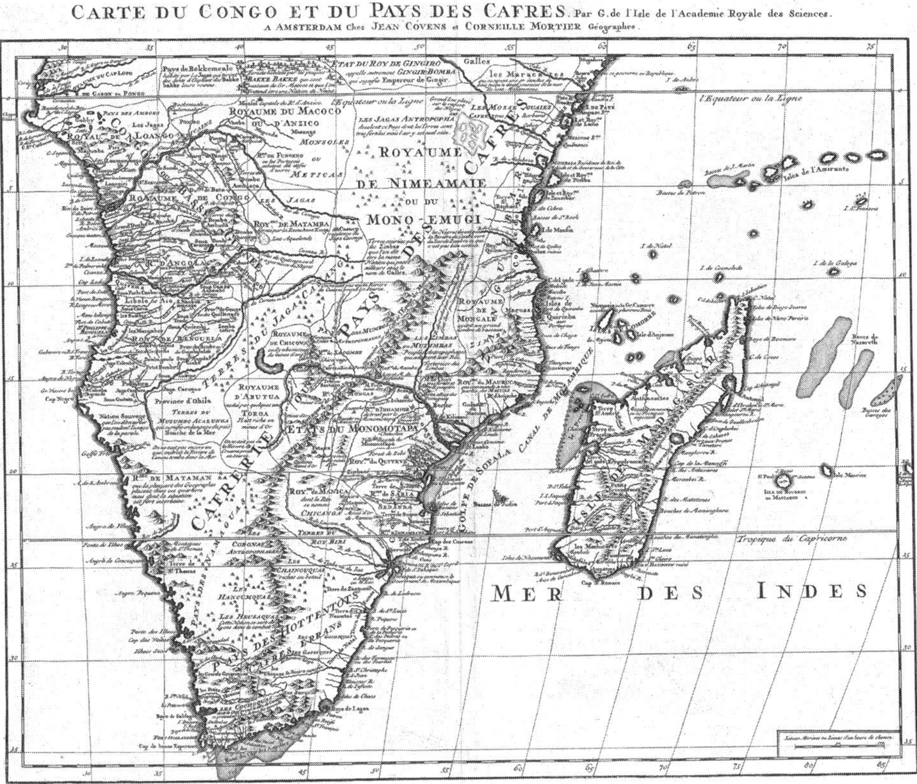

Figure 8. Map of Southern Africa (de l'Isle), ca. 1739, Wikimedia Commons

that Dumas had since left the island, in 1769 Filet replaced the royal ships with his own ships in Madagascar, including one outfitted by a Sieur Glémet (a *régisseur de traites*), who had written a personal letter of recommendation for Filet to Dumas, whom he knew. Filet obtained approximately two thousand slaves and sold them in Île de France for his own profit, using the funds to pay off substantial debts he had incurred on the island.

Despite his illicit dealing, Filet was sent back to Madagascar the next year for more slaves, this time under the assurance that the governor would protect him; he also got an "immense quantity" of beef to supply the colonial troops. Upon arriving in Foulepointe, Madagascar, he declared that he was going to make war against the Amores nation (a hundred leagues into the interior) and forced the young warriors of Foulepointe to go with him. He continued to complicate local politics and provoke more fighting over the winter of 1770–1771, destroying a decade-long relationship with the Foulepointe people, who (as Poivre explained in a letter to the government in France) had previously furnished the army with substantial portions of rice, but who would not now follow through on their deal to supply approximately three thousand beef cattle (living and salted) to the Mascarenes. As a result, Île de France was "blighted" with food shortages. Upon hearing that Filet had died in Foulepointe in 1771, Poivre remarked: "Happily for our colony, Providence has made such a dire project vanish." Filet's death resulted in the dispersal of the Foulepointe warriors and the renewal of possibilities for trade.[74] Officially, Filet was serving as a royal interpreter when he died, but these off-the-books transactions no doubt tarnished his status in the wake of his death.[75]

Filet's meddling in Malagasy politics brings one more kind of conseil supplicant to light in the form of Malagasy tribal leaders who took advantage of frequent transit (whether officially sanctioned or not) between Madagascar and the Mascarenes to pursue their own agendas.[76] Neighboring Malagasy residents sometimes sought out Mascarene legal entrepôts, especially as portals through which they could access French royal authority and, potentially, aid. Marie Elisabeth Sobobobié-Betty was the daughter of Transimalo, the king of Foulpointe, Madagascar. Foulpointe, on the island's eastern coast, operated as an important trading entrepôt and a portal for European incursions into the island. Foulepointe's leaders thus tended to get caught up in local fights between Malagasy and European groups—as with those provoked by Filet.[77] Following her father's death and subsequent political upheaval in 1757, Sobobobié-Betty had traveled in Île de France "with the debris of her fortune."[78] As a baptized Catholic, she had acquired official permission to move to Île de France.

After arriving, however, she sought further political asylum in the form of the king's good favor, citing her good standing as a Catholic and her ability to do everything French people could do. She made a point of asking for both local goodwill, which could be provided by the conseil, and royal patronage through registration in the king's administration (through the *bureau au domaine du roy*), presumably to secure property and title claims. Conseil approval could provide immediate unspecified aid, but this meant sending letters all the way to France and waiting to find out whether the king and his ministers would reply (a process that could take several years). Nevertheless, Sobobobié-Betty added the stipulation that upon receiving a positive reply from the king, her new status would be registered in the records (greffes) of the Île de France conseil.[79]

Meanwhile, Filet's intrusions into Malagasy politics raised the possibility of new alliances between Sobobobié-Betty's nephew and the French, so she felt compelled to return to Madagascar in 1770 as Filet began to make war on the island and draw Foulepointe warriors into the interior. Officially sent by one of the administrators who had sponsored Filet, Sobobobié-Betty sought to take captives in the fighting who could be sent back Île de France as slaves upon her account, a strategy likely meant both to secure her status within the Foulepointe community against her nephew's claims and to strengthen her leverage with French officials in Île de France. Amid this multivalent calculus, not all French officials trusted her. Poivre, realizing that she and Filet had both been sponsored by his colleagues (Filet at least without his knowledge), worried that her additional presence in Madagascar would serve only to slow or stall efforts to provision Île de France (and likely supply slaves as well).[80]

Personnel files for both Filet and Sobobobié-Betty fall silent at this point, but by 1780 Sobobobié-Betty had been compromised in her desire for direct royal aid and entered a request with the Île de France conseil supérieur for naturalization as a French subject.[81] Again, she appealed to both the king in France and the conseil magistrates, recognizing that her claims in Île de France could not be guaranteed, given internal dissent in the conseil, without more durable legal backing from the king and his ministers.

These snapshots of French subjects interacting with conseil officials in the Indian Ocean underscore the entrepreneurship—social, political, and economic—that characterized the patterns of legal practices in this region during the mid-eighteenth century. Rose became the commercial expert in Île Bourbon and Île de France through a classic family business career. But he first leveraged a minor position as a magistrate into a more powerful political role. This Mascarene political standing allowed him to broker directly with the royal government in France about monetary policy and the entire trading strategy for the French Indian Ocean.

Filet's duplicitous and risky efforts to profit off government provisioning contracts exhibited a similar boldness in approaching the Mascarene conseils, but with poorer results as insider politics provoked enemies in both Île de France and Madagascar. The efforts of Sobobobié-Betty to transform herself from Malagasy royalty into French subject walked a fine line between Rose's success and Filet's failure, as she initially won the political protection she desired but was eventually tempted by the prospect of regaining her former status in Madagascar and—presumably failing that— finally applied for French naturalization.[82]

Though Rose, Filet, and Sobobobié-Betty all appealed to the king in France as the ultimate arbiter and guarantor of their claims, their attempts served more immediate goals within the Indian Ocean region. First, petitions to the king alerted the conseil administration that their claimants were serious and presented the possible threat of royal reprisals if the conseil sided with the wrong person, as illustrated by the stark disagreement between Poivre and Dumas over Filet's plan. The urgent reports from Poivre to the ministry of the Marine regarding Filet underscore his fear that a competing report from Dumas might reach France first and win approval against his.

Second, regional—not just local—political and economic calculations frequently lay at the heart of matters placed before the conseil. Relations between the Mascarenes and Madagascar were the catalyst for Filet and So- bobobié-Betty's proposals as the two petitioners sought to capitalize on opportunities in both places. Relations with Madagascar were continuing sources of difficulty for Mascarene administrators as they tried to maintain food supplies and satisfy demand for slaves. Plenty of illicit traffic passed between the Antilles and the Americas, but North American colonies did not form the object of legitimate plans (commercial or otherwise) in the way that Madagascar continually did, as seen throughout Mascarene conseil records and other archival materials, such as Alexis Rochon's scientific expedition report. The Mascarene-Pondichéry relationship and the Lesser

Antillean-Saint-Domingue (or perhaps Louisiana) relationship share distinct similarities, but Madagascar has no clear complement for the Atlantic.[83]

Finally, the Mascarene economy in the eighteenth century operated within global and imperial frameworks shaped by the Antilles as well as by France. Île Bourbon's early economy depended upon Martinique as a market for slaves, a resource for ship repair and provisions, and, eventually, a model for developing a cash-crop plantation economy. Pondichéry and Chandernagor sat amid densely populated regions of South Asia, but they increasingly used the Mascarenes as provisioning sources.

Though scholarship on smuggling and piracy has recently reinvigorated debates about the power of transactions conducted outside official forms, the conseils supérieurs offered unique and exclusive access to forms of power such as lucrative trading contracts (for Filet and Rose), Indian Ocean–wide (and potentially global) political protection (for Sobobobié-Betty and Rose), and monetary policy including credit (for Rose).[84] Filet, for example, might easily have turned to a career in Malagasy piracy, as had many free agents before him, but instead he believed it might be more lucrative to gain the explicit backing of (at least some members of) the Île de France administration, including the military governor. This evidence validates and extends calls for historians to flip their telescopes from looking outward from imperial metropoles and instead to stand anchored in colonial contested spaces, such as the Mascarenes, and their regional counterparts, such as the Indian Ocean.[85]

Conclusion

Conseils occupied a central position within colonial societies because French subjects depended upon them to provide justice through the cooperation of magistrates and court users. Unlike the common-law system applied throughout British Empire, France's civil-law system depended upon the adjudication of cases by panels of magistrates, rather than a combination of judges and juries. In the French system, local opinions about justice were accessed informally in the courtroom through practices like the interrogation of witnesses. Outside the courtroom, French subjects publicly debated laws about court etiquette and public speech, as in the Bordenave and La Grange cases (considered in this chapter) and through the convergence of local assemblies against royal administrators in both Martinique and Île de France (discussed in chapter 3).

The conseils facilitated the feedback loops between colonial and metropolitan subjects, which were reinforced by informal associations like interjudicial correspondence and kinship networks. Conseils supérieurs sat at the heart of France's ancien régime imperial constitution, between these extremes. Judicial processes tended to push cases toward the conseils from lower jurisdictions (as appealed cases) and from higher courts in France (as colonial administrators often sent appealed cases back to the conseils for final judgment).

All court participants paid attention to changes in the law that governed them, taking advantage of opportunities they perceived in the conseils specifically. Within the conseils, court users such as Blot and Sobobobié-Betty used their knowledge of the law and legal process to defend their positions and they did not hesitate to appeal conseil decisions when they received unfavorable judgments. Women and enslaved defendants pushed back against courts dominated by those magistrates and a legal system that offered them few protections by appealing to higher courts that were (but sometimes proved not to be) more sympathetic to their arguments. Though enslaved people, nonelite whites, and planters entered courtrooms with vastly different expectations about the kind of justice they would receive, they shared common spaces and confronted a predictable set of magistrates who held the power to determine their cases.

Magistrates also sought to manipulate this choreography through their decisions, as in the criminal punishments that publicly defined the boundaries of acceptable behavior and physically sanctioned the bodies of those who transgressed them. Local magistrates in the Antilles and administrators in the Mascarenes with connections to royal court society mustered a combination of colleagues and legal experience to pursue debtors and enemies through the courts.

Between *"Île Deserte"* and *"Île de France"*

There is going to be a great misfortune, the creoles [*bequets*]
are going to make an uprising [*gaoulé*] like the blacks.
—Cornette de Saint-Cyr, 1718[1]

All I could see around the harbour was a rugged coast,
stripped of trees and covered in yellow grass. . . .
We learned from the pilot that things on the island were ablaze,
with two warring factions headed by the intendant and by the governor,
and that there was only paper money.
—Jacques-Henri Bernardin de Saint-Pierre, 1768[2]

ON 5 MARCH 1768, Jean André de Ribes waited nervously to board a
ship anchored in Île de France, destined for a "deserted island" somewhere
in the Indian Ocean. In the interim, he dashed off a letter to the minister of
the Marine in Paris begging for assistance. Ribes served as attorney general
for the island's conseil supérieur, and he had infuriated the governor, Jean
Daniel Dumas, by disagreeing with him over whether conseil members
were required to attend parish church services. Dumas responded in fury.
He put Ribes under house arrest, then banished him from the island. Ignor-
ing the timing—it was the season for bad weather—Dumas forced Ribes
and another court official to board. Ribes found himself, as he waited on the
ship, untethered between metropolitan France and Île de France legal resorts, with the prospect of an "île deserte" as a solution.[3] Interjudicial correspondence, however, offered Ribes a way to eclipse this physical and legal
distance. Ribes realized that if he could get his account of the fight with

Dumas to Marine officials in France first, he could get the fair hearing he could no longer expect in the Île de France conseil. Ribes faced three pressing problems: weather, isolation (banishment), and sanction (Dumas's anger). But correspondence allowed him to advance his legal case even while he was physically restricted.

Previous chapters have emphasized the community cohesion and problem-solving fostered by the conseils through legal rituals, court personnel, and interjudicial correspondence. This chapter highlights how moments of crisis revealed vulnerability and sometimes resilience within a global French legal culture. Tensions among personnel stationed at legal entrepôts like the Île de France conseil could erupt dramatically. These conflicts highlight the vulnerability of legal entrepôts to personal conflict, whether based in petty enmity or deep-seated disagreement. Knowledgeable subjects like Ribes used tools that complemented the conseils, such as interjudicial correspondence and advocacy through local assemblies, when conflict within the conseils made traditional judicial methods unfeasible. Though the French colonial patterns of justice centered on the conseils, Ribes's path from the Île de France to the deserted island and finally to France shows that rituals of justice acted out within and adjacent to the conseils interfaced with empire-wide legal trajectories that included the metropole as well as the colonies.

In Martinique, a similarly dramatic event known as the Gaoulé (uprising) had occurred in 1717. It, too, originated in a contest between conseil members and administrators. It, too, led to the banishment of some participants.[4] In Martinique, a crisis had erupted over long-standing provisioning shortages on the island, and so colonial residents had resorted to illicit trade with their Dutch, English, and Spanish neighbors. When a new governor and intendant arrived in Martinique with instructions to stop the illegal trade, they were met by a restive assembly of local elites (*notables*) who had overtaken the conseil supérieur. Skeptical of the new administrators' intent, the *notables* quickly packed them onto a boat headed back to France and sent a packet of evidence to the Marine ministers explaining their actions. As in the Dumas affair, internal conflict within the conseil (which included the administrators and magistrates) prompted the employment of complementary tools like local assemblies and interjudicial correspondence. Like Ribes, the administrators were not allowed to stay within a colonial jurisdiction but instead were forced back out of it into a watery space that lay in between. French subjects depended upon physical access to legal entrepôts but could use interjudicial correspondence and ties to global themistocrats to overcome these distances, as Ribes did when he was banished by Dumas.

When extraordinary local and imperial pressures converged on the conseils, they became key sites for debates about legal and political power for local and metropolitan, elite and nonelite players. The Gaoulé and the Dumas affair testify to the unsustainable pressure that extraordinary circumstances like food crises and personal disputes could put on the conseils and cripple the entire legal machinery and leave some, like Ribes and the Martinican administrators, stranded between "îles" of France. The actions of local elites in both Île de France and Martinique show, however, that the conseils were enmeshed in a legal culture that included informal local assemblies and transimperial correspondence networks. These coexisted with the conseils during times of peace but could function in place of the conseils during times of conflict until the conseils could be restored.

This chapter explores the conseils during moments of crisis. Both the Antilles and the Mascarenes experienced periods of local resistance to imperial authority in the form of revolts by local elites in the eras of colonization. In both places, local controversies were concentrated in the forums of the conseils supérieurs as debates about the validity and appropriateness of colonial rule. Conflicts usually erupted as personal contentions: Dumas versus Ribes, coalition of Martinican elites versus new administrators. They often stemmed, however, from long-standing feuds about how to deal with colonial problems like provisioning and defense.

These moments exposed weaknesses within France's ancien régime empire. But they also proved the resilience of its global legal culture, linked together by the conseils, as subjects employed interjudicial correspondence and networks of themistocrats as antidotes to conseil crises. Assumptions about jurisdictions and legal practices were revealed in cases like the Gaoulé and the Ribes controversy precisely because they were moments in which the colonial legal machinery broke down. The Gaoulé and the Dumas affair also illustrate that these forums were complemented by another space—the ocean—into which the losers of colonial fights could be thrown, set adrift from the protection of French law as maintained by both colonial conseils and the metropolitan government in France.

The Gaoulé, 1717

The 1717 revolt in Martinique known as the Gaoulé marked the successful cohesion of a local elite against metropolitan administrators. It also demonstrated that local elites were not tied to the decisions of the governor and intendant as the sole leaders of the colony. Instead, the colonial order forged in and maintained by the conseil supérieur could be ripped apart across, not just within, the hierarchy of elites. Jacques Petitjean Roget has argued that the Gaoulé happened as a result of a conjuncture of events, drawing on the Annaliste concept, but he neglects the judicial context in which the revolt occurred. A subsistence crisis and weakened defenses combined with recalcitrance—whether real or perceived—on the part of the administrators in charge created a perfect storm in which the governor and intendant became vulnerable to these events rather than being at the helm of them.[5] The eventual banishment, however, of the administrators Antoine d'Arcy de La Varenne and Louis Balthazar de Ricouart from Martinique was a rejection of judicial negotiation within the conseil and between the colony and the Ministry of the Marine. Instead, local elites chose to push the administrators outside French jurisdiction entirely by banishing them. This challenged the constitution of the French Empire itself and put Martinican elites in a position to determine what the modified structure would be. Gaoulé participants eventually won the pardon of the king for their actions (if not an overturning of the legislation that prompted it) and thereby won an argument for local authority that was centered on the conseils but shared by associated assemblies of *notables* (local elites, such as merchants, military officers, and lower-status planters).

The epicenter of the Gaoulé lay in the specific incident of Ricouart and La Varenne's capture in Martinique, but the conflict had regional dimensions that signaled a more widespread discontent among Antillean planters with royal authority. An incident on Guadeloupe in 1715 precipitated the Gaoulé. Following the seizure of an English ship as a prize on the Guadeloupean island dependencies of Les Saintes, officials found evidence of illegal trade between some Guadeloupeans and the English. The neighborhood's military commander, Pierre Gilbert de Crapado, sent four Guadeloupeans to Martinique to be put into the nearest prison and then fined, but local inhabitants resented the commander's actions.[6] A group of nearly four hundred of them went to the commander's house to petition him for a reprieve, citing their misery due to a food crisis as the reason for illegal trading with the English. Finally, they decided on a plan to present the petition to the head of the regiment and reassured the commander of their loyalty by yelling "Vive le Roi" five times.[7] Here and in Martinique, a pattern was established in which colonial residents repeated the cry of loyalty to the king while simultaneously demanding different conditions.

In the meantime, Martinique and Guadeloupe awaited the arrival of a new governor and intendant, the latter of whom occupied an important local judicial and administrative post as the official presiding over the Martinique conseil. On 3 May 1717, the intendant, Ricouart, finally arrived in Fort Royal, Martinique, and met with the conseil in the presence of the governor-general, the marquis de Feuquières, as well as the conseil members and greffier.[8] The conseil registered a royal edict from 18 November 1716 concerning new currency valuation.[9] Ricouart and La Varenne also made sure to register the new laws against foreign commerce. Both of these matters were considered essential to preserving and protecting the island's valuable sugar production for France.[10] Then they set out on a tour to see the island's various militias and administrative districts (*quartiers*), both to check on fortifications and to get a sense for the state of local unrest (Figure 9).

First they traveled south from Fort Royal around the bay of Cul-de-Sac. Pentecost fell on 16 May 1717, and so they stopped at a Jesuit chapel in Cul-de-Sac à Vache before proceeding south to the Ilet à Ramiers across from Fort Royal, a favorite port for illicit traders that they planned to replace with a military base.[11] Next they traveled across some low mountains to the somewhat isolated southern coast. Near the shore, they were greeted by the

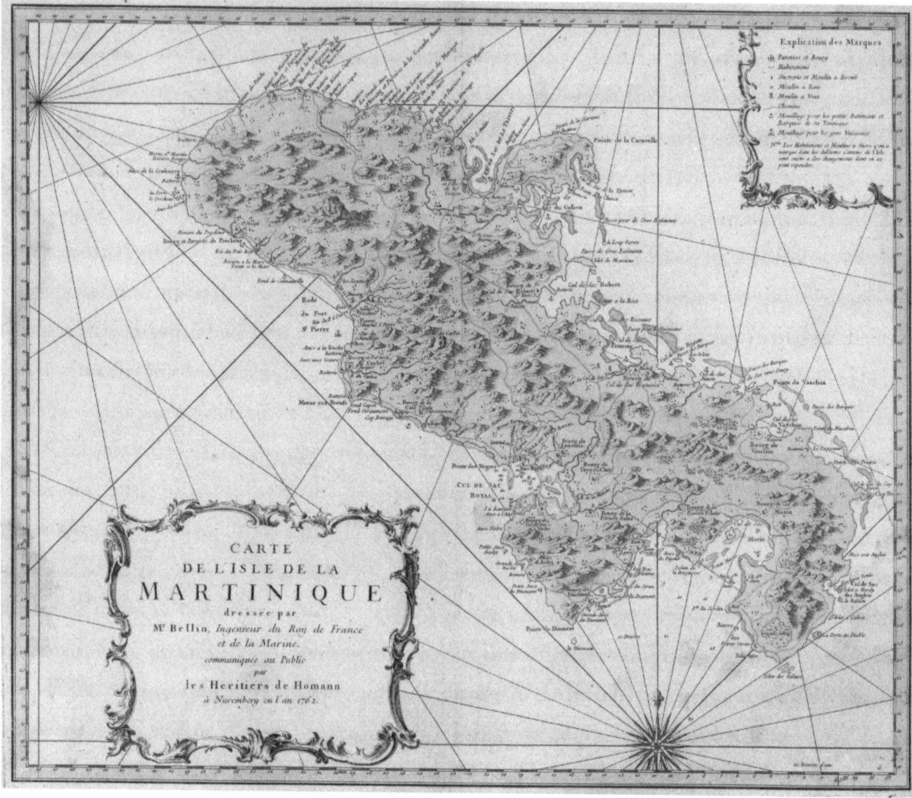

Figure 9. *Carte de l'Isle de la Martinique* (Bellin), 1762, John Carter Brown Library

tailor-turned-planter Étienne Bourgeot, who held a dinner in their honor at his plantation house. The terrace of Bourgeot's plantation house looked out onto the water toward the south, with the rock of Le Diamant jutting out in the near distance. The island of Saint Lucia was also visible just twelve miles away. As a site of frequent illicit trade that contravened measures like the recent currency and foreign trade acts, it was a reminder of the brewing conflict between Antilleans and administrators.

Though the arrest itself came as a surprise to many witnesses (many of whom noted that the target was the governor, not the intendant), local forces hostile to La Varenne and Ricouart had been massing near the official procession as it moved through the colony.[12] On 17 May, the delegation went south toward Le Diamant, where an assembly of more than thirty militia soldiers, foot soldiers, and cavalry officers had gathered the day before. The soldiers had met in front of the Macouba church before the Pentecost mass and then had gone from one plantation to another, adding people to their group. They had even enlisted a conseiller, Pocquet, as they traveled south (parallel to the official delegation).[13] Key dinner guests, like Hauterive, the conseil's attorney general, had also planned to do something drastic all along—though perhaps not make an arrest. When that assembly arrived at the Bourgeot plantation and met with the official delegation, they stated that the governor and the intendant had to go with them, on pain of death if anyone resisted. Hauterive did not make a move to stop them.[14]

Weeks of brewing conflict exploded as royal representatives and the colonial faction finally met up at Bourgeot's plantation, but even this confrontation emphasized questions of legitimacy over personal politics. The group of militia officers and soldiers led by Collart and de Roussel, including militia captains, stormed the house in the middle of the official dinner, saying: "We're under orders from the Colony to kill you if you run off, to break your head if you resist." They put a pistol under the noses of the administrators and threatened an attack by five hundred men who were purported to have surrounded the house. Hauterive, the attorney general, had been a dinner guest, but it turned out that he was one of the arrest's architects along with Collart and de Roussel.[15] La Varenne and Ricouart were put under house arrest before being transported back to Fort Royal and finally sent on a ship back to France. The weeks of assembling and frustration also broke out into some violence outside the plantation. Collart attacked a cavalryman (*cavalier*) in front of the governor and the intendant soon after leaving Le Diamant. Meanwhile, a curate arrived because he had heard people in the distance yelling "Vive le Roi" and wondered what the matter was.[16] This latter anecdote points out that the entire controversy was still carried out under the purported auspices of royal authority, but the actions of Collart, de Roussel, and their colleagues signaled an appropriation of royal protection against what they perceived as the unjust actions of the governor and the intendant. Intendants had varying levels of authority over local police forces because militias were managed by the (military) governor but run by the planter elite who controlled the conseil. Here, again, conseil members mediated royal power, but in their capacity as militia leaders.

Fewer sources for the Gaoulé than for the Dumas affair emphasize the maritime aspect of local action, but in both cases the drastic step of banishment depended upon one party having the power to demand and enforce the absence of the other by pushing the opponent out into the empty space of the Atlantic and Indian Oceans, respectively. Putting La Varenne and Ricouart on a boat was an important step beyond their initial arrest because it indicated the Gaoulé rebels' desire to be rid of the administrators, rather than to deal with them on local terms in Martinique. The logic of the Gaoulé after the confrontation at Bourgeot's plantation thus had two parts. First, participants constrained the movement of La Varenne and Ricouart by physically isolating them through house arrest. This step asserted local power over the metropolitan administrators in a very tangible way, overriding their superior authority as representatives of the French monarchy. Second, Gaoulé rebels banished La Varenne and Ricouart from the island. This action made an even stronger statement of local control but denied the administrators any kind of hearing within the French jurisdiction held by the Martinican conseil. While on the island, La Varenne and Ricouart could have attempted to find a sympathetic audience for their mistreatment from local residents more willing to accept royal authority (even when it was accompanied by distasteful edicts) and, especially, judicial recourse via the conseils. As captives, however, La Varenne and Ricouart became impotent and lacked any protections until they reached another French jurisdiction.

The events of the Gaoulé illustrated a confident, even brazen, rebellion against unwanted metropolitan authority by local elites. In the aftermath of the Gaoulé, however, local elites were more circumspect, especially as they sought to avoid charges of treason. Following the arrest of La Varenne and Ricouart, Martinicans compiled evidence that they had acted with reason and purpose. On 22 May, deputies were sent to interrogate La Varenne and Ricouart, who responded to nearly every question by saying that they would give an account to the king and the conseil (not the deputies). Meanwhile, the members of the local assembly met to compose a report of their deliberations. They described themselves as militia officers, nobles, conseil and jurisdiction officers, traders, and *notables* (a catch-all term) of Martinique, assembled in a room of the Jacobin monastery to discuss an earlier report given by Dubucq (the leader of the mob from 18 May), who had been chosen in an informal plebiscite by "several cries of 'Vive le Roi,'" a move that asserted civic cooperation and royal deference in the midst of political protest. Dubucq reinforced this posture in an acceptance speech: he stated that he would not stand for attacks on clerics or military officers, nor would he allow disrespect toward La Varenne and Ricouart.[17]

The conseil's report articulated alternatives to metropolitan laws while asserting the right to adjudicate the administrators' case. It included immediate reforms for the colony as well as instructions for dealing with La Varenne and Ricouart and specified that they would be sent on an armed convoy from Martinique, forbidding the ship captains on pain of death to stop at any of the American islands. They also made plans to send for beef and grain from foreign territories, especially from English ships navigating the waters around Saint Lucia. The latter articles of the report concerned the conseil specifically. One limited magistrates from putting planters (*habitants*) in prison unless they had broken royal ordinances (that is, not ones given by the intendant or governor), while another required that justice be administered without delays and excessive cost.[18]

The assembly also composed a letter to the regent and the maréchal d'Estrées, the viceroy of New France, that provided the testimony of the island's religious leaders, including Jesuits and Dominicans, as confirmation that the assembly had not done anything wrong. Conseillers compiled evidence showing that they knew how to provision their own colony, in contrast to the misguided plans of the administrators. They also emphasized their own competence in restoring civil order by dealing with what they considered to be rogue administrators in a logical, if not approved, manner. They backed their actions with the testimony of religious authorities, a strategy that played to the monarchy's synthesis of political and religious ideas as the foundation of civil society and also reflected deep cultural assumptions about the terrestrial and divine dimensions of imperial authority that had been vested in the conseil. Conseillers presented a multifaceted body of evidence to the Marine designed to show that they—not La Varenne and Ricouart—held legitimate authority over the colony, building a case for local autonomy that simultaneously reassured the Marine of their loyalty as French subjects.

The number of Martinicans—more than four hundred—involved in the Gaoulé made it difficult to discern who was directly responsible for the banishment. In the aftermath, participants sought to obfuscate the record to conceal their potentially treasonous behavior. In the Gaoulé, a few ringleaders were singled out and convicted on criminal charges, while the general inhabitants were granted general amnesty. The Martinique conseil judged (in absentia) on 4 and 8 October 1718 regarding the revolt on 17 May 1717, condemning Belair and Cathier to be burned alive and the three others to be hanged.[19] Michel Labat, one of the five Martinicans condemned to death for his collusion, cited the other participants as evidence that a large group had accompanied the administrators around the island.

Though most of the local assembly members had been dissatisfied with La Varenne and Ricouart, only a few had dared to attack them. Several affidavits were made in favor of Labat and Dorange at the request of Mademoiselle Labat and the new governor-general, Pas de Feuquières.[20] They collected statements made and recorded in the Fort Royal register, or greffe (which included the conseil), in March 1719 by different Martinicans in support of the convicted Gaoulé participants and approved by Michel Labat, who signed this set of affidavits. They were sent to France as evidence along with an impassioned letter written by Labat himself.[21] As they had done with the conseil's report, conseil members and Gaoulé participants worked together to draft a history of the revolt that played to their original political purposes but kept them from being punished for thwarting French law and the king's instructions.

This collection of evidence persuaded Marine officials and the king, even if it minimized the Martinicans' defiance. In September 1719, the king gave amnesty to the Gaoulé participants Belair, Cathier, Dorange, Labat, and Bourgelas. The new Martinican intendant and governor (favorable to the rebels) had petitioned on their behalf, as they had been excluded in an earlier general amnesty issued in March 1718. The amnesty restored their good reputations ("leur bonne fame"), returned all goods that had been confiscated from them, and quashed any other rulings (unspecified, but including those decided in absentia) that had gone against them on this matter. The amnesty also imposed "perpetual silence" on royal attorneys general, their substitutes, and all other defendants against Belair, Cathier, Dorange, Labat, and Bourgelas to conduct any legal proceedings against them.[22]

The favorable judgment rendered by the Marine validated the Gaoulé participants' decision to use interjudicial correspondence to rewrite the Gaoulé as a reasonable protest. It played to the monarchy's desire for loyal subjects and helped the rebels avoid severe punishment from the king (via the Marine). It did, however, forbid the defendants to participate in illicit assemblies and to take arms against the orders of governors and "major" officers of the military who commanded the districts of the king's territories "against the enemies of the State," reiterating their duty to obey and be loyal to royal representatives. The amnesty then instructed the conseil to register it in its records to make it active as part of the law of Martinique (as well as France).[23] The Martinicans used the conseil as a vehicle for allying local elites. Through the conseil, they articulated a unified interpretation of the Gaoulé that was difficult for the Marine to challenge.

This process also happened individually as conseil members followed a similar pattern of rebelling and then requesting the king's pardon. As the conseil's attorney general, Hauterive, had helped orchestrate the Gaoulé, he wrote a pleading letter to the king later that year to request clemency. Hauterive claimed to have had nothing to do with either the arrest or the banishment and that, instead, his enemies or misinformed people had conspired against him. He also called the deportation of La Varenne and Ricouart an "embarkation" (*embarquement*), implying that it was a matter of course for the administrators to travel to France rather than a concerted effort by local elites to force them to return.[24]

This chain of reports and letters to the Marine reestablished links to metropolitan authority that had been temporarily severed by the Gaoulé but sought to expand local power by reframing the revolt itself as a justified action (and perhaps even repeatable precedent) in the face of ill-advised instructions from the king. Underlying this strategy was the assumption that the king would not (perhaps because he could not) enforce severe punishments. By taking initiative and then asking for forgiveness later, the Martinican officials put themselves in a position of power. This way, they could argue that they were loyal to the king while simultaneously justifying their own autonomous actions.[25]

This line of argument reappeared in Antillean rhetoric throughout the eighteenth century, but the strategy was not carried out continuously. Though the assemblies organized by nonelite whites, militia captains, and conseil members had dominated the Gaoulé itself, in its aftermath they rapidly gave way to the conseil. Local groups had expanded in response to conseil weakness and internal conflict but devolved their new authority back to the conseil after the crisis had passed. The assembly dissolved after a final meeting on 25 May, and Pierre Bègue took over from Dubucq as governor. The conseil began meeting again on 7 July in Fort Royal. Martinicans were worried that another revolt might break out, but the conseil actually registered two edicts it found among the papers of Ricouart: one regarding the number of admiralty court officers, another about monetary policy. The conseil also wrote a letter to the Marine stating that it had not participated in banishing La Varenne and Ricouart.[26] This was another political move designed to reframe the planter revolt as a respectful negotiation with the king, sidelining the expulsion of La Varenne and Ricouart as an unfortunate accident rather than a premeditated challenge to royal authority.

The political protest encapsulated in the Gaoulé resulted directly from a Martinican tradition of local political organization concentrated in the conseil. By the early eighteenth century, the conseil already had a distinctive character dominated by local families who had been in the area since at least the mid-seventeenth century. These local families would, by the end of the eighteenth century, form the core of an Antillean themistocracy with global reach. *Notable* inhabitants of the Antilles had also begun assembling as early as 1665 in Martinique, a year after the conseil was established. These local elites included planters, merchants, and military men of more minor rank who deliberated on legislative matters even though the conseil was the only body authorized to collect laws (which had to be given by the king or the intendant and the governor).

The assembly, a more locally oriented counterpart to the conseil, was so strong that upon arriving in 1717 La Varenne and Ricouart instructed the governor-general of the Antilles to turn the local assembly into a forum for dealing with local issues like fortifications and the quartering of troops.[27] Metropolitan administrators were reluctant to support provincial assemblies (and even less inclined to convoke the Estates General), but they had little power to overcome the Martinican organization.

Most of these locally born leaders had served as conseillers in the decade or two before the Gaoulé. Many came from families who had lived in the Antilles for generations. Michel de Clermont began as a lieutenant judge in Martinique, then joined the conseil in 1708. An eloquent speaker, he had gained the governor-general's respect as in the years before the 1717 revolt. Clermont had been born in Saint-Christophe in 1663, and like many early Caribbean settlers had migrated from the small island to Martinique in the mid-seventeenth century.[28] Guillaume Dorange's family had arrived in the Americas in 1628 and aided the colonial founder Pierre Belain d'Esnambuc in chasing the English off the first French Antillean colony of Saint-Christophe.[29] He was a key participant in the Gaoulé, one of those named in the royal ruling that in 1719 finally pardoned several people who had initially been convicted.[30]

Petitjean Roget has defined the Gaoulé as fundamentally a Martinican revolt, calling it "the crisis of adolescence for this first generation of Martinican creoles." While most instigators had parents who had emigrated to Martinique as the first generation of planters, the Gaoulé participants had not been born in France. They had, however, been born into the island's elite. At least two dozen participants who were locally born, most of whom had names like Le Vassor de La Touche, Cacqueray de Valménières, and Cornette de Saint-Cyr, which appear repeatedly in conseil records for the duration of the eighteenth century.[31] The Gaoulé was an opportunity to test and stretch the limits of local authority within the French kingdom as a whole, to see whether the Marine administrators at Versailles would accept the autonomy claimed by the Martinican local elite.

The label "gaoulé" attached to the 1717 revolt has a history that encapsulates the complexity of the event itself and the various tensions

Martinican residents and French authorities sought to work out during the revolt. Though the term originally referred to a group of indigenous people assembled to go to war, by the nineteenth century it had a much wider meaning.[32] Petitjean Roget also speculated that it might have been a reference to African dances observed among slaves in Saint-Domingue or Brazil.[33] Before 1717, ideas about a gaoulé were strongly tied to practices Europeans saw among groups they saw as inferior, but after 1717 the meaning changed to refer to this Antillean uprising rather than to resistance by indigenous or African groups. This pattern indicates an appropriation of an American phenomenon by European-descended Antillean elites as a way of arguing that their own revolt (and the colonial concerns it reflected) was distinctive.

The term first appeared in reference to the 1717 revolt in a letter by the Martinican conseiller Cornette de Saint-Cyr in 1718, when he wrote: "There is going to be a great misfortune, the creoles [*bequets*] are going to make an uprising [*gaoulé*] like the blacks."[34] This phrase brought together ideas about the three groups who lived together in the Antilles: white Europeans, indigenous Caribs, and enslaved Africans. In Cornette de Saint-Cyr's usage, the meaning of "gaoulé" had slipped from its origin referring to Carib warfare to designating local rebellions by slaves, signaling a demographic shift, as Caribs had been essentially wiped out from Martinique by the end of the seventeenth century, replaced by growing numbers of enslaved Africans. Defensive efforts made by local elites like Cornette thus shifted in focus from skirmishes with indigenous groups to attempts to squelch slave resistance in forms like marronage and slave revolts. Cornette's statement indicates that ideas about local cases of resistance (Carib and slave revolts) become integrated with and mapped onto French conceptions about royal authority (assertions of loyalty to the king, complaints against his ministers).

Terms for local revolt that linked white rebellion to revolt by indigenous and enslaved populations were present in both French Atlantic and Indian Ocean domains. In the Indian Ocean, a similar Carib word, "guivi," was used in Île Bourbon to refer to white settlers who deserted other colonists to join maroon communities in the hills of the island. They were said to "faire le guivi," or "go native," in a travel account from 1671. "Guivi" was perhaps a corruption of "gaoulé," a possible sign that the language of revolt transferred between French colonies in the Indian Ocean and the Atlantic.[35]

More generally, eighteenth-century usage of the term "gaoulé" resembled the concept of a "fronde," or "revolt of lords" (*seigneurs*), generally applied in the seventeenth and eighteenth centuries to conflicts between monarchs and their noble subjects, named after the Fronde revolt between roughly 1648 and 1653 in which nobles had revolted against growing royal power in France. By the early nineteenth century, the term "gaoulé" had widened in definition to become a general term for revolt. This change in meaning over time points to a gradual conflation of specific types of civil disorder into a more general idea of local revolt against imperial power. The persistence of the term "gaoulé," however, linked it inextricably to the 1717 revolt as an important instance and even model case of this kind of conflict.

The Gaoulé was a flashpoint for tensions between Antillean and metropolitan elites at a moment of imperial weakness and Antillean confidence. In the Atlantic Ocean, long-standing experience with local governance had imbued local elites with the confidence to counter new royal instructions that seemed to go against their own interest. Having already worked out solutions to problems like provisioning by finding illegal but adequate sources in territories owned by different empires, local elites also believed that they could counter royal administrators by pointing out their own, locally achieved success. When their arguments proved problematic, they improvised the solution of banishment, which the royal government eventually pardoned following the pleas of Gaoulé participants.

The great distance separating Martinique from Versailles proved to be a buffer that Martinicans assumed (rightly, in this case) the royal government was hesitant to cross in order to pursue punitive measures. The conseils increasingly became sites for legal debates about the status of Antillean governors that would eventually take the form of written debate as colonial promoters and lobbyists like Petit and Dessalles made increasingly historical cases for their expertise by compiling legal codes that tracked local jurisprudence from the earliest years of colonization to the present, establishing a pedigree of legal competence. Though some Gaoulé participants, like Labat, argued that the arrest of La Varenne and Ricouart had taken the protest too far (implying that it did not fit his conception of the proper choreography of justice), the muted response from Versailles indicates that the Martinicans had successfully shifted the steps in imperial dimensions of that choreography.

The Dumas Affair, 1767–1768

Though French administrators were pushed out of a colonial jurisdiction during the Gaoulé as Antillean elites claimed authority for themselves, royal administrators barely responded. The Dumas affair, by contrast, illustrated a different dynamic, in which a resident metropolitan administrator (Dumas) sought to dislodge a member of the local elite (Ribes) by sending him out of French colonial jurisdiction, and it was the latter who resorted to metropolitan forums for remedy. The Dumas affair, though centered on a personal dispute between Ribes and Dumas, was also marked by greater attention from metropolitan audiences.

While the Gaoulé occurred at a moment of imperial indifference, the Dumas affair occurred at a moment of imperial renewal.[36] In 1767, French administrators had renewed their attempts to develop the Mascarenes into flourishing colonies, taking over from the bankrupt Compagnie des Indes orientales and installing direct royal rule, which was vested in Pierre Poivre as intendant of both islands and Jean Daniel Dumas as the Mauritian governor. The Mascarene conseils were also dissolved and reconstituted in 1767 as part of the royal takeover. This marked a decided expansion into the Indian Ocean, following a pattern of tentative settlement, territorial defeat against Britain in South Asia, and (more recently and painfully) global setbacks via the terms of the Treaty of Paris in 1763 that drastically reduced French territory in North America.[37]

It was also a period of renewed interest in the natural resources that could be exploited in the Mascarenes and Madagascar, attracting scientific research expeditions by well-known botanists (Figure 10). The years 1767 to 1768 included the arrival of the governor and explorer Louis Antoine de Bougainville (coming in from the Pacific while circumnavigating the globe)

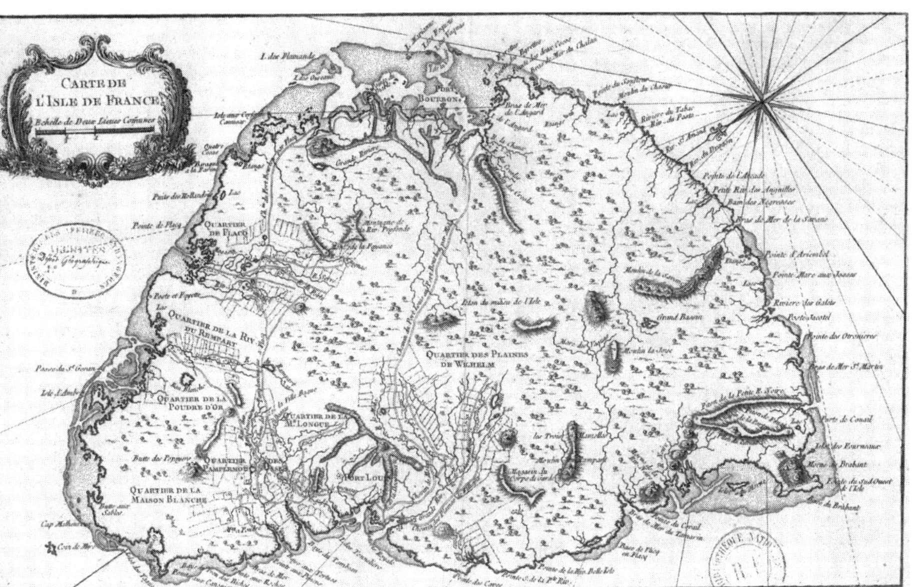

Figure 10. *Carte de l'Isle de France* (Bellin), 1764, Gallica, Bibliothèque nationale de France

and the travel writer and engineer Jacques-Henri Bernardin de Saint-Pierre (who arrived from the west). The naturalist and academician Pierre Poivre was likewise installed as the intendant, with a goal of revitalizing the Mascarenes' agriculture through new crops and better conservation.[38]

The political power, centered on the conseil supérieur, governor, and intendant, did have other more grassroots iterations in the form of municipal governments and militias. Under company rule, the Île de France conseil had established local representatives, known as *syndics*, to manage community affairs.[39] *Syndics* were often Europeans who had migrated to make their fortunes but had achieved neither the spectacular economic success nor the metropolitan offices and patronage connections held by most conseil members. In the Mascarenes, *syndics* were most often minor landholders and soldiers. Edmé Charles Yardin embarked for Île de France in 1739, replacing a soldier (somewhat forbiddingly named Brisetout, or "Break-all") who had just deserted. Yardin received an advance of thirty livres at Lorient, France, and left for Île de France in April.[40] By 1764, a

Charles Yardin (Edmé Charles or his son) was a *syndic* of the Montagne Longue district (canton) and was wealthy enough to purchase a plantation for seventy-four thousand livres.[41] By the late eighteenth century, the Yardins appear to have become landed and somewhat *notable*: Jean Baptiste Yardin was a notary in the Plaines-de-Wilhems district of Île de France from at least 1797 to 1806.[42] As community leaders, *syndics* formed a crucial point of connection between the planter class that tended to dominate the conseils and other layers of colonial society.

Yardin the *syndic* held this role during the transitional era from private company to direct royal rule, which coincided with the existence of a distinct assembly of *syndics* (*chambre syndicale*) from 1762 to 1768.[43] According to the conseil's attorney general and the *syndics'* sponsor, Jean André de Ribes, the syndics could assemble in front of the governor, who could approve their initiatives and examine reports on their conduct. This was meant to acknowledge the oversight of the administrators, but it ultimately left significant power in the hands of the *syndics*. They received statements regarding slaves who had become maroons, conducted annual censuses, and managed the *corvées* (road taxes and maintenance). In the tropical heat, the bodies of people who died often deteriorated too quickly, so the *syndics* were also entrusted with carrying out some of the procedures regarding estate successions, as conseil officials could not get there fast enough.[44]

The *syndics* were also in charge of local militias gathered to hunt maroons. Local planters wanted increased compensation for the extra effort they exerted in capturing maroons, so the local assemblies of syndics were a way to organize these forces more effectively. The government paid *syndics* in the company's paper money, however, a currency widely considered worthless. This factor, not articulated by Ribes, also seems to have contributed to local discontent because it meant that even increases in payments resulted in little actual change in compensation. Ribes had requested a new payment system to be implemented that would follow the goal of the royal orders to pay the *syndics* but not be limited to the specific provisions for payment. Even though the governor and intendant had suspended the new payment system, however, the syndics had continued to meet.[45]

Ribes had a track record as an advocate of local political power. He had started his career in Île de France in 1754 as the chief greffier for the island's conseil. He became a conseiller in 1763 and then the conseil's attorney general in July 1766.[46] This meant that he was part of a generation of conseil officials who had been in place for at least a decade under company rule. They were part of the conseil that was suppressed and then recreated in 1767 as the island came under direct royal rule. The fact, however, that he was chosen as attorney general in July 1766, with the creation of a new conseil, showed that he did have clout within the metropolitan administration (where these decisions were made).

By contrast, Dumas had worked his way up through the military, serving first in Canada before being appointed to run the military arm of the Mascarene government under new direct royal control.[47] While Ribes supported the *syndics*, Dumas had established militia commanders for each neighborhood (quartier), who were given authority to police the coming and going of residents. Dumas had instructed the commanders to make sure that planters did not leave their plantations without their permission. Ribes explained in his report that he would have managed this differently. He would have assured the citizens of their freedom of movement, something he feared bringing up with Dumas.[48] The conseil officials, represented by Ribes, counted Dumas's militarization as a "perpetual shock" against the power of the conseils, which focused on law as a means of managing the colonial order. The refusal by Dumas to rescind his order to the conseil brought this conflict to a head because it meant that he insisted on using the conseil for his own ends, without consulting the conseil officials.[49]

If the *syndics* were an ongoing site of contention between Ribes and Dumas, then a second area of conflict, official ceremonies, brought their disagreements into even sharper relief. The official processions and ceremonies of the conseil and wider colonial government were designed to illustrate the imperial hierarchies that governed specific colonial spaces, so ad hoc gatherings by local *notables* formed a threatening alternative to these ritualized events. Besides the *syndic* payments, Ribes had also asked the conseil about rank and precedence in church and public ceremonies, including a query about which days the conseil would meet as a body in the church. Ribes had shown the conseil, including the governor and the intendant, the royal ordinance given to Martinique regarding the festival of Saint Louis. The practice had been for the conseil to accompany the governor in a procession as a celebrant led singing of a holy hymn (*hymn du saint*). The governor led the way to the church to light a ceremonial fire (*feu de joy*). The procession then went to the church, and the *Te Deum* was sung there.[50]

Ribes's remarkable awareness of Antillean processional regulations likely reflected Martinican habituation to these practices, which can be documented as early as 1664.[51] In the newly royal Mascarene islands, however, there was confusion over which colonial elites were required to attend this procession and ceremony. Some, including the intendant (Poivre) and the head of the conseil (the *doyen*) thought that this was a purely military ceremony, so they had skipped it. Dumas, however, assumed that the ritual fire alerted the conseil members that they should attend. He asserted, citing information from local priests, that this ceremony was part of a fundamental rite of the parish church of the island. In this case, Dumas was angered that he had been in the procession and then found himself unexpectedly alone when he arrived at the church. Though his personal pride was no doubt wounded, too, Dumas accused Ribes and the conseillers of having snubbed the king, whom he represented in the colony as the governor.[52] Dumas's authority was called into question without the presence of the conseillers to present a unified community of local elites to observers. Ribes, Poivre, and the conseillers countered that there was no act that specified that they had to attend the *Te Deum*. Dumas responded by drafting an order to the conseil that required the conseillers to retain the dignity of their places and prevent personal conflicts from disturbing the public order. Ribes responded again with a legal measure. Since the Île de France conseil lacked a law for this ceremony, Ribes wrote to France to request one.

At stake in this fight was a question of legislation versus custom. Ribes, the prosecutor, insisted on following only the instructions that had been received as law from the king. Dumas cared more about whether general principles were followed, especially regarding deference to the king. Political and religious ideas were thus merged for military administrators like Dumas in a way that they were not for the legal and financial administrators of the island like Ribes and Poivre. Where Dumas believed that he had brought royal authority to Île de France in his role as governor and stand-in for the king, Ribes believed that royal authority could only be brought to Île de France in the form of legislation. Dumas insisted on the presence of royal authority as vested in a person, while Ribes insisted upon law, especially written law, that had come from France.

The clash of Dumas and Ribes over the *Te Deum* captured a whole set of tensions and assumptions about how royal and local authority worked in a setting that was already a scripted portrayal of these ideas. This custom was, by Dumas's arrival, more than a hundred years old in colonial practice. Upon the arrival of a new Martinican governor in 1664, several officers and planters went out to escort him from his ship, proclaiming that they had "found an incomparable man" under whose leadership the islands would flourish. Following a procession through Fort Royal, complete with a cannonade and military regiments lined along the streets, he was taken to the Place d'Armes at the heart of town where locals (habitants) again saluted him among a growing throng of bystanders. The governor, accompanied by local officials, including conseil personnel, then went to the church, where the *Te Deum* was sung "in thanksgiving" (*en action de graces*).[53]

The *Te Deum* itself was a hymn of divine praise that dated to the fifth century, possibly earlier.[54] In the seventeenth century, however, it had been appropriated by the French monarchy as a symbol of royal power backed by divine authority. The *Te Deum* focused on the stability and protection of the king for his subjects, saying that he "represents the necessary stability for the perpetuity of the kingdom [*royaume*] of France."[55] It merged ideas about deference to the king with worship of God. The twenty-nine lines of text that formed the *Te Deum* called upon God and the king as sovereign protectors and affirmed the loyalty of the king's subjects. The members of the king's court were likened to Christ's apostles, characterizing them as disciples of the monarch, who was simultaneously a political and a religious leader. Adoration of God by singing the psalms also counted as adoration of the divinely appointed king by his loyal subjects.[56] The *Te Deum* was exclusively reserved for events related to the king, such as baptisms and marriages. Versions of it often referred specifically to military victories and peace treaties, too. These factors made it the most common hymn during the ancien régime.

Because of its constant association with the French kingdom and royal power, Jean-Paul C. Montagnier has likened the *Te Deum* during the ancien régime to the centrality of the *Marseillaise* for the republic.[57] It was always publicly performed and singing it was often a required ceremony specified by royal decrees, which were sent to the colonies as well as throughout France's mainland provinces. A letter from the king in April 1713 required the governor of Saint-Domingue to have the *Te Deum* sung in commemoration of the peace treaty signed at Utrecht, which ended the War of the Spanish Succession.[58] In 1749, another royal letter instructed the Martinican governor to have it performed to celebrate the end of the War of the Austrian Succession.[59]

Ribes was aware of these decrees, even ones that had been sent to Martinique, showing that he understood French law in contexts outside the Indian Ocean. It is unclear how he knew about colonial law in the Antilles, but there is the intriguing possibility that conseillers were communicating with each other among colonies rather than strictly through the metropole as a mediator. Ribes was in communication with other conseillers in France, including a Moydieu in the Grenoble Parlement.[60] The *Te Deum* symbolically connected these disparate colonies and regions within France as processions were performed nearly simultaneously across France's ancien régime empire.

Thus, the contest over the *Te Deum* is a reminder that conseils, and colonial societies, were not strictly defined by the state. Instead, colonial life (even that centered around the conseils) involved a range of activities that were religious and social in nature, not just political. The procession of colonial officials from the parish church to the palais de justice made this connection explicit by the line it drew between these two places.

The requirement to sing the *Te Deum* in the colonies as well as in France expanded the idea of the kingdom (*royaume*) in the same way that the conseils expanded the judicial definition of the kingdom so that it was conceived as one unified entity. The Dumas affair shows that on the one hand this was true: the *Te Deum* was performed in an Île de France that lay several thousand miles away from the Île de France that was centered on the court at Versailles, where Lully and Lalande's music that expressed ideas about royal hierarchy would have been performed more regularly.[61] The *Te Deum* required local elites to gather and articulate ideas about royal authority, whether by following the hymn's script or by working out hierarchies by talking to each other. Only once Dumas had banished Ribes did the conflict take on a new form through the correspondence that both men sent to the metropole in their defense.

The procession itself, however, constituted a moving community, not a unified form. The squabble between Dumas and Ribes showed that participants could have very different ideas about how religious, military, and civil authority should be constituted, even while agreeing with the general assertion of the procession and the singing of the *Te Deum* that religious and royal authority were tightly knit. Both Dumas and Ribes wanted to use public ceremonies to set precedents for their visions of royal authority and colonial governance. They both saw that these were models that signaled to colonial residents how they should act toward them: with deference to the administrators, king, and God simultaneously.

On 23 February 1768, Dumas put Ribes and a colleague, Raymond Rivals de Saint-Antoine, under house arrest. On 5 March, Dumas escalated his "despotic vengeance" by banishing them from the island. He ordered them to embark on a ship in the season of bad weather ("la saison la plus critique") for an uninhabited island ("île deserte") until he decided otherwise. He thought that by his ferocity he could make everyone believe that the actions that he had imputed to Ribes were atrocious. Ribes dissented. He insisted that even if he had done something wrong he had not deserved this punishment, assuring the minister: "My heart is pure, my hands clean, and my conscience tranquil, victim for the moment of the intrigues of M. Dumas, I will find in you the avenger of an unjust oppression."[62] Ribes thought that he could count on the help of the minister of the Marine, who was (nevertheless) a six-month voyage away by ship.

This counterintuitive decision encourages a reframing of eighteenth-century ideas about space and time. By Ribes's calculation, nothing lay between Île de France and France except the "île deserte," so his next and best hope lay in accessing people in France. This solution became overwhelmingly necessary as his efforts failed to persuade Dumas to let him off the ship in Port Louis harbor. The Marine minister lived six months away at Versailles, a definition of time that elided descriptions of the water over which they would traverse and the intervening ports that they would visit, but Ribes believed that he had a better chance of receiving aid via this letter than from any other means of communication. The wording of the letter, emphasizing the bad weather and poor timing of the voyage, implied that Ribes thought that the letter might even make it to France before he did. This possibility was further encouraged by the presumed destination of a desert island, giving Ribes little hope that he would even make it to France.

The testimony of the letter was thus as important to Ribes as its destination. His account gave a counterargument, in writing, to any slanderous dispatches that Dumas might send to his immediate boss, the Marine minister, who was also Ribes's intended recipient. This factor points to Ribers's apparent rush in writing the letter. Ribes wanted to make sure that *his* side of the story reached Versailles first, especially since Dumas had the higher position in the colonial government. If Ribes could get his letter there first, he could appear to be a loyal subject and prosecutor who alerted the monarchy of a perversion of justice by the king's own representative, Dumas, rather than the other way around if Dumas's letter arrived first.

Governors represented the king symbolically and had greater practical powers in terms of managing military fortifications and other island defenses as well as controlling the entry and exit of people to and from the colonies. They often saw themselves as the de facto guardians of the colonies and resented the conseils (and their chiefs, the intendants), whose legal and administrative power they saw as insignificant compared to the governors' access to force.[63] Attorneys general had a role as gatekeeper within the legal regime, however, because they brought and prosecuted criminal cases (sort of like modern district attorney), whereas conseillers tended to deliberate and decide on cases only. In biannual assemblies called *mercuriales*, they were also responsible for calling out their peers in cases where justice had been unfairly rendered. Both Dumas and Ribes appear to have seen themselves as guardians of Mascarene civil order, each citing the other for misconduct based on a wider social understanding of their official roles within the French kingdom.

Dumas and Ribes were forced to work out their differences directly with each other, but Dumas used his power as governor (and stand-in for the king) to force Ribes and Rivals off the island. Ribes and Rivals were then forced to seek the aid of metropolitan authorities, but from outside the bounds of the formal legal system, on a desert island. Dumas's actions removed Ribes and Rivals from the jurisdiction of the conseil by physically sending them away, kicking them out from under the protective barrier of conseil procedure. Aligning himself with royal authority by claiming his symbolic role, Dumas exerted royal authority over the conseil in a way that mirrored royal orders from Versailles that could quash conseil rulings.

The letter took on a life of its own, as Ribes dispatched it ahead of his own voyage. One can imagine the letter itself on a tumultuous journey, stuffed away in a sack deep in a ship's hold as it tumbled through the waves down to the Cape of Good Hope, up the African coastline, across into the Caribbean, and back across the Atlantic to France. It is also possible that people on the ship read Ribes's letter as they tried to pass the time on the long voyage. A man named Tiver wrote to the Marine in 1771 complaining that mail normally entrusted to ship captains was frequently opened by them when they got bored and curious on long voyages. Tiver cited family secrets and commodity prices as two kinds of sensitive information that could be distributed unknowingly via unscrupulous ship captains. He proposed a specific maritime postal service to connect the Antilles and France, hoping to get the contract himself.[64] Ribes's letter might have suffered a similar fate, but it did eventually reach the Marine, where it is now in his personnel file.

For Ribes himself, however, the journey ahead seemed much less certain. With the only destination labeled a desert island, Ribes did not know whether he would make it back to France at all. He spent the next several years banished from Île de France, traveling a circuitous route to France to appeal directly to the king against Dumas. Ribes faced a conundrum familiar to many colonial residents in the eighteenth century: the distance of Île de France from France's imperial headquarters at Versailles meant that colonial residents had to work out their own dispute resolutions or wait for letters or their own bodies to travel the great distance to France.

Ribes was not alone in his fight against Dumas, however. He had been accompanied by Raymond Rivals de Saint-Antoine, another conseil official, while under house arrest and banishment. Supporters of Rivals and Ribes also sent letters to persuade Marine officials in their favor. Rivals's brother, Rivals de Perles, wrote from Lorient on 5 February 1772 to the Marine to request its protection for Raymond against the suffering incurred by the animosity and hate of Dumas. Rivals de Perles claimed that Dumas had always abused the authority of his place, misusing the power entrusted to him by the king. This argument implied that Dumas had cast aspersions on the king, whom he represented in Île de France. Dumas's unjust rule had rightly prompted the response of Rivals (and Ribes) as leading members of the conseil.[65] Like Ribes, Rivals interpreted Dumas's actions as violations (and even a betrayal) of royal authority and the king's responsibility to provide justice for his subjects. Ribes and Rivals's arguments against Dumas cut into the core message of the *Te Deum*: that the king was a divinely inspired magistrate worthy of thanksgiving, and identified Dumas as a false personification of that message.

A number of strong personalities like Ribes and Dumas have stood out in the history of the Mascarenes during the eighteenth century, obscuring the role of a wider community of inhabitants who negotiated ideas about justice and authority.[66] Ribes's fight with Dumas was accompanied by a similar personality conflict between Dumas and Poivre, which was observed by the travel writer Bernardin de Saint-Pierre and others. In the latter case, Dumas accused Poivre of financial crimes, while Poivre thought that Dumas was incapable of doing his job. By the time Bernardin de Saint-Pierre arrived in mid-1768, the Île de France government, especially its judicial machinery, had ceased to work entirely. His description noted a dismal natural environment mirrored by a chaotic civil order: "All I could see around the harbour was a rugged coast, stripped of trees and covered in yellow grass. . . . We learned from the pilot that things on the island were ablaze, with two warring factions headed by the intendant and by the governor, and that there was only paper money."[67] Bernardin de Saint-Pierre recognized the schism that divided Mauritian society even as a new arrival, though he did not see inside the conseil politics of which Ribes was part.

The conflict between Ribes and Dumas spanned France's ancien régime empire: from the local *syndics* to French parlements. Though predicated upon a personal fight, it signaled a divergence in ideas about colonial order that ran across society and lined up *syndics* against militia leaders, conseillers against marine officers, and intendants against governors. This conflict converged on the conseils because these were the state-sanctioned forums in which competing groups (and colonial elites) gathered. Ribes was required to work with Dumas, who symbolically headed the conseil as a royal representative. Dumas had to rely on Ribes and the conseil to confirm his orders and to act as guardians of the king's laws. But Dumas and Ribes had different ideas about who should run local politics and how royal authority should be distributed. Dumas favored the militia commanders, while Ribes supported the *syndics*. Dumas favored a military regime of which he was the head and royal representative, while Ribes desired a legal regime built on local political participation and a rule of law based on the conseils.

The Ribes and Poivre faction won this conflict and the power of the *notables* grew, sheltered under the conseils and lower courts. At the end of 1768, Dumas was recalled to Paris and replaced by a temporary governor named Jean Guillaume de Steinhauer until 1769, when the new governor, Chevalier Desroches, arrived.[68] In the second half of the eighteenth century, increasing numbers of *notables* were integrated into the judicial framework of Île de France. A conseil ruling from Île de France executed letters patent from the king from July 1776 allowing the conseil to name five *notable* residents (habitants) to assist the royal judge and his lieutenant in criminal cases.[69] An additional regulation by the conseil of 10 July 1778 added a sixth *notable* to help the royal judge, who could act as a substitute for the others.[70] A third conseil regulation of 5 July 1782 let *notables* supplement officers on the local jurisdictions, including replacing them if they were unavailable for some reason, pending royal approval.[71] The Île de France conseil took the initiative to hire extra magistrates but recognized that they would have to submit to the king's will. The delay in passing the law and having the king confirm it (accounting for an ocean voyage of at least six months in each direction) implied, however, that the conseil could at least have enough judges to clear a backlog of cases well before the king could stop them.

This pattern indicated an expansion of judicial personnel at the most local level—the royal siège—by the highest local court, the conseil. It also signaled a growing inclusion of local leadership into the legal apparatus of the kingdom, recognized both by the king at Versailles and by the conseil, which added another person in recognition of its own expertise on how many people were needed to adequately dispense justice in the court.

Ribes's case became expensive over time. It continued in France for several years as Ribes traveled around France to seek a final judgment from the Marine and gather the resources and permissions to return to the Indian Ocean. In a letter dated 7 May 1775, he explained to the minister of the Marine, Antoine de Sartine, that he had been out of Île de France for three years (since April 1772), during which he had been visited the royal government several times (at court) to advocate for his reinstatement. He had made three trips to request aid in person: once to the royal palace at Fontainebleau and twice to the French court at Compiègne. This may not count as a typical court case involving a cause, depositions, and witnesses, but it was a court case in that he presented his problem directly to the French court—as a conglomeration of officials and nobles—in person with the hopes that they would, like a judge, decide on his situation.

These face-to-face interactions with royal officials had not worked, however, so in the letter Ribes requested royal payment for him to return to Île de France with his two island-born daughters, as he had no means with which to establish himself in France. Within France, Ribes wandered from court to court to try to recover the employment he had lost when Dumas had banished him, but he does not appear to have had much of a hearing. France proved to be an unsatisfying and insecure place. Ribes sought the help of his brother, based in Paris, but even then he could not find the adjudication and employment that he sought.

Paradoxically, then, the only "île" of France on which Ribes could finally settle was the one in the Indian Ocean, not Europe, from which he had been originally expelled. The island, unidentified in the correspondence, may have been Rodrigues, an uninhabited Mascarene dependency. Though

Ribes had earned around forty thousand livres in profits from his plantations, he found it difficult to convert this income into money that could support his legal difficulties while he was in France.[72] Liquidity was a constant issue for participants in the emerging global economy. In the Indian Ocean world (more even than in the Atlantic), specie in the form of silver Spanish *piasters* was the preferred, but scarce, currency. New experiments in paper money issued by the monarchy, as opposed to privately issued paper, emerged by the mid-eighteenth century. Colonial residents distrusted paper money for its volatility, however. Paper money lacked the intrinsic value of precious metal specie. Paper was delicate, especially in wet tropical environments, as court clerks attested for their paper registers, which deteriorated even without leaving court offices. Paper money values could thus fluctuate wildly across time and space, between France and sites around the Indian Ocean.[73] These transactions, which depended upon the success of communication networks and maritime travel, were further complicated by frequent changes in French monetary policy, particularly in the 1770s and 1780s. Within French territories in the Indian Ocean, however, Ribes could at least consume and sell the products of his plantations and gain a measure of financial security, linking him to the land in both tangible and symbolic ways.

Ribes also sought to reestablish himself among the planter elite with privileges that allowed him to participate in the colony's governance. He explained to Sartine that he did not want to be reinstated as attorney general, partly because the conseil had been suppressed and presumably partly because of his own disastrous experiences in that role. He did want to practice in the new conseil, noting that M. Du Verdereau (formerly his substitute prosecutor) had requested to return to France, vacating his old position as conseiller. He also requested honorary status with the right to *séance* and voix deliberative in consideration of his twenty years of service on conseils successively established on the island: as greffier in chief from 1754, conseiller from 1763, and attorney general (procuréur général) from July 1766. A report from 16 April 1775 recounted his actions since he had been banished from Île de France three years before. He asked the Marine to rule in his favor and quash the conseil ruling against him, as well as to grant him honorary status in the conseil. He repeated what was in the previous report and itemized his requests, of which there were five. The Marine acquiesced in two of the requests, one for honorary status and the other for passage back to Île de France.

The Marine objected to his request for honorary status on the same conseil from which Ribes had been banished, predicting that it would encourage him to renew the troubles that had started this issue. They did, however, recognize his long-standing service in the conseil, so they awarded him honorary status without the right to attend and participate in hearings (privileges of *séance* and deliberative voice). These rights gave Ribes the rank of conseiller without any of the power that typically went along with it, allowing him to rejoin the community of elite planters who ran the conseil but limiting his ability to influence them directly. This punishment may not have limited Ribes in practice, as his return to Île de France, and to the conseil specifically, would surely have led him to seek informal influence by virtue of his connections and experience.

Metropolitan administrators did recognize that some remedy (if not recompense) was due for the treatment Ribes had suffered under Dumas.[74] The Marine granted him passage back to Île de France, along with his domestic and two daughters. It also authorized the cashing of letters of exchange so that he could have money for travel and to set up his new career in Île de France. On 28 May 1775, he wrote to Sartine to thank him for giving Ribes and his daughters passage back to Île de France and also the balance of his appointments ("solde de mes apointemens") that he had requested, though he renewed his request for a position in the conseil.[75]

These "appointments" were legally binding instructions designated for the conseil greffe that would have specified the terms of his reinstatement, assuring that the Île de France community would have to recognize his status.[76] Ribes, like the Gaoulé participants, successfully lobbied the Marine as a conseil member for favorable instructions that were guaranteed by the conseil as a legal repository, winning a conflict with metropolitan administration through the persuasion of interjudicial correspondence and the authority of conseil rulings.

Together on Île de France (far away from their superiors in metropolitan France), Dumas and Ribes were forced to work out their differences directly with each other and within the local community. Dumas employed the strategy of banishment to end the confrontation, leaving Ribes with no option but to seek the aid of metropolitan authorities, but from a sort of no-man's-land outside the bounds of the French kingdom, on a desert island. Ribes reached out for supporters in France via interjudicial correspondence as a countermove to banishment. Though the stakes of political exile were different from those for banishment that originated in familial and community disputes, this case shows that the strategies were very similar. Exile constituted a very direct action designed to end conflict by separating warring parties, while interjudicial correspondence acted as an informal workaround to restore communication and continue conflict negotiations.

Between Îles de France

In both the Gaoulé and the Dumas case, conflict was played out as a contest between royal and local power. Once French subjects stepped off the land onto a ship (whether freely or under duress), they were effectively cut off from political communities centered on the conseils that included local *notables*, magistrates, and administrators. Lauren Benton has argued for "the sea as a space of intersecting corridors" among early modern colonies and metropoles, in which common shipping routes became legal spaces themselves.[77] Evidence from the Gaoulé and the Dumas affair points to a different conclusion, however: that the Atlantic and Indian Oceans were understood as empty spaces, in which French jurisdiction was absent, not present. Though the ship captains for their respective forced voyages may have asserted a kind of sovereignty over these displaced administrators, in practice all of these people were dislocated from the French royaume as a whole, caught in a legal void from which they could only recover by reestablishing their links to a French jurisdiction (usually imperial jurisdiction by contacting Marine officials at Versailles) via interjudicial correspondence that could only be renewed by confirmation from the Marine.

This pattern is also analogous to Sue Peabody's portrayal of slaves arriving in France, equipped to use French law in metropolitan courts, even though they came from a differently defined legal space outside it. Peabody has shown that though France and its colonies seemed to be separated by an impermeable legal barrier of the slave codes for the colonies and the free soil principle, there was actually important traffic across this divide as slaves challenged their status in France.[78] In this case, however, French subjects who found themselves outside any French jurisdiction sought to work their way back in by accessing the nearest courts that they could find. The global array of conseils offered, for subjects like Ribes, the nearest option. Subjects like him worked within France's *royaume* by hopping from one forum to another, whether in person (as when he traveled from court to court in France) or via correspondence (like the letter he first sent while under house arrest).

In addition to the exceptional cases of La Varenne, Ricouart, and Ribes, the coerced movement of people from one colony to another marked out a pattern of transit in the Atlantic and Indian Oceans that encompassed enslaved people, soldiers, and indentured servants. In French colonies, colonial governors oversaw this traffic: the travel writer Bernardin de Saint-Pierre attributed a delay in his voyage between the Mascarenes to the absence of the Île de France governor, who was at Île Bourbon and could not give the order to allow him to travel.[79] Dumas was in a particular position to control people when they were under French jurisdiction. He had also added to this power by making the militia commanders police the movement of planters even while they were on their plantations. Cases like the Gaoulé show, however, that local elites could force governors to relinquish that power by co-opting the power of banishment for themselves.

Banishment was a common punishment in early modern France and its empire. Families in particular sought this remedy when dealing with violent or recalcitrant relatives. Voltaire was nearly arrested on a warrant sent by his father, a lawyer in the Paris Parlement, who sought to disown him and send him to the French Antilles in the first decade of the eighteenth century. Banishment in a colonial setting carried the same cultural assumptions and social outcomes. By putting people on a desert island or out to sea, colonial elites (whether the Martinican planters or the Mauritian governor) physically, symbolically, and legally put them outside the jurisdiction of—and therefore the protection of and recourse to—French laws and personal ties within the French political community.[80]

Banishment from the colonies, however, carried a much stronger sense of removal from society. An asymmetry characterized understandings of colonial and metropolitan spaces: the colonies most often characterized as disorderly and degenerate, the metropole most often seen as the source of civilization and legal order. The banishment of royal officials in the Gaoulé inverted this trend by assigning the metropole the role of chaotic destination and the colonies the role of the place in which order needed to be (and could be) reasserted through drastic measures. In the Dumas affair, however, Dumas claimed his role as the stand-in for the king against Ribes (and, in a complementary case with slightly different dynamics, Poivre) and drew upon the metropolitan pattern of banishment by sending Ribes to a desert island—with no reference to a return to France or another French colony.

The age of each colony and the geopolitical timing of the Gaoulé and the Dumas affair made a difference in the rationale and success of these episodes. The Gaoulé occurred at a moment in which a set of Antillean families had been in place for nearly a century since the colony's founding in 1635, and so they argued that their experience in local governance in the conseils made them better equipped to handle local crises than new governors sent from France. This convergence of local dissatisfactions had inordinate influence, however, because the French monarchy was also in a precarious position. Louis XV had only recently come to power: he was just five in 1715 when he acceded to the throne, the same year troubles first emerged in Guadeloupe. He was seven when the Gaoulé broke out in 1717. The monarchy, in a transitional regency period, had less interest in dealing comprehensively with colonial issues than it would have during an era of muscular imperial expansion like the 1680s or later, in the 1760s, as it reevaluated and redeployed imperial resources following major territorial losses.

Like the Gaoulé, the Dumas affair brought debate about the colonial and metropolitan dimensions of imperial rule to the foreground, but it occurred at a moment in which the Mascarenes needed the injection of royal support to renew the colonies' development as trading and agricultural centers. Following the loss of France's North American possessions at the end of the Seven Years' War in 1763, French personnel were sent from North

America to the Indian Ocean colonies in an attempt to revitalize the East Indian sphere of French colonial interests. The Dumas affair coincided with the arrival of scientific expeditions, like Bougainville's global expedition, and engineers, like Bernardin de Saint-Pierre, who wrote a critical narrative about the Mascarenes. As the monarchy rolled out new initiatives for economic and imperial growth in the Indian Ocean, the character of colonial governance was hardly predetermined, and efforts by members of local elites like Ribes indicated their desire to have a voice in the process by which those initiatives would take place.

Both the Mascarene and the Antillean revolts were remarkable in the degree to which the colonial legal order based on the conseils returned after the conflicts subsided. Colonial revolts were not unknown in other parts of the empire, but they tended to occur on imperial frontiers. As late as 1768 and 1769, revolts erupted in Saint-Domingue, France's late-developing but precocious Antillean plantation colony.[81] They were especially prominent, however, in the frontier regions of the island's western and southern provinces, areas that were still quite rural and isolated from the densely populated sugar plains of the northern province. Charles Frostin has argued that these chronic revolts indicate that Saint-Domingue's white population, from planter to wage laborer, exhibited "constant insubordination" throughout the ancien régime.[82] The Gaoulé and the Dumas affair, however, were characterized by calculated, not constant, defiance that relied upon alternative and complementary methods of legal and political protest, like the local assemblies and interjudicial correspondence, that existed alongside the conseils.

While planter revolts in the first half of the eighteenth century constituted serious threats to the colonial order, the intensification of imperial wars by the middle of the eighteenth century meant that conseillers' interest began to align more and more with royal authorities who had the money and the manpower to defend the colonies (and thus the conseiller's plantations). Revolts like the Gaoulé and the Dumas affair can thus be seen as formative periods in which colonial elites—especially those who had been born in the Antilles and Mascarenes—defined the limits of their autonomy to a larger degree, while having it simultaneously challenged by an encroaching (but not always powerful) monarchy.

These two case studies illustrate large-scale debates about royal authority and local power on a very human scale. The Martinique *notables*, the Mascarene *syndics*, and Ribes resented overbearing military governors and sought to build coalitions of local elites who could counter misguided royal instructions. Though correspondence linked Martinique and Île de France to metropolitan France, personal interactions among local elites in and around the conseil setting were ultimately more important. Ribes's alliance with the Mauritian assembly and the unification of conseillers and *notables* like Labat in Martinique created forces (often armed) that constituted practical and serious threats to administrators, whose resources lay back in France.

In both the Gaoulé and the Dumas affair, a striking number of local participants emerge from the archival shadows, revealing the reliance of high-profile actors upon grassroots support. Repeated references are made to many local *notables* as being involved in these contentions, even though the records tend to emphasize disputes between a few key players: Le Vassor de La Touche versus La Varenne and Ricouart; Ribes (and Poivre) against Dumas. Le Vassor de La Touche was only one of several Martinicans who had accompanied the administrators on their tour. Ribes was only the attorney general who objected to Dumas's instructions to a variety of Mauritian notables (mostly conseil members) who were supposed to participate in the *Te Deum* processions. Colonial revolts were community events that centered on the conseil members but were connected to municipal and militia organizations as well as to networks of parlements and court officials in France.

In each of these cases, conflicts revolved around questions of precedent that were symbolic and processional, not just legal and procedural. Dumas cared about the *Te Deum* ceremony because it symbolized his role as king-by-proxy. Ribes cared because it interfered with the power of the conseil and its constituent *notables*. La Varenne and Ricouart sought to follow the stipulations of the legislation with which they had been entrusted by registering and enforcing it via the Martinican conseil, but Le Vassor de La Touche and the other Gaoulé participants saw these actions (and the administrators' rejection of their petitions and peaceful, if armed assembly) as misappropriating royal authority and overturning a local pattern of assembly and hierarchy that was working without royal assistance. Evidence like the pardon issued to Belair, Cathier, Dorange, Labat, and Bourgelas indicates, however, that these conflicts took place in a community setting, especially among the elite planters who ran the conseils supérieurs.[83] In both the Gaoulé and the Dumas affair, local coalitions of *notables* and *syndics* formed groups corollary to the conseils. They exerted pressure on the conseils via direct petition, as in the Gaoulé, and indirectly, through the support of conseil members like Ribes. In each colony, the conseils were embedded in a wider community of elite and nonelite whites, whether metropolitan or colonial in origin.

Conclusion

Within and adjacent to the conseils, legal personnel and local elites forged justice via creative solutions to such problems as personal competition, provisioning crises, and unwanted trade restrictions. In Martinique, the uprising of local elites known as the Gaoulé culminated in the expulsion of the island's governor and intendant. In Île de France, resistance by conseil officials like Ribes sparked the rage of imperial officials, prompting their banishment.

Mutinies on land (as well as at sea) were a continual risk for new colonies that often depended upon the abilities of a designated leader, usually the governor, to help deal with the significant threat of natural disasters, hurricanes, and volcanic eruptions in both the Antilles and the Mascarenes. In the Antilles, local revolts were endemic in the seventeenth and early eighteenth centuries. Early participants in revolts were frequently pardoned and given general amnesty.[84] Revolts grew less frequent as the colonies became increasingly dependent upon French military support and as colonial elites grew more and more enmeshed in Atlantic networks of political power through patronage, education, and transatlantic legal careers. Colonial demands for autonomy became bound up in a transatlantic conversation about colonial law, articulated by jurists like Dessalles, Petit, and Moreau de Saint-Méry that circulated beyond the Antilles in the form of printed legal codes and commentaries.

In the Indian Ocean, the Mascarenes were isolated enough that local disputes could break out as in the Antilles, creating situations in which local elites had to work out solutions to their problems, even if it meant simply banishing whoever lost in the conflict. They were more isolated than the Antilles, however, in that victims of the conflict like Ribes were forced to call upon royal aid, even waiting for a letter to reach Paris (a six-month journey away). Local elites thus depended much more on royal ties, lacking the local legal community that was large enough and self-sufficient enough to counter royal claims in a similarly strong fashion. Instead, they preferred to work with royal connections at Versailles.

Conseils were separated from each other and the king's court at Versailles by thousands of miles. In between lay vast, often maritime, spaces in which subjects became vulnerable to weather, to exile, to isolation from legal resources, whether accessed in person or via correspondence. Though personal and political contests, like the Gaoulé and the Dumas affair, often centered on the conseils, they could also spill out into other judicial spaces (like metropolitan parlements and royal offices) or into a different kind of space that lacked any legal community or jurisdiction, the desert islands in between. People like the Martinican administrators and Ribes linked these distant pieces together through their correspondence and physical movement among them, motivated by their knowledge of how the France's ancien régime empire worked. They understood that the legal forums that could deal with their problems lay in specific places, like Martinique, Île de France, and France, but they used correspondence as a way of accessing those distant channels until they could arrive in person, whether in the conseil or the king's court, to make their case. Le Vassor de La Touche and Dumas likewise understood that they could use the ocean to detach their opponents from the French jurisdictions, making them powerless to use formal legal channels.

Whether located in Martinique or Île de France, the conseils supérieurs were fragile institutions that depended upon the cooperation of a group of local elites and metropolitan administrators. Individuals involved in the conseils were vulnerable to personal attacks and disaster. Fractures within the conseils pointed to wider fissures extending throughout colonial society, especially over questions of membership. When that happened, colonial society depended upon the ability of people like Ribes and Dumas, Le Vassor de La Touche and Ricouart, to work out their differences and define local rules of civility. Otherwise, each of these parties (and, in a way, colonial society as a whole) risked being cast onto a lonely "île deserte," with a real prospect of death, not just the loss of a court case.

Entrepôts in a Changing Empire

The port of île de France is the arsenal of our forces and the
entrepôt of our commerce.
—Alexis Rochon, *Voyage à Madagascar et aux Indes orientales*[1]

It is in these [Antillean] Islands that one sees accomplished this wish
of nature and politics, that ensures that no man is useless in society. . . .
Some are destined to be armed. . . . Others are charged with
the maintenance of laws and public safety.
—Jean-Baptiste Thibault de Chanvalon, *Voyage à la Martinique*[2]

ON 5 MARCH 1729, the French ship the *Jason* arrived in Île de France from China and appealed to the conseil for help. For the previous four days it had gone without a "single pound of flour nor a single grain of rice" despite the great economies those onboard had made with their food on the voyage, and they had feared starving. On their journey they had stopped at Pondichéry, only to find a famine going on. Passengers reported that in Pondichéry many settlers had abandoned their plantations to live in the woods and hunt. Île de France, despite its great distance from Pondichéry, was the closest French port and the passengers' best hope for aid.

Though the hunger faced by the *Jason*'s passengers was not specifically a legal issue, the conseil deliberated upon their problem. It determined that it could not offer material support. Instead, the conseil directed the passengers to stand by for the arrival of another ship, called the *Aleyon,* due to arrive soon from the East Indies. Île de France magistrates planned to send the *Aleyon* on to Madagascar to collect more slaves and rice, which could be used to aid the passengers of the *Jason*. The magistrates also noted that since Île Bourbon was closer than Madagascar, they would also appeal to the Île Bourbon conseil for help. The conseil doubted that the new arrivals were well equipped to start new plantations in Île de France and contribute to the island's economy, but the magistrates noted that the *Jason*'s passengers could form a useful workforce in the meantime to harvest coffee and help clear land (though clearing land was considered too laborious for them and, by implication, better suited to enslaved laborers). The conseil sent the arriving passengers to cultivate some newly transplanted coffee plants while they waited for a shipment of provisions.[3]

The primary objectives of French activity in the early modern Indian Ocean world may have been commercial, but they were anchored by the legal institutions of the conseils supérieurs. Sea-tossed subjects, such as the passengers of the *Jason*, recognized the services that imperial institutions, such as the conseils, could provide. They also understood that Pondichéry and Île de France, though separated by the Indian Ocean, lay within the same institutional framework.

This chapter unravels such regional dynamics, locating the Antillean and Mascarene conseils within distinct (though interconnected) Atlantic and Indian Ocean worlds. The unique position of conseils as entrepôts at the center of a global ancien régime empire derived from the convergence of colonial expertise, emphasizing cash-crop production and trade, and military skills, regarding colonial defense. This chapter demonstrates how the conseils supérieurs gained strength over the course of the long eighteenth century in the Antilles and the Mascarenes. This happened through a combination of colonial vulnerability, which generated a need for local institutions, and professional opportunities, which enabled aspirant legal and military officials to advance their careers through the conseils. Finally, the conseils supérieurs were concentrated sites for *legal* expertise, through personnel such as the lawyers, bailiffs, and magistrates discussed previously. Their increasing influence also depended, however, upon their role in fostering several kinds of expertise, including military and commercial knowledge. These characteristics remained dominant throughout the long eighteenth century, though the relative strength of these dynamics ebbed and flowed with changing conditions.

French trading entrepôts on the subcontinent of South Asia, such as Chandernagor and Pondichéry, offered far more than just sites of commercial exchange. Rather, these complex and dense urban areas commingled communities of diverse religious, political, social, and economic origins.[4] Islands such as the Mascarenes had lain unoccupied for most of Indian Ocean history. Later, they became oceanic entrepôts for maritime journeys to more densely occupied continental entrepôts, such as Muscat or Chennai, until Dutch settlement in the seventeenth century.[5] Substantial migration and settlement did not begin until the cultivation of cash crops by enslaved laborers under French company rule in the 1730s.[6] The Mascarenes under French rule (beginning around the turn of the eighteenth century) were from the beginning enmeshed in networks of correspondence among merchants and colonial administrators, however, which reflected their central position within a French Indian Ocean system. Ships and messengers were essential as carriers of these messages, but they also marked out their own distinct trajectories as they moved around the Indian Ocean.

Change over Time

Antillean and Mascarene colonies became more and more intertwined as imperial conflicts, such as the Carnatic Wars in South Asia, intensified by the mid-eighteenth century. Both sets of islands hosted thousands of soldiers on the move. Both grew rapidly into colonies with economic interests dependent upon volatile global markets. Leading up to and during the Seven Years' War, officials at the Ministry of the Marine assigned substantial naval resources to defend the Antilles. By 1757, an array of these ships were transferred to the Mascarenes to fight on behalf of the Compagnie des Indes orientales against the British East India Company. According to Jonathan Dull, Marine officials intended to buy time until they could force the British to the negotiating table.[7]

The career of Armand François de Maizière de Maisoncelle tracked with these developments. Born in a village in France's Champagne region in

1724, according to his service record, he entered the military as a cadet in Canada in 1738. By April 1750 he was a lieutenant "on foot" in Île Royale, Canada. By 1760, he achieved the military honor of the Cross of Saint Louis and in 1761 began receiving a three-hundred livre annual pension. His retirement was short-lived, however. He rejoined the military in 1765 as a captain in the Volontaires d'Afrique, with promotion to lieutenant colonel in the Île Bourbon regiment in 1772. By 1775 he had become the commander of a battalion in a new Île de France regiment, where he died on 17 July 1777.[8]

In the 1670s, the Antilles underwent a rapid development into cash-crop sugar economies. New officials, such as the intendant Jean-Baptiste Patoulet, selected notaries and other officials as they built a legal infrastructure to support new colonial and transatlantic businesses and facilitate trade. In 1767, royal administrators arrived to oversee the new direct governance of the Mascarenes and to replace the Compagnie des Indes orientales. Led by the intendant, Pierre Poivre, they reorganized and reconstituted the Île de France conseil supérieur and hired new clerks (greffiers) to organize and oversee the creation of official records.

Saint-Mâlo in France was known in the sixteenth and seventeenth centuries as the birthplace of important Atlantic explorers, such as Jean Cabot and Jacques Cartier, and as the home port of successful corsairs, such as René Duguay-Trouin. Bertrand-François Mahé de La Bourdonnais, a governor-general of Île de France and Île Bourbon (and president of the conseil supérieur) was also from Saint-Mâlo and married into the prosperous Malouin family of Le Brun de La Franquerie, bringing his own fortune of three hundred thousand livres (including *lettres de change*, gold, and diamonds) to a bride who was similarly wealthy. La Bourdonnais's father-in-law had made his fortune by transporting silver from Peru to France. This pattern of Malouins in the Indian Ocean continued despite the creation of Lorient in France as the primary trading entrepôt between India and France via the Compagnie des Indes orientales, for which it was established (hence the name "Lorient"—"l'orient"—or "the east").[9]

In the first half of the long eighteenth century the Antilles and Mascarenes developed local legal cultures that were embedded in and reflected Caribbean and Indian Ocean economic concerns. The benign royal reaction to the Gaoulé in 1717 and the blasé accommodation of pirates in Île de France in the 1720s (such as those who sometimes employed Pitre Paul noted in the Introduction) seem to have coincided with a period of general flexibility within France's empire early in the reign of Louis XV, from his accession in 1715 under a regency to 1723 when Cardinal Fleury took over for a much longer term as regent (until 1743). The colonial government was also in the process of being reorganized at this time. The Marine was formally established in 1715. Subsequently, a new wave of judicial reforms emerged, beginning in 1723 with the promulgation of the second version of the Code Noir (issued to Île Bourbon and Louisiana) and the replacement of Île Bourbon's conseil provincial with a conseil supérieur.

During the first half of the eighteenth century, Pondichéry and its adjacent trading *comptoirs* were almost always at the center of colonial objectives in the Indian Ocean as French traders organized under the Compagnie des Indes orientales sought to take part in the South Asian textile and spice trades. The Mascarene islands, midway between Pondichéry and the Cape of Good Hope, acted as France's Asian redoubt: places in which to amass resources and house military regiments. From the islands, French commanders could protect and secure Asian commercial ventures as well as East African slave-trading routes. So, like Martinique and later Saint-Domingue for the Caribbean, the Mascarenes formed a regional center for France's widely dispersed overseas empire.

Fewer French families appear to have settled permanently in the Indian Ocean colonies than in the Caribbean. Most often, employees of the Marine or local government were posted in various places in this region over the course of their careers with little reference to the kinds of family networks that existed in the Caribbean region. For example, Jean Baptiste Nicolas Claude Lefebvre served as attorney general for Pondichéry's conseil and was later promoted to king's attorney for Île Bourbon's jurisdiction, while families like the Baleine du Laurens dominated a single council, in Pondichéry (similar to the Assier, Petit de Viévigne, and Dessalles dominance of Martinique's council).[10]

In the Indian Ocean, the slower development of conseils (see Table 1) indicates that the Mascarenes remained important primarily as trading entrepôts and only secondarily as colonial producers, in contrast to Caribbean islands' larger and more interconnected regional trade and family networks. The lack of a developed mainland colony for which Bourbon could act as a trading center limited Bourbon's growth as a conduit for trading and retrading goods. Indian ports like Pondichéry and Chandernagor channeled Asian goods to Île Bourbon but remained seaside ventures that had more in common with African slave trading comptoirs than with settler colonies.[11]

As the slave trade accelerated in the 1720s and 1730s, ships also began to arrive from West Africa. One set of instructions to the Île Bourbon conseil noted that the company had sent the *Vierge de Grace* and the *Diane* to buy slaves in Juda and Senegal, respectively, along the West African coast, to be sent on to the Mascarenes, leaving the majority at Île de France. After these ships arrived, the Île Bourbon conseil was to send them on to Pondichéry by August 1730 to collect shipments for a return voyage to France by the end of September.[12]

The same missive from the company directors told the conseil that according to messages they had received in Paris from the Pondichéry conseil, the Mascarenes could expect the *Syrenne* to stay until the next November so that it could facilitate communication between Île de France and Île Bourbon while also making runs to Madagascar for slaves. Further instructions told conseil members where and how to direct several other vessels to the Sofala Coast (in modern Mozambique around the mouth of the Zambezi River; see Figure 1 and Map 2) and China, trading primarily for slaves but also for unspecified goods along the Indian Ocean and western Pacific littorals.[13]

The rise of French participation in the Indian Ocean slave trade is apparent in the intensified discussion of slave-trading company ships circa 1728–1732 that appears in the Bourbon conseil correspondence, but so too is the strength of intercolonial ties between the Mascarenes and the Antilles (though still moderated by company directors in Paris).[14] In October 1732, the directors wrote a short but dense letter to the Bourbon conseil members that again outlined the trajectories of several company ships. This time, however, they focused on the haste with which they hoped that Île Bourbon administrators would reequip ships soon to arrive from the Cape of Good Hope for a series of expeditions to Madagascar.

Upon acquiring at least 350 enslaved Africans (two-thirds male, one-third female, desired ages specified) in Madagascar, one ship was to set sail directly for Martinique, where it would resell and unload the slaves. Meanwhile, two other ships were instructed to meet a Sieur Bart at a new slave-trading port along the Sofala Coast (here identified as the Coste des Caffres) or, if that was not possible, in Bengala (presumably Benguela, along the Angolan coast).[15] The company directors underscored their instructions for the ships to head straight to Martinique as soon as possible, not wanting to risk losing such valuable cargo.[16] For the main slave-trading ship, the *Vénus*, they reiterated the trajectory again at the end of their short letter: Mascarenes to Madagascar, Madagascar to Martinique, Martinique to France. In some cases, the trajectory went back to Île Bourbon from Madagascar and then directly to Martinique as a way to be sure the transactions were done correctly ("en droiture"), presumably a measure to curb illicit trading.[17]

The correspondence itself created the illusion of direct transit and communication between company directors and Île Bourbon administrators, but the content of this letter highlighted a different trajectory in which regional entrepôts, primarily Martinique and Madagascar, played crucial and unavoidable roles. Without the supply of slaves in Madagascar and without the demand for them in Martinique, company directors had no reason to write this letter to Île Bourbon.

Even as slave-trading routes shifted, however, the links between Martinique and Île Bourbon remained strong. Île Bourbon sought to copy the success of Antillean coffee growers: its conseil members recognized that their early coffee cultivation efforts put them at a disadvantage with other French islands. Citing a drop in the price of Bourbon coffee in Holland and Hamburg, they requested samples of Martinican coffee so that they could compare its (superior) quality to theirs.[18] While company directors and the king himself (to a certain extent) sought to manage the affairs of burgeoning colonies such as the Mascarenes, their main contribution was to establish—and sometimes maintain—the legal and institutional vehicles through which Indian Ocean participants could act on a regional scale.

Sanctioned royal and company ships, for example, carried correspondence between Île de France and Île Bourbon. These letters (cited throughout this book) defined Indian Ocean legal culture, which depended more heavily on interjudicial correspondence than in-person litigation and court proceedings. For the French Atlantic, Kenneth Banks has argued for the weakness of both imperial communications and the state.[19] This evidence, however, suggests that even in a more distant oceanic system (thereby more fraught with the dangers of shipwreck and other disasters) such as the Indian Ocean, *enough* correspondence was able to get through via imperially maintained routes to allow a simultaneous (if sometimes time-lapsed) functioning of individual entrepôts.

Legal infrastructure thus developed to support the growing economies of these slave societies and trading entrepôts: the Antilles matured first, then the Mascarenes.[20] Geopolitical objectives also mattered. The small and previously uninhabited island colonies of Île de France and Île Bourbon in the Indian Ocean occupied a strategic location for military and commercial endeavors, as they were located along major oceanic trade routes between Europe and Asia. As French interests in India shrank in response to British dominance, the Mascarenes became centers of colonial trade and defense, developing a thriving coffee and sugar culture. As ships frequently stopped at Île de France to for repairs and provisions, they also traded some of the goods they carried, enabling links to develop between the Mascarenes and many other Indian Ocean ports.

These commercial and military activities also created the need for judicial institutions that could manage conflicts and complications that arose over such issues as trading rights, successions, and personnel disputes. Indian Ocean conseils became key sites in which French participants in international trade could access the French legal system for arbitration and judgment without having to travel all the way back to France. The wide physical distances between the Indian Ocean colonies (and therefore the conseils) meant, however, that the courts were somewhat more isolated both from each other and from metropolitan oversight than were the courts in the Atlantic. In the Indian Ocean, Mascarene courts were critical because they provided access to French legal services that were difficult to access elsewhere.

The Seven Years' War (1754–1763) brought about renewed and reinvigorated colonial advocacy, channeled to metropolitan audiences through *conseil* members. These changes also affected the Antilles and Mascarenes directly, as the British occupation of Martinique and Guadeloupe during the war temporarily cut off their sugar exports, threatening a valuable component of the French colonial economy (if increasingly outpaced by Saint-Domingue). In the Antilles, the war prompted vociferous political engagement by local elites, primarily through the legal and administrative vehicle of the *conseils*, through which these elites exerted political power as colonial magistrates, an extension of their economic power as planters.

The career of Antoine Mercier coincided with the Seven Years' War. It illustrates how conseil-based themistocrats latched onto metropolitan legal networks to survive. His career bridged an early pattern of local investment and loyalty, characteristic especially of the Antillean themistocracy, and an emerging pattern of conscious metropolitan engagement that emerged in both the Antilles and the Mascarenes. Born in Guadeloupe, Mercier had devoted his early career to law through informal local training, having been "deprived, at 1500 leagues from the Kingdom [metropolitan France], of all the resources that the Public Schools offer for instruction," and served as a lawyer and supervisor of notaries (*doyen des notaires*) in Guadeloupe.

Guadeloupe's chief administrator (*ordonnateur*) chose Mercier to assist in the island's defense when British military forces attacked in 1759. Mercier won distinction during a siege of three months. He boasted to the Marine that he had not "taken any of the king's treasure," despite what he implied were massive temptations to profit off war shortages. Instead, he gained the confidence of several colonial investors (*plusieurs capitalistes*). During this period he also spent eighteen months in France, where he participated in weekly conferences designed to reform colonial legislation, which he brought back to Guadeloupe.[21]

Building on this pattern, which had emerged by the early eighteenth century, magistrates from prominent Martinican families, such as Emilien Petit and Pierre Dessalles, launched codification projects designed to articulate the particulars of Martinique's legal history and its current jurisprudential culture to Antillean and metropolitan audiences. This strategy, accompanied by the emergence of a planter lobby in France itself by the 1770s and 1780s, served to attain political influence in Paris and at the king's court directly, beyond the regional port cities like Bordeaux and Nantes that had previously been the key metropolitan nodes of the Atlantic colonial enterprise.

The Seven Years' War, through its Carnatic dimensions, similarly demonstrated the vulnerability of Indian Ocean colonies (such as Pondichéry—besieged twice in this era and twice soon after: 1748, 1760–1761, 1778, and 1793). Mascarene legal elites responded in a strikingly different pattern, one that is initially much more perplexing because of its lack of sources and scholarly attention. In the Mascarenes, a dearth of archival sources for the period 1740 to 1766 indicates a more local approach—perhaps of survival most of all—especially in an era in which the finances of the first Compagnie des Indes orientales spiraled into bankruptcy.[22] The few records that exist within Mascarene conseil correspondence for this period emphasize South Asian trade. A missive from the minister of the Marine, the duc de Choiseul, to all of the company-managed conseils occupied with Indian trade (Pondichéry, Chandernagor, and Île Bourbon—which oversaw Île de France, too) specified company priorities in the acquisition of textiles and precious metals.[23]

By the early 1760s, however, the company's financial position had deteriorated. Mascarene conseil records for this transitional era are spotty at best. As military units were reassigned to the Indian Ocean, however, as part of Marine Minister Choiseul's new strategy to counter British economic hegemony in Asia, the Mascarenes appear more and more as sites for both colonial and local military forces.[24] Île Bourbon conseil registers (greffes) reflect this change, as the number of ordinances concerning military units—national or local—increased rapidly after 1768. For example, militias were established in Île de France and Île Bourbon on 1 August 1768, though not registered until 2 January 1770.[25]

By the mid-1760s, it became clear that the remaining Indian Ocean colonies at Pondichéry and the Mascarenes could no longer be administered by the company, and thus they became the cornerstones in the new, directly administered strategy against Britain. This transition was accompanied by the monarchy's takeover of colonial administration in the Mascarenes and Pondichéry from the (by this point) failed Compagnie des Indes orientales, which also ushered in a new administrative regime, and consequently a new corps of legal administrators, in 1766–1767. Thus, legal sources for the Mascarenes, such as Delaleu's comprehensive legal code, most often begin in 1766 and offer little evidence for the period beforehand aside from mentioning key features of the pre-1766 legal regime, which included the Code Noir (issued to the Mascarenes in 1724) and the Custom of Paris (applied to property and family-law matters).[26] Similarly, none of the administrative decisions or regulations compiled in 1859 by Bonnefoy from the compagnie era 1722–1767 for Île de France mentions the backdrop of global conflict.[27]

This pattern would be extended in the mid-eighteenth century when Guadeloupe fell rather easily to British occupation during the Seven Years' War. Like Île Bourbon with Île de France, Guadeloupe became a subsidiary colony to Martinique by the mid-eighteenth century as Martinique became the central hub for regional governance and commerce (though, again like Île Bourbon, its larger arable land area enabled it to produce more sugar). Thus, by mid-century it had become reliant on illicit trade, especially with English traders in the Antilles and New England to make up for provisioning and other supply deficits.

Few, then, were surprised when the island surrendered to the British in 1759. Some observers in France assumed the takeover had occurred via "treason en masse," convinced of Guadeloupean affinity for the English. This was not exactly true. Having endured the brunt of English attacks, including burned towns and sugar mills and mass killings of slaves, Guadeloupeans had simply lacked the resources to fight harder. English forces had also singled out Guadeloupe (and Martinique) as colonies that could overcome slowed agricultural growth in Jamaica and the Leeward Islands.[28]

The terms of the 1763 Treaty of Paris averted permanent British occupation in the Antilles, restoring Martinique and Guadeloupe to French possession. But the treaty cost France its entire territory in Canada. Subsequently, Marine officials moved military regiments that had been stationed in Canada in large numbers to the Indian Ocean, where many of them decamped at the Mascarenes while awaiting reassignment to South Asian conflict zones, chiefly Mysore and the Coromandel Coast.[29]

Military Aspects

Colonies, especially the Antilles and the Mascarenes, were much more militarized than metropolitan France for two reasons. First, they were garrisons for troops moving back and forth between Europe and the other main theaters of imperial warfare in the eighteenth century, South Asia and North America. Second, these islands were home to enslaved majorities (more than 80 percent by the 1780s). The planter elite, who dominated the conseils, dreaded slave revolts and welcomed military support as an alternative to militia service, which took up valuable time otherwise spent on agricultural production.[30] Though conseils often sparred with governors over conflicting royal and local interests on issues like taxation, they supported the governors on these matters of defense.

Because of this military component to Antillean and Mascarene colonization, governors played a decisive role in colonial administration—in contrast to British colonies, whose governors tended to have civilian origins.[31] In a century of prevalent imperial wars, French colonial governors prepared fortifications against foreign attackers and managed land and naval troops, including the provisioning and housing of regiments en route to other theaters of conflict. Locally, they helped manage militias alongside the same colonial elites who ran the conseils. From the mid-seventeenth century into the first half of the eighteenth century, the Antillean judicial elite was made up nearly entirely of families who had made substantial military careers as well. Founding Antillean families like Collart and Goursolas pop up frequently in both militia and conseil records. This pattern existed in the Mascarenes, too, but was much less pronounced.[32]

France's commercial and agricultural ventures were established simultaneously as military outposts, serving both geopolitical and economic purposes. Colonial military officers, like earlier colonial proprietors, bought plantations and royal offices as they developed diversified careers as planters and merchants. Over time, such officials built distinct social and political networks in and among the colonies. Military service was thus a primary foundation for social and economic mobility in ancien régime France, as wealth derived from successful missions could be used to invest in colonial plantations or to purchase government offices, such as seats in the parlements. The Order of Saint Louis, for instance, was an honorary title given as a reward for military service that was also a key step in obtaining letters of nobility.[33] Similarly, free people of color sought to prove their loyalty to France and thereby establish political rights through military service, especially in colonial militias.[34] As imperial wars continued to break out in the later decades of the eighteenth century, sons of families based in colonies flooded new military academies established in and after 1776, likely capitalizing on such long-standing family experience fighting wars along France's borderlands.[35] Military families provide some of the best-documented cases for the history of France's early modern empire, though they have been overlooked in literature that artificially distinguishes between commercial, agricultural, and military occupations. In the Antilles and Mascarenes, as in other slave societies, cash-crop production and trade depended upon defensive and punitive regimes supported by local militias and imperial armed forces.[36]

Military families overlapped with planter and merchant families throughout the early modern era of colonization, but initial patterns of colonial family networks were established from the seventeenth century. The Valmeinière and Hurault families of Martinique, for example, dominated the island's political and economic elite throughout the colonial era in large part because they had a dual heritage of military service and plantation interests.[37] Members of these two families had originally settled in Saint-Christophe and then moved to Martinique in the late seventeenth or early eighteenth century and had served as lieutenants, commandants, and other officers in the royal military. Valmeinières witnessed Hurault weddings and marriage contracts, while members of both families served on Martinique's conseil supérieur.[38] Another family from this era (which was associated with the previous two families), the Goursolas, survived in Martinique well into the nineteenth century. Adrien Claude de Goursolas appears in Marine personnel records after having been given the honorary title of chevalier de Saint Louis on 28 April 1821.[39] The continuity of these family relationships across the colonial period counteracts a tendency to see Antillean history as a series of dramatic episodes, from colonization to revolution and (for Saint-Domingue) independence.

In the Indian Ocean, distinctions between military and commercial ventures (and families) were less conspicuous as the Compagnie des Indes orientales often contracted its own military defense, until 1715 in Île de France and 1767 in Île Bourbon. The most stable family networks extended from Pondichéry, such as those of the Baleine Du Laurens family, which included at least two generations of men who served as council magistrates on the Pondichéry conseil supérieur.[40] Several families, however, were spread out over several Indian Ocean colonies, such as the Rivals. Antoine Rivals de Saint-Antoine was a council magistrate in the Île de France conseil supérieur in the 1770s. After having been dismissed from service by Governor Dumas, several of his family members, including Raymond Rivals, who lived in Pondichéry, and Sieur Rivals de Perles, who lived in Lorient, France, wrote to various governors and administrators on his behalf.[41] This collection of family members, dispersed across the Indian Ocean colonies as well as the French metropole, illustrates both the distances which separated family members and the lengths to which they were willing to work together to aid each other.

Personnel assigned to Africa and India often overlapped with those stationed in the Mascarenes via the Compagnie des Indes orientales even before the transition to direct royal rule in 1767. Blaise Estoupan de Saint-Jean became a conseiller in Île de France after having first gone to Senegal as an attorney general and then to Pondichéry, the seat of the company's business in the East Indies and later a seat of French royal government in Asia and the Indian Ocean. His career from 1746 and 1770 followed the trajectory of French attempts to establish slave-trading entrepôts in Africa (especially in the first half of the eighteenth century), to recover South Asia in the 1760s (unsuccessfully), and finally to retrench their efforts in the Mascarenes, where they invested more fully in the islands' agricultural prospects from the late 1760s.[42]

Governors-general headed French establishments in Africa and India under the rule of royal companies in addition to colonies, like the Antilles (after 1674) and the Mascarenes (after 1767), under direct royal rule. For Mascarene governors the most important task was to ensure that French interests in India and the Indian Ocean region as a whole were adequately supported. Pierre Félix David rose through the ranks of the Compagnie des Indes orientales in Senegal and other parts of West Africa, then served as governor of Senegal. These African dimensions of David's career should not be obscured, because they highlight the fact that the African slave trade supplied both the Antillean and the Mascarene markets for plantation labor.[43]

Governors traveled farther across and beyond France's ancien régime empire than their fellow conseil administrators. Their experience tended to reflect a background in engineering, construction, and other military sciences, coupled with assignments in key imperial hotspots. In June 1746, David left for Île de France to replace the previous governor, Mahé de La Bourdonnais, and arrived in October. David disembarked in Port Louis to find a chaotic situation. The French fleet had just been defeated in India (having besieged Madras) and had sent its shattered forces back to Île de France to recover. David managed to salvage four ships, however, and send them on home to France.

This was an important, if small, victory, as ships in the Indian Ocean were often beset by terrible storms and the seasonally shifting winds of the monsoon, so those damaged by warfare were at a double risk of sinking. As an entrepôt between South Asia and the Cape of Good Hope, Île de France often served as a waystation for battered ships that needed repairs as they traversed the Indian Ocean between the two, an area which has notoriously difficult currents and is subject to frequent cyclones (known as hurricanes in the Atlantic). David's ability to organize and reform the ailing vessels and their crews served as a testament to his resourcefulness, a key trait for administrators far from the Marine's headquarters at Versailles.

Local colonial governors had played a similar role in Martinique under an attack in 1674, again by a Dutch force (of forty-five ships this time). The Martinican governor, Monsieur de Saint-Marthe, had cooperated with the governor-general, Monsieur de Baas, to rally the local militias at Fort Royal and in neighboring towns. The Dutch did make landfall in this instance and were less easily defeated. The arrival in port of a French naval ship and the heroic stand of an old Martinican colonist named Sieur d'Orange on top of the fort contributed to the final defeat of the attacking force.[44] Several other participating officers, such as Valmeinières, Cornette, and Amblimont, later went on to become conseil members or governors. Here, too, the governor's attention to detail in terms of fortifications and the chain of command made a huge difference for French military forces defending seaborne attacks.[45]

Governors, like most colonial residents, were eager to profit from local plantations, and like the intendants they were instrumental in making colonial economies viable. From 1750 to 1752, David devoted his energies to more domestic matters, encouraging the new attempts to produce cash crops on the island. He supported the planting of cotton and indigo, as well as wheat. He bought so much wheat flour to feed the military troops that the price dropped by one-quarter. This move prompted a growth in the production of wheat, which precipitated a surplus that was then sold in Pondichéry.[46]

The ability to make the islands self-sufficient through engineering and construction projects and the support of imperial campaigns in India marked a successful governor in the Indian Ocean. Between 1747 and 1748, David remodeled the defenses of Île de France, establishing new batteries on the windward and leeward sides of the island. He also reorganized both naval and land forces so that the whole island could be ready to defend itself within two hours. In 1748, David sent Dupleix, the governor of French India, a squadron of six royal fighting ships with 450 men and three million livres, which Dupleix said were crucial for the defense of Pondichéry. A second force subsequently followed to relieve the siege of Pondichéry in 1749, only to find that the siege had already ended. This massive movement of resources across the Indian Ocean left Île de France vulnerable, however, and the island was attacked soon after by six Dutch ships. David's foresight in developing the island's batteries and militias paid off: the Dutch forces abandoned their advance after two attempts to come near enough to fire on the islanders.

Jean Daniel Dumas—of the Dumas affair in chapter 3—was the commander of the Mascarenes from 1766 to 1768 during the transfer of the islands from company rule to direct royal control. He had served in Canada during the Seven Years' War and requested a new posting in Martinique following the war but was sent to the Mascarenes instead.[47] In fact, the loss of Canada in 1763 prompted a massive redeployment of Marine personnel from North America to the Indian Ocean. Some, like Dumas and Antoine de Bougainville (who circumnavigated the globe in the 1760s), had second careers in the Indian Ocean that charted the change in French imperial priorities from Atlantic to Indian Ocean spheres on an individual scale.

In between their activities as planters and military strategists, governors like David also presided over the conseil supérieur as the king's representative. David had previously served as governor and president of the council in Senegal, so by this period he had had ample experience in colonial jurisprudence as well as being a commander of military troops.[48] His previous role as governor under the Compagnie des Indes orientales seems to have made it easier for him to be promoted to another governorship under the rule of the company. He was named president of both Mascarene conseils supérieurs as part of his duties as governor-general; being president fell to him within his nomination for the latter title.

Mechanisms of Aggregation

In France's Antillean colonies, the dispersion of judicial sites formed regional networks of courts and personnel in a pattern that contrasted with the more isolated (and fewer) Indian Ocean conseils. Cases tended to aggregate toward colonial administrative centers such as Fort Royal in Martinique from agricultural areas scattered across many islands. Guadeloupe's council was inaugurated in 1664, at the same time the king issued letters patent for Martinique's conseil, while Saint-Domingue's conseils dated from the seventeenth century (see Table 1). Even isolated and sparsely populated Guyane had a conseil by 1701.[49] Martinique's conseil played an important role as a jurisdiction for several small island dependencies, such as Grenada and Saint Lucia.[50] Martinique, however, was the seat of government for all of the French Antilles until 1714 (for Saint-Domingue) and 1762 (for Guyane and Guadeloupe). Guadeloupe illustrates this regional arrangement, as cases came to its conseil and then were sometimes sent on to Martinique's conseil rather than the metropole.[51] Administrators tried to keep, and clear, cases in colonial settings rather than let them be appealed to metropolitan jurisdictions.

There were some asymmetries in this arrangement, especially when conseil members were themselves involved in litigation. In these cases, the availability of several colonial jurisdictions within a region created opportunities for plaintiffs and defendants to resolve conflicts through local courts rather than having to travel to France. Metropolitan officials likewise could review cases to make sure they followed royal orders, but they could delegate the final judgments and details of cases to the colonial judges.

Cases ricocheted among colonial and metropolitan courts through the appeals process, demonstrating an empire-wide entanglement of courts that dissolved distinctions between "colonial" and "metropolitan" jurisdictions. In the late 1720s, Sieur de Rez, who was a conseiller in Guadeloupe, and Pierre d'Espert, a Guadeloupean planter, went to court in the Guadeloupe conseil over a property dispute.[52] The local nature of the dispute— over property on the island—highlighted the value of having a local forum in which to resolve conflicts rather than having to resort to metropolitan courts (in port cities, for instance) or to wait on correspondence with imperial officials in France.

These local circumstances created other problems, however. Rez had a conflict of interest as both a member of Guadeloupe's conseil and a litigant. As a conseiller, he had a deliberative voice in conseil meetings (*séances*) and the right to convene with other council members while they decided his case, giving him a right to judge his own case. When the Ministry of the Marine reviewed the case in 1731, it issued an arrêt to overturn a decision by Guadeloupe's conseil in 1729, but instead of making a ruling itself, it sent the case to the Martinique conseil for a final decision. The final referral of this case to Martinique indicated a desire on the part of colonial administrators in France to invest local authorities with the practical details of colonial governance. It also, however, signaled the ever-present power of the Versailles ministers to intervene if local magistrates made ill-favored decisions.

Conseils often dealt with cases brought to them from afar as ships arrived full of passengers, like the *Jason* described above, or the passengers of the *Sirenne*, who alerted the Île Bourbon conseil to Pitre Paul's alleged polygamy. Passengers brought their problems to the conseils as French jurisdictions. Court users, in turn, maneuvered among the conseils via interjudicial correspondence. This informal legal lever worked especially well in the Indian Ocean, where the Mascarenes formed strategic trading entrepôts for the French subjects operating around the entire Indian Ocean littoral.

Correspondence along the Pondichéry-Chandernagor and Île Bourbon–Paris axes marked out two crucial pathways within the French Indian Ocean that were reinforced by the frequent crossings of the ships that carried these letters.[53] In contrast to Atlantic conseil communications, these letters focused less on legal, and especially judicial, matters raised by local events such as crimes and litigation, but rather emphasized logistical and administrative challenges to trade. One likely explanation for this difference lies in the fact that French subjects in Indian Ocean territories, such as Rose discussed below, were, until the establishment of cash-crop agriculture in the Mascarenes, overwhelmingly more likely to represent trading ventures based in France in coastal cities like Saint-Mâlo and Lorient, which had their own long-standing legal infrastructure.

Practical considerations, such as travel times, strengthened specific legal and travel routes in the Indian Ocean. Travel times between Île de France and Île Bourbon were asymmetrical: to reach Île Bourbon took one day, but it often took a month to return to Île de France due to the prevailing monsoon winds (see Map 2).[54] The difficulties of travel between the island and mainland France made Île Bourbon popular as a waystation for ships traveling from the East Indies toward the Cape of Good Hope and around Africa back to France. Its coffee industry proved vulnerable to more competitive suppliers like Moka and Java, so conseil personnel tried to control its price by negotiating with the Compagnie des Indes orientales.[55]

In addition, French Indian Ocean territories were held under company, rather than royal, rule for much longer than their Antillean counterparts, which had transitioned to direct royal governance by the end of the seventeenth century. Royal oversight was generally exerted in the form of the conseils supérieurs, with a governor and intendant to supervise the conseils and manage military matters and justice, police, and finance, respectively. The Mascarenes, however, were under conseil administration from 1711 for Île Bourbon and 1723 for Île de France, which reported to the company until it was replaced by direct royal rule in 1767.[56] Mascarene conseils thus shared a commercial orientation with their South Asian equivalents but began to look more like Antillean conseils in the mid-1760s as their plantation economy became mature.

The Chandernagor and Pondichéry conseils naturally focused on topics most pertinent to South Asia. Even more than the letters between the company and the Île Bourbon conseil, their letters largely elide judicial issues, such as criminal-case proceedings. These letters focus almost entirely on trade. Dominant themes include shipwrecks, the quality of wheat coming from the South Asian interior, and reports about local negotiations with South Asian rulers, while raising the occasional concern about competing Europeans in the area. These included the Ostendois, from the Flemish (now Belgian) port, against whom the French often sought British support. Correspondence between the Bourbon monarchy and the company similarly emphasized commercial concerns over judicial matters.[57]

In October 1776, a small ship called the *Pondichéry* left Lorient, France, for China. On board were several passengers, including a man named Salavy and a newly married couple, Monsieur and Madame de Chaux. Their passage was uneventful until 16 February 1777. As the ship crossed the Indian Ocean, Chaux challenged Salavy to a duel, acting on suspicions that the latter had made several secret rendezvous with his new wife of six months, who was only sixteen. That evening, while the rest of the ship's passengers listened to a service of evening prayers (vespers), Salavy stabbed Chaux in the chest. Chaux died instantly. Occupied with their prayers, no one on board heard the duel, reported the ship captain, Querangal, until "the moment of the cry of death." At sea, the captain could do little to prosecute Salavy for murder except collect testimonies from various passengers and an autopsy report from the ship's surgeon. Now in need of a criminal court, the captain changed course and made for the Île de France and its conseil supérieur. Upon arrival in Île de France in March, he wrote to the island's governor and intendant to request permission to deposit a report of the duel with the island's conseil, which was received and signed by the attorney general and registered in the conseil, which prosecuted, but eventually pardoned, Salavy.[58]

In one snapshot from a route traversed many times during this era, this case crystallizes some of the key logistical and legal dilemmas that ancien régime subjects faced as they sought to navigate the dispersed sites of France's first global empire, which lay both in Europe and beyond. Oceanic voyages were fraught with danger both physical (storms and shipwreck) and personal (as in the duel aboard the *Pondichéry*), so French subjects needed safe havens on their journeys in which to repair damage. For matters like duels that had legal implications, the conseils supérieurs constituted essential forums for legal remedies.

Ship captains like Querangal traveled across large distances empty of French jurisdiction in order to find judicial resorts like the Île de France conseil, but French subjects also participated from a distance through letters. Imperial subjects like Querangal sought to record criminal activity and other legally actionable cases with the conseils, devolving his authority as a ship captain to a more secure form of justice as soon as he arrived in Île de France, armed with several testimonies from passengers and an autopsy report by the ship's surgeon. Upon finally arriving in Île de France after a cyclone damaged the ship, Querangal requested permission to deposit a report of the duel with the Île de France conseil, received and signed by the attorney general, and to anchor there for repairs. He requested the greatest "precautions" by the conseil for "conforming to the ordinances of the king for crimes [*délits*] committed at sea" and asked for orders on how to proceed. The captain assured the administrators that Salavy was very honest and had a reputation for good conduct, having been "generally loved and esteemed." The captain noted that the duel had caught him by surprise, as he had observed Chaux and Salavy working together. They had appeared to have great candor and openness with each other.[59]

Querangal worded his report to persuade the conseil to take the case. He reinforced the legitimacy of his own actions against the illegality of the duel between Chaux and Salavy. "After having received aid on land,"

Querangal planned to return to sea as soon as possible. He promised to work hard to put his ship back in order ("en sureté") and make a speedy departure from Île de France. Above all, he underscored the risk of losing his ship to the next storm, an outcome that would strand him and his crew on the island—and leave them dependent upon the care of Île de France administrators, including the conseil magistrates.[60]

Querangal's strategy worked. Court magistrates sought to extend their jurisdiction to people such as Querangal by welcoming their cases and using them to claim a central role for the conseils in adjudicating matters that occurred at sea as well as those on land. Ailhaud reviewed the Chaux and Salavy case, and he granted amnesty to Salavy (as a *brevet de grace*). He then requested that the Île de France conseil confirm the ruling by issuing its own arrêt.[61] Ailhaud insisted on making a decision on the case, seeking a central role for the conseil. The royal jurisdiction, a lower court, officially had jurisdiction as an admiralty court, but the conseil claimed precedence and insisted on liaising directly with the metropolitan government. Ailhaud requested a copy of a similar ruling (arrêt) so that he could model the conseil's version on a precedent. This implies that the Salavy case was somewhat extraordinary: Ailhaud was willing to wait on new instructions, even though he wanted to push the case rather than let another jurisdiction decide on it. Accuracy and jurisdiction were priorities for him.[62]

French subjects such as Querangal became aware of the conseils as they traveled from one place to another through their careers that contributed to the growth of colonial trade and agriculture. The proximity of his ship to Île de France en route from France to the East made the island a convenient stopping point for legal services in addition to the repairs that initially encouraged Querangal to stop there. It also made sense for people who were from a particular colony to be heard in that colony's courts if possible. Chaux came from Île Bourbon, and Salavy was the nephew of Île de France's chief munitions guard (*garde-magasin général*), so they both had relations and other contacts in the Mascarenes.[63] Courts such as the Mascarene conseils might have appeared to be isolated from the more contiguous parlements in French urban centers such as Paris, Bordeaux, and Toulouse, but they were very strategically located for traders, ship captains, and other imperial participants. French subjects were drawn into the global network of legal entrepôts and specifically into conseil courtrooms by events, such as Salavy's killing of Chaux, that required adjudication even if those subjects happened to be navigating the Indian Ocean far away from metropolitan France.

Information traveled along the same circuits as slaves and sugar. In 1771, Hugues Tiver submitted a report to the Marine suggesting a new way to manage correspondence between the Antilles and Europe because the current method of transporting letters was "uncertain, slow and subject to multiple abuses." He explained that ship captains often got bored and curious on the multiweek voyage, and so they often read the mail as a diversion, discovering family secrets as well as other privileged information like commodity prices and production rates (facts commonly considered trade secrets now). Ship captains, he contended, profited from insights (*lumières*) that they acquired and sometimes intentionally suppressed important information by neglecting to deliver letters.

Tiver proposed a central maritime post office that would create a surer method of handling correspondence. A central bureau of correspondence in Paris would act as a clearinghouse for court orders and other critical correspondence, while an in-house cashier (*caissier*) would receive funds and dispense them. In each port, post office directors would collect and manage correspondence to and from the colonies. They would register and stamp letters, enclosing them in a specific tamper-evident envelope that could be opened only by the postal director in each port city. Tampering with maritime mail could be punished, as within France, and postage would generate an estimated two million livres over fifteen years. This scheme primarily accounted for correspondence between the capital and the colonies, but it also provided for correspondence among the islands: a letter sent between Martinique and Guadeloupe, for example, could travel for ten *sols*.[64]

Tiver's proposal implied a high demand for secure mail between port cities, which was often routed through the conseils as the primary administrative and legal entrepôts. Such correspondence can be examined collectively as interjudicial correspondence. This layer of France's imperial justice system included rulings and instructions given by ministers in

France at Versailles rather than locally in the colonies, including pleas to governors for economic assistance, requests for exemptions, and other attempts to bypass or appeal the decisions of the conseils. These sources enrich individual court cases by giving a more detailed view of the concerns of litigants and their connections to other parts of France's empire.

Tiver had not been the first to notice problems with the mail and to seek solutions that would support the webs of correspondence. A 1765 ordinance registered in Guadeloupe created several offices to secure the mail, noting numerous complaints about letters having gone astray throughout the colonies. This new regulation specified its intent to protect commerce, perhaps alluding to the malfeasance of ship captains asserted by Tiver in addition to the more quotidian challenge of lost business correspondence. A year later, a royal edict established a postal system in Martinique.[65] A Mascarene ordinance required ship captains to give the post office director a month's advance notice of their destination, so that they could gather mail to be carried.[66] For nascent colonies in the Indian Ocean, administrators sought to create a repository that would preserve copies of conseil business, despite the fears of local officials that this was a hopeless task—presumably given the difficulty of ensuring that such registers successfully traveled to France.[67]

Vulnerability and Opportunities

In 1727, the *Triton* stopped in Martinique for repairs on the way from France to Île Bourbon. The *Triton's* crew transferred its cargo to the *Hercule,* which finally made its way to Île Bourbon. With logistical support in France too far away to supply the Antilles and the Mascarenes, colonial administrators encouraged Martinique and Île Bourbon to work together.[68] Expressing surprise that Île Bourbon residents found it hard to find trees suitable for building large canoes (*grandes pirogues*) for local transit around the island (which has no natural harbors), company directors noted that the *Sirenne* had reprovisioned in Martinique by permission of the company, emphasizing that Île Bourbon residents should collect timber to make masts and yards for ship repairs.[69]

The option of Martinique as a stopover provided additional security for cargoes that might otherwise be lost or delayed on damaged ships as they traveled between Atlantic and Indian Ocean destinations. Ships arriving from Île Bourbon, like the *Hercule*, brought full cargoes of East African and Malagasy slaves to Martinique's booming plantation economy before reloading with Atlantic goods destined for Indian Ocean ports.[70]

This coinciding of interests was further supported by the custom of ships anchoring at Martinique to reprovision on their way back to France, beginning in the early eighteenth century. Specifically, the already-strong demand for African slaves in the Caribbean created opportunities for Mascarene residents to profit from their easy access to Mozambique and Madagascar, which were slaving economies that were relatively underdeveloped in comparison with the booming and competitive trade in West Africa. As French colonies, they could also avoid transimperial trading restrictions and supply slaves directly to their Antillean counterparts, such as Martinique, an easy target along trading routes from the Indian Ocean.[71]

The fact of colonial vulnerability for the Antilles and Mascarenes—each situated at the heart of a dynamic and contested oceanic system—meant that residents faced two important challenges: volatile populations and warfare. The conseils maintained personnel, military and civilian, charged with guarding against this problem. The conseils' survival throughout the long eighteenth century created an institutional continuity that mitigated against rapid personnel turnover.

A major problem faced by local administrators was a chronic shortage of capable personnel, especially as tropical climates contributed to high incidences of disease and mortality. Administrators confronted a multitude of hazards, such as tropical diseases, long travel times, storms, warfare, and uncertain food supplies. Much of the correspondence between the Ministry of the Marine and the colonies concerned requests for leave (*congé*) to return to France to recover from poor health. Several people who requested employment noted that they sought an office that was currently vacant, while other records mention the illness of council members and other employees as a factor in replacing personnel.[72] In 1717, the Martinican conseiller Major de Laguarigue de Savigny finally returned to France to recover his health after having been ill and unable to fulfill his duties for some time.[73] In 1727, François Le Sauvage was granted one year of leave by the Martinique conseil from his post as substitute attorney general (procureur général) to recover his health, following the certification of an unspecified illness by a local surgeon.[74] Claude Albert Borde served as a judge in the local jurisdiction of Fort Royal, with prior experience as a Paris Parlement lawyer. In 1767, he was nominated to take over the day-to-day duties in the jurisdiction, as well as a simultaneous post on the island's admiralty court, and be ready in case of illness or absence to succeed the Martinican conseiller Jean Médéric Moreau (father of Moreau de Saint-Méry) if he died.[75]

Colonial revenue problems were rooted in these staffing problems. Royal administrators at Versailles understood that vacant positions could mean that taxes went uncollected and—worse—that valuable cash crops and trade could go unprotected. As one solution, administrators designated extra officials to take over in case a key colonial governor left the colony on business or died in office. The chief magistrate of the conseil supérieur, for instance, would sometimes be next in command if the intendant was absent. In 1742, the nomination papers for Saint-Martin as chief magistrate (*premier conseiller*) for the Île Bourbon conseil supérieur specified that he would be in charge of civil and military affairs in the absence of Mahé de Labourdonnais.[76] As the administration of the Mascarenes shifted to direct royal control, three separate orders were created regarding the single office of intendant between 1766 to 1771. The first, in 1766, gave the duties of intendant to the oldest marine *commissaire* in the islands, while a second order, from 1770, designated a specific commissaire, Étienne Claude Chevreau, to replace the intendant (Poivre at the time) in case of death or absence.[77] The last order, in April 1771, named Léonor Claire Potier de Courcy (the *commissaire général de la marine*) to replace the intendant in case he was absent or died.[78] Military officers like Chevreau and Potier also frequently left the islands on various missions, and so an apparently clear chain of command could become uncertain, especially if a colony faced a convergence of crises. Chevreau's job as commissaire included responsibility for the island's food provisions (*vivres*), and he took at least two trips between 1769 and 1777 to inspect Madagascar for its food resources.

Such plans contributed to an institutional continuity, and other offices existed to provide extra personnel. In 1709 in Martinique, the governor-general and the intendant created the role of assesseur in order to permit the conseil to meet despite the absence of enough judges to form a quorum. The king had previously refused to increase the number of conseillers but required that five out of the seven conseillers be present for the conseil to meet. Assesseurs had a deliberative voice only in these cases and could go to regular meetings. If the conseil had enough regular meetings, the conseillers did not have deliberative voice and then would act as *rapporteurs*.[79] A general edict issued by the Marine office in August 1742 specified that conseil assesseurs would be named by colonial governors.[80] Similarly, a regulation for Île de France named several *notable* inhabitants as assesseurs to assist royal judges in criminal matters.[81] This last provision, which encouraged the participation of long-term residents, usually planters and prominent merchants, encouraged ongoing engagement with the conseils by imperial subjects.

The fortune of commercial entrepôts was also tied to the success of the conseils as legal entrepôts. August Toussaint has argued that by the time the ancien régime ended with the French Revolution, the Mascarenes had become the headquarters of France in the Indian Ocean. In 1789, the seat of government was transferred from Pondichéry to Ile de France: "After the War of American Independence which, in spite of Suffren's successes, had not much improved the position of the French in India, many far-seeing Frenchmen felt that the hope of an Asiatic Empire should be given up once and for all and that the development of the Mascarene Islands should become the main objective of the French policy in the East."[82] Waning French holdings in South Asia, lost through decades of imperial warfare, muted some of the grander objectives for Asian expansion, but simultaneous increases in plantation development strengthened the Mascarenes' relative power in the Indian Ocean region.

According to the calculations of the trader Rheims Rose, he had sent more than twenty-eight million francs (considered the same as livres) worth of goods back to Saint-Mâlo during his career by 1777. As a négociant, Rose was an expert in the dynamics of colonial commerce. He wrote a report for the Marine in which he explained the circulation of currency in the Indian Ocean, indicating how specie (especially in the form of Spanish silver *piastres*) never stayed in the Mascarenes but always migrated to Africa and South Asia.[83] Louis XVI had tried to solve this problem by issuing paper currency, but Mascarene residents knew that the rarer silver piastres were worth more (due to their scarcity), further complicating exchange rates. Travelers visiting the islands thus had difficulty making transactions. Bernardin de Saint-Pierre had been greatly disappointed to learn that Île de France only had paper money when he arrived in 1768.[84] As a solution, Rose suggested that the minister of the Marine send a ship loaded with a hundred and fifty thousand or two hundred thousand piastres to the islands and to exchange these for lettres de change (bills of exchange) that could be sent back to the central French treasurer, as they were more acceptable to consumers in France than to colonial inhabitants who were stationed at the epicenter of the prosperous and chaotic Indian Ocean trading system.[85]

Distance was the central challenge for colonial administrators and court users in each legal entrepôt, too, as even the area under a single jurisdiction could be huge. The Îles du Vent, a regional governing category in the Antilles managed by a governor-general, included Martinique, Guadeloupe, and several other islands known as "dependencies," including islands, like Saint Lucia and Tobago, that switched possession from French to British and back again several times between 1680 and 1780.[86]

Frequent cases of shipwreck and capture on voyages between colonies and France posed challenges for all maritime voyagers. Jean-Baptiste Du Tertre reported from his 1640 journey to the Antilles that, upon sighting land, everyone would sing the *Te Deum* and quickly rinse their ragged clothes and dress themselves to become presentable for landing, "as if they were going to be married."[87]

In the Indian Ocean, larger distances and political and economic asymmetries characterized the dispersal and functioning of local jurisdictions. Until France's efforts in South Asia were decisively supplanted by the British in the mid-eighteenth century with the defeat and recall of Governor Dupleix from Pondichéry by 1754, the strategic value of the Mascarene islands lay in their ability to support the South Asian comptoirs with military regiments and to provision and repair ships that were traveling to and from Asian coastlines. Travelers dreaded the passage around the Cape of Good Hope, due to the frequent storms that affected the area and pirate nests in Cape Town and Madagascar. French passengers and crew customarily sang the *Te Deum*, the hymn of praise associated with French royal authority, after successfully passing the Cape and the Mozambique Channel, especially during storms. Other rituals accompanied milestones along these long voyages: sailors and officers would plan for and celebrate crossing the Tropic of Cancer with marine symbols such tridents and harpoons, special food, and by decorating their faces with soot. They got very drunk ("ou plutôt quelque Baccanale"). Various members of the crew and passengers would be dunked or "baptized" with sea water.[88]

In 1782, François Michalet arrived in Bordeaux on an English packet boat, following a grueling journey to the Indian Ocean and back. Michalet had headed to Île de France to take up a post as the intendant's secretary there, but he never actually made it to the island. Instead, his ship traveled all the way around the Cape of Good Hope only to be taken as a prize by an English ship. From there, the ship had taken him to Saint Helena, where he had been imprisoned for a month and then finally released onto another English boat headed to San Sebastián in Spain. Finally arriving in Bayonne, France, Michalet traveled by land to Paris, where he requested royal support for his voyage back to Île de France and a one-time payment (*gratification*) to cover the cost of his losses.

Free passage to and from the colonies was a perk enjoyed by government employees and frequently requested by those, such as part-time conseil employees, who could claim that their work benefited the kingdom.[89] Royal officials, however, argued (as they often did) that Michalet was not an official royal employee, and so he could not be reimbursed. As consolation, they allotted him a *gratification* of 185 livres to cover his expenses between Bayonne and Paris, recognizing his journey *within* French territory while denying recompense for any of his travails in foreign or unclaimed regions.[90]

Michalet, like the Mascarene attorney general Ribes and the Martinican administrators Ricouart and La Varenne discussed in chapter 3, spent considerable amounts of time on the exposed waters of the central and southern Atlantic. Michalet's close, but not quite direct, ties to the global network of royal personnel created a similar problem to the one faced by Ribes. Without the kind of personal ties that guaranteed royal recognition through employment or patronage, even people who worked directly for colonial government (whether as a prosecutor or a secretary) could find themselves disconnected from those channels of communication and aid. Michalet's case also works as a foil for the spatial dimension of Ribes's dilemma. Like Ribes, Michalet spent a considerable amount of time in the southern Atlantic, at sea, as he tried to get into contact with metropolitan officials who could help him reach both dry land and French judicial services.

Unlike Ribes, Michalet got reoriented toward Île de France very quickly. By 15 May 1782 a letter written from the French port of Lorient instructed Michalet to return to Île de France as Chevreau's secretary (not as a key conseil official). On 18 December 1782, Chevreau encouraged Dumas to go ahead and send Michalet on to Île de France.[91] Whereas Michalet could simply return under the approval of Chevreau, Ribes needed a superior of Dumas (in France) to request his reinstatement in Île de France. This contrast highlights some of the differences in the channels through which colonial participants moved: Ribes moved in more elite circles than Michalet, such as his contacts at Fontainebleau and in the Parisian legal community, but in some ways these contacts were actually restricted. Michalet, on the other hand, was more vulnerable—he seems to have had fewer official contacts in Paris (instead working through connections on the ship from Pondichéry)—but it was easier for him to be returned to his original goal.

Environmental Factors

In the Atlantic and Indian Oceans, prevailing winds and currents defined which maritime routes were accessible between legal entrepôts. In the Indian Ocean, sailors had relied upon the monsoons for predictable sea lanes for millennia. In the Atlantic, winds and currents made Martinique an easy target for ships coming from Africa, whether carrying West African slaves or trade goods from the Indian Ocean via the Cape of Good Hope. Slave-labor shortages in colonies such as Louisiana and Guadeloupe could often be attributed to ships having first sold their human cargo in more accessible sites, such as Martinique and Saint-Domingue.[92] Such environmental factors also helped generate cycles of interjudicial correspondence as ships carried mail and the letters of passengers.

The environmental challenges that helped precipitate the Gaoulé and the Dumas affair defined life in the Antilles and the Mascarenes during the eighteenth century. Hurricanes and provisioning crises could prompt colonial residents to seek legal recourse, to stave off bankruptcy for example, in the conseils. They also appealed to colonial administrators, such as conseil magistrates and associated legal personnel, through personal appeals and petitions gathered by local assemblies.[93] On some issues, like nobility and tax exemptions, local elites needed royal approval, but colonial investors and residents were willing to submit to metropolitan rules (and delays).[94] On other matters, particularly the issues of provisioning, defense, and slavery, colonial elites argued that they were the only ones who had enough local knowledge to properly ensure and govern enslaved and free subjects.

These issues were interconnected. Provisioning undergirded the survival of nonslaves, and to a certain extent of slaves, too, keeping the island populations high enough to sustain the plantation colonial economy. Defense took into account concerns about outside invasions but prioritized local threats, such as revolts sparked by enslaved people and maroons. Slavery permeated social, economic, and political calculations: expeditions to Madagascar were almost always both for new supplies of food and for slaves, linking provisioning and slavery into a single enmeshed economy.

Local crises were the most likely to prompt local resistance to metropolitan governors or conseil authority. The best agricultural regions in the Antilles and the Mascarenes also tended to be the most under-provisioned, as land was devoted to cash crops like sugar and coffee rather than food staples.[95] Food shortages were constant threats in both the Antilles and the Mascarenes. It was no accident that governors were frequently responsible for bringing new food crops to their colonies for slaves. For example, the Île de France governor La Bourdonnais introduced manioc to the Mascarenes in the 1740s for slave consumption. He also revitalized colonial agriculture with the aim of making the islands a provisioning station for military units traveling between France and South Asia.[96] Water scarcity (or abundance, in some cases) may have also figured into contestations between Antillean (in this case, Dominican, Martinican, and Guadeloupean) planters and enslaved people.[97] The French Navy was good at building forts and roads, but it was terrible at ensuring the safety of trade routes and food supplies, so in an odd way it acted more like an army than a navy.

Colonial residents devised makeshift tactics to compensate for their consequent vulnerability, such as flying neutral or foreign flags (*pavillons*), arming corsairs, and breaking blockades—strategies that help explain both local outbursts of autonomy as expressed in political revolts and chronic patterns of smuggling.[98] Martinique and Île de France straddled vital Atlantic and Indian Ocean trading routes, respectively, but they were both outproduced by their complements of Guadeloupe and Île Bourbon. Higher population densities and established plantations made it difficult to add provisioning grounds in places like Martinique. In both the Antilles and the Mascarenes, frequent legislation on the cultivation of lands granted by the king pointed to an inadequate supply of staple food crops as well as a possible reluctance on the part of planters to make concessions profitable quickly enough.

Provisioning and defense had been issues in the domain of French royal authority, but colonial residents increasingly saw themselves as on their own when it came to planning for hurricanes and other crop disruptions as well as for external attacks, from which military strategists at Versailles were little help. The organization of local assemblies in both the Antilles and the Mascarenes reflected grassroots efforts to deal with these challenges, while their interactions with the conseils showed that local initiatives could be met by a range of reactions, from the support of Ribes and Hauterive to the dismissal of Dumas and Crapado.

The Gaoulé and the Dumas affair illustrate two different logics for dealing with colonial crises. In the Gaoulé, a coalition of local elites aligned against imperial administrators as they arrived from the metropole. This strategy favored cutting off metropolitan control of the colonial political economy completely, rather than negotiating with imperial representatives.

Major conseil and planter families like Le Vassor de La Touche did not hesitate to question royal authority and to assert their autonomy. The Le Vassor de la Touche family and the Dubuc family were the two most powerful Martinican clans. Though they sometimes allied with the conseil as part of the island's local elite, as in the Gaoulé, they could also act independently of the rest of the chief plantocracy and themistocracy.[99]

In the Indian Ocean, the Dumas affair erupted from a similar conflict between local and metropolitan elites, but local members of the elites like Ribes chose to circumvent rather than defy the metropolitan representative by appealing directly to ministers in Paris. There administrators like Dumas (and Poivre) thought their decisive and aggressive tactics were appropriate as they sought to create a roadmap for new crops and trade and a reinvigorated French military presence in the Indian Ocean. Local elites gathered support from the local assemblies (as in the Gaoulé), but when this strategy proved inadequate with the banishment of Ribes, they drew upon their knowledge of the empire as a whole to find alternative forums, even appealing personally to ministers at Versailles.

The extenuating circumstances in the background of these crises were peculiar to the colonies—both the Mascarenes and the Antilles—and distinct from metropolitan problems. Provisioning crises did affect metropolitan France throughout the eighteenth century (bread riots famously figuring in the early stages of the French Revolution), but they never erupted out of the same kinds of physical and imperial isolation faced by the colonies. Likewise, the constant threat of imperial takeover that motivated such independent actions by the Martinican *notables* and such heavy-handed rule by Dumas were unique to islands that were at the center of busy, rich, and constantly disputed regions of European imperialism. In these areas, such conflicts were specifically colonial and reflected local fears about becoming isolated, hungry, and defenseless against nearby opponents and a faraway imperial defensive force.

Planter revolts were persistent though unpredictable features of Antillean and Mascarene history during the eighteenth century, much like the hurricanes and cyclones that frequently ravaged the islands. A lack of imperial support pushed administrators and local elites—usually constituted as conseils supérieurs—to act independently. In the Antilles, these assemblies had the critical mass of *notables* needed to counter royal instructions from Martinique and Guadeloupe. In the more isolated Mascarenes, interjudicial correspondence was a more important factor that extended local complaints as conseil members like Ribes sought outside support for their actions and against royal administrators.

These conflicts, however, also tracked with metropolitan concerns about the dimensions and quality of French political power. In both the Dumas affair and the Gaoulé, colonial participants sought audiences in Paris to protest their treatment and insist upon their innocence. The Gaoulé participants (unlike Ribes) did not visit the royal court themselves but used the interjudicial method of correspondence with the Marine to introduce a competing narrative to the report of insurrection that La Varenne and Ricouart were certain to give. Ribes, too, used interjudicial correspondence to forestall accusations from a metropolitan representative, Dumas, and to jump across jurisdictional boundaries to reach a metropolitan audience. He supplemented this strategy by visiting the royal court as it moved between Versailles, Compiègne, and Fontainebleau, circumnavigating France's ancien régime empire in person as well as via letter.[100]

More than the Gaoulé, the Dumas affair can also be interpreted as a metropolitan controversy, especially as three individuals (Dumas, Ribes, and Poivre) battled each other over competing claims to royal authority. Gaoulé participants started from a position in which they were less tied to the court in France and law courts like parlements, so their strategy was to make their own informal assembly as an alternative to the conseil. This move kept the affair within the realm of the colony, the local setting, rather than reaching across the Atlantic. The banishment of Ricouart and La Varenne also enforced a boundary between the metropole and the colony that Ribes spent his time trying to break down. In the Dumas affair, however, all three officials had significant experience in the highest circles of French royal authority, and all three had contrasting ideas about how their share of that authority should be enacted in Île de France.

The existence of local assemblies in both Martinique and Île de France does, however, point to a long-standing pattern of homegrown forums that were designed to deal with the problems that colonial notables thought were important. The movement of people like Ribes and Le Vassor de La Touche from the assemblies to the conseils and back indicated not that the assemblies were meant to replace the conseils but rather that they could be called in to provide an unsanctioned (by the king) though locally legitimate forum when conseils did not do the job that the *notables* expected of them.

The difference was whether metropolitan administrators would be included the conseils. As the official heads of the conseils, the governors and the intendants were required to be included in their proceedings. Locally organized assemblies, however, could draw upon the legal expertise of people like Ribes and the other magistrates, but they could exclude administrators whom they saw as blocking judicial and administrative processes.

Death: Unwitting Participants

Many colonial residents became the subject of conseil proceedings, but only after they had died, as conseils sought to clear the estates of those who died intestate. Because they controlled the outcome of probate cases, conseils held significant power as arbiters even over people who did not initiate or participate in court cases. The conseils managed the personnel, such as bailiffs and clerks, who processed successions. But they also adjudicated vacant successions in which colonial subjects died intestate, often without known kin. Thus unwitting court participants influenced how the conseils practiced law, as deceased French subjects whose unclaimed estates came under conseil jurisdiction.

Gabriel Labour died unexpectedly in Île de France in 1774 when the powder mill in which he worked as a carpenter caught fire. His tragic death brought together many local residents—including officials as well as his friends—to gather and distribute the few possessions he had left behind. He lacked any known relatives in the colony, and so his estate was considered vacant. Vacant successions were fairly easy cases to complete, requiring only a few conseil employees to inspect the deceased's estate and complete the paperwork.[101] The Île de France conseil's attorney general, Jean Marie Virieux, presided over the proceedings for Labour's succession and signed off on the guardian's appraisal and distribution of the estate, accounting its total value at 1,081 livres. Though the succession was not completed until 1782, it involved only three conseil employees and appears to have been quite simple to manage. The eight-year delay most likely signals the time taken by conseil employees to try to find Labour's next of kin—an effort that leaves no trace of success.

Upon tallying Labour's possessions, the clerk valued the estate at 1,859 livres. For the colonies, this was a very small estate. A typical sugar plantation was valued at a hundred thousand livres, though the value could range enormously. Most of the value of the estate Labour left behind was attributed to his single slave: a Malagasy woman named Angelique. Debts included expenses for food for Angelique as well as fees incurred by conseil officials, including the notary and the guardian, which were paid out of the estate. Labour's possession of a single female slave implies that she may also have been his mistress, as women were scarce in the Mascarenes, and men often cohabited with enslaved women.[102] The succession record does not, however, give any details about Angelique's life or relationship with Labour. Instead, it lists her value at 800 livres and notes that the guardian, Jean Louis Suerto, and notary, François Pelte, sold her for 1,010 livres, making a profit of 210 livres. Out of the whole estate, the colony collected 1,081 livres, since Labour lacked a known extended family; vacant successions could yield a welcome windfall.[103] Though Labour never knew about it, he too was a conseil subject as the court tallied up these few possessions and sold them to the profit of the colonial government.[104]

Vacant successions such as Labour's imply some ambivalence toward the conseils and legal services by those who could not afford to access them. Their existence attests to the power royal representatives, whether *curateurs* or court magistrates, exerted even over people who did not choose to use them. Wills could be drafted by notaries or procureurs but cost money to commission. For colonial residents of humble means, like Labour, drawing up a will likely seemed pointless and inefficient given a lack of nearby kin and substantial property. Labour does not appear to have ever entered the conseil chambers himself. But successions were a key mechanism by which conseil members exerted local power, especially regarding property.

Thoughout France and its empire, property transactions fell under civil jurisdiction and had to be discharged locally by assessing a deceased person's possessions and debts, tracking down any possible heirs, and auctioning off unclaimed goods. Successions occupied a substantial percentage of the conseils' time, wherever they were located. Occasionally, the Chandernagor and Pondichéry conseils also reported to each other on successions. The number of unclaimed estates grew large enough by the mid-eighteenth century to warrant the appointment of specific officials to manage them. This change reduced the workload for conseil magistrates but added new officials for them to oversee. The state also had a strong incentive to manage successions, as it could charge large fees and claim assets for which no heir could be found. Here, the additional distance from Europe made it exceptionally difficult to identify and notify potential heirs even with the frequent correspondence between Pondichéry and Chandernagor about pending estate cases.[105]

Conclusion

The late eighteenth-century scientist and traveler Alexis Rochon worried that Madagascar and the Mascarenes were too isolated to be useful to French imperial and commercial projects in the Indian Ocean, but he ultimately concluded that with the right investment of resources, one of those islands, Île de France, could form "the arsenal of our forces and the entrepôt of our commerce."[106]

When Rochon called Île de France the "arsenal of our forces," he identified it as a strategic site for the French in the Indian Ocean. Military regiments frequently stopped there on their way to India to protect French trading centers like Pondichéry. During the eighteenth century, Île de France was largely a military base, a lot like the modern U.S. military base at Diego Garcia, also in the Indian Ocean. From Île de France, French naval officers could organize fleets to go to Madagascar, India, or East Asia.

When Rochon wrote of Île de France as the "entrepôt of our commerce," he referred to the island's strategic significance along Indian Ocean trade routes. Soldiers, sailors, and traders stopped there to repair their boats, buy new supplies, and even deal with legal matters. Successful traders like Rheims Rose used Île de France as a staging area for trading expeditions throughout the Indian Ocean. He sold coffee from Île de France to France, he shipped slaves from Mozambique to Île de France, and he brought back porcelain from China. As the Dutch had discovered in the seventeenth century, and as Rochon agreed, Île de France was ideally located as a base for trade around the Indian Ocean littoral (and beyond).

This chapter has clarified some of the mechanisms by which an interconnected early modern French Atlantic and Indian Ocean world developed. Geopolitical and military developments over the course of the long eighteenth century unfolded in tandem with transformations in Antillean and Mascarene legal cultures. Such a century-long perspective changes understandings of an interconnected early modern Atlantic and Indian Ocean world in two ways.

First, French Atlantic and Indian Ocean colonies were embedded in many of the same global rhythms. British imperial scholars, especially South Asianists, have long noted the connections between a British Atlantic and Indian Ocean during the long eighteenth century. Their Francophone counterparts, however, have been much slower to recognize these reverberations, with the exception of work that has incorporated Mascarene slavery into more familiar narratives of Atlantic slavery.[107] This story, however, follows a full cast of legal personnel across the long eighteenth century, as the conseils, and by extension Antillean and Mascarene legal cultures, changed over time. The consolidation and expansion of regional imperial conflicts into the truly global Seven Years' War by the mid-eighteenth century prompted both Antillean and Mascarene legal participants to adopt more defensive postures aimed at securing metropolitan attention and aid. This change took several forms, some of which were unique to the Atlantic and Indian Ocean arenas.

Second, in the archives, and subsequently in the secondary literature for the Indian Ocean, the regional dimension easily falls out of focus for the Seven Years' War. Older histories detail military maneuvers, while newer works favor a comprehensive approach to this "first" global war, giving detailed analyses of major engagements between British and French forces in North America, Europe, and South Asia.[108] Scholars have explored the

aftermath of the decisive victory of the British in the war, but they emphasize the immediate impacts of the war rather than considering this era as a
critical turning point *within* a long eighteenth-century process of European
imperial intervention in the Indian Ocean and the Atlantic.[109] For the Atlantic, historians have investigated post-1763 designs for new colonies, but little scrutiny has been brought to bear on Antillean and Mascarene zones of
occupation during and immediately after the war itself.[110]

Through the migration of court users such as the passengers of the
Jason to the island's courtrooms, Île de France also became a legal entrepôt
that linked continental entrepôts like Pondichéry and insular hinterlands
like Île Bourbon and Madagascar. Rochon had been half right when he said
that the Mascarenes could become "the arsenal of our forces and the entrepôt of our commerce": he overlooked the legal and political forms that
such an arsenal and entrepôt took.[111] Letters migrated between these locations, as did individuals, but via the vehicle of conseil-sanctioned transit.

Conclusion

IN 1668, JEAN de Lacombe, sieur de Quercy, departed from the French port of Bordeaux to travel to Île de France (now Mauritius) in the Indian Ocean, beginning nearly a decade, from 1668 to 1676, as a captain in one of France's many military regiments. At times working specifically for the Crown, at other times protecting valuable cargo for state-sanctioned companies, he served in England, the Americas (including Brazil and Québec), Batavia, and Java as well as Île de France. Lacombe's travels highlight the circuits of trade and far-flung military operations of France's late seventeenth-century colonial apparatus.

Lacombe's description of six months touring in the Americas, then his service in European wars, and finally his travel to the East Indies are emblematic of the three spheres in which France's first empire operated: the Atlantic, Europe, and the Indian Ocean. Lacombe's travel through and among these spheres documents their permeability and interlocking relationships. Continental wars in Europe were concurrent with the expansion of American empire. French administrators and investors undertook American and Asian projects simultaneously, especially between roughly 1680 to 1780. French subjects like Lacombe initially made global careers through the opportunities afforded by military service in imperial wars, but the political upheavals generated by such wars also created massive opportunities for legal professionals to make careers in new overseas territories, chiefly by obtaining posts in the colonial law courts known as conseils supérieurs.

Lacombe's travels demonstrate that the Atlantic and Indian Oceans, though distinctive, were never separate spheres of French imperial activity. Instead, these spaces formed a coherent whole as they were traversed and connected by the constant movement of French subjects and their correspondence. These movements were often channeled through the global network of legal entrepôts, especially the conseils supérieurs. If colonial and imperial

170

history has most often been told as the history of spaces in between—and of links and movement and migration and travel—then the conseils give us sites in which to observe various colonial movers from a single vantage point.

Seaborne travelers marked out global circuits among these sites. Others sent letters carried on ships, building a global community. Their inter-judicial correspondence traced a global legal network, akin to a Republic of Letters. Some routes stand out, more deeply inscribed and reinscribed with multiple succeeding journeys. Intense connections tied the Antilles and the Mascarenes to the metropolitan center at Paris, via Le Havre, and to Atlantic entrepôts such as Bordeaux and Nantes. Conspicuous and long-standing connections also developed between colonies, as between Martinique and Île de France.

State-dictated pathways of communication aimed to ensure colonial cooperation with metropolitan schemes, but litigants, like the free woman of color Magdeleine Françoise, and overseas traders, like Rose, could navigate these routes in the opposite direction—toward France—in search of legal protection or state patronage. Such cases, often preserved as the metropole-directed side of a two-way conversation, suggest that the overwhelming dominance of direct communication between Paris and individual colonies reflects more the temperate (not tropical) archival conditions in France than a fully realized Colbertian information state. The intercolonial relationships and regional analysis (as briefly attempted here) documented in cases such as Martinican dynastic rule in the Antillean conseils and the adventurer Fi-let's western Indian Ocean slave-trading designs build out this critique fur-ther, hinting at a *polycentric* global empire, modifying revisionist models of a weak state (as proposed by Kenneth Banks and James Pritchard).[1] In these cases, regional hubs like the conseils in Martinique and Île de France offered sufficient access to both royal and local power.

Empire's Legal Archipelago

In the eighteenth century in France, an unknown artist imagined the French empire as a sun shining over an immense but calm ocean: a landscape drawn of France's ancien régime empire (Figure 11). The imperial sun is emblazoned with three fleurs-de-lis, symbols of the Bourbon monarchy, and flanked by transparent clouds. The viewer stands on an unknown shore, surrounded by some of the tools of empire building: two cannon and some cannonballs, a ship's anchor, sails, a drum and some trumpets, and a banner. A ship of the line is moored to the right. Two other ships sail in the middle distance. The proximity of these two ships to the sun to indicates that they, like the ship closer to land, remain under French guardianship even while at sea. To the left, a town—small in proportion to the ship—sits just beyond the jumbled assortment of sails and munitions. Is the onlooker standing in a colony newly brought to heel by the conquering sun? Or perhaps the jumbled materiel is evidence that those ships have just departed, loaded with ammunition, to conquer a new distant territory. The onlooker's perspective is ambivalent. The town (like the ships) is dwarfed by the sun, which presides over the entire landscape. Rising from far away, the sun exerts an inescapable power over all.

Encapsulating ideas about imperial power and place, this image was placed above a royal edict issued at Versailles, the capital and epicenter of France's empire, which created a central repository for documents created in overseas colonies. This edict created part of the archive that has since become the Archives nationales, section outre-mer, now based in Aix-en-Provence, whose holdings form the basis of this book.[2] In the universalized setting of this imperial clip art, the setting could be France. It could be Martinique. It could be Île de France. The image emphasizes the scope of French sovereignty held in the person of the king and symbolized as the sun. The sun shines over a town full of people and an emptier ocean containing scattered ships that meet at the shoreline, where an assortment of maritime equipment lies on the land. In the image, the sun is the center point for all activity. In the text of the edict from 1776 in which the image appeared, establishing a central depot for legal papers from around the empire, Versailles is the central point to which all subjects—even those who inhabit colonial margins like the image's seashore—must direct their accounts.

As this book demonstrates, however, France's ancien régime empire was constituted by French subjects, not by cannon and ships, in distinct sites around the globe.[3] Royal power concentrated at Versailles and, for the

Figure 11. Illustration in *Édit du Roi, Portant établissement à Versailles, d'un Dépôt des papiers publics des colonies,* June 1776, Gallica, Bibliothèque nationale de France

colonies, in the Marine office, was diffused to overseas territories not by a sun but by the movement of people and paper. One can imagine Jean de Lacombe, for example, disembarking from the moored ship in the image and leading his soldiers toward the town. Perhaps it was his men who left the cannonballs. Perhaps Pitre Paul, the sailor and sometime polygamist from the beginning of this story, laid out the ship's rigging to dry on shore. On the walk into town, we can imagine meeting the ship captain Querangal, rushing to tell the conseil registrar about the duel (or murder) that happened at sea. We might bump into Magdeleine Françoise and her children, coming toward us to catch a ferry to a neighboring island. As we enter the town, we might stop as a *Te Deum* procession traces the distance between the parish church and local government offices. (Can we notice Governor Dumas fuming, plotting to exile his attorney general Ribes, as he trades dirty looks with Indendant Poivre?)

This image also encourages questions about the imperial power itself that emanated from France and was centered on the monarchy at Versailles, symbolized by the sun and fleurs-de-lis. France's ancien régime empire spanned Europe, the Americas, Africa, and Asia, but this global state depended upon a configuration of legal entrepôts set up in key parts of the European and overseas empire. In between these entrepôts, French subjects and court participants could fall, or be pushed, into legal lacunae that were both real, like Ribes's dreaded desert island and the Martinican administrator's Atlantic banishment in chapter 3, and symbolic, like the punishments of La Grange and Bordenave in chapter 2. Without the court magistrates and other participants (or in cases where there was a refusal to participate, like the Gaoulé), parts of France's overseas empire could become disconnected from the whole. This framing challenges us to rethink categories of globalization and migration to account for the absence as well as the presence of unifying forces like law. Conseils were staging areas for conflicts between (and among) local and metropolitan interests that could extend into the countryside, as with Ribes's connection to Yardin and other Mascarene *syndics* and La Touche and Hauterive's ties to both the Martinican conseil and the local assembly. Conseils were also gateways to metropolitan France, as conseil membership gave Ribes and the Gaoulé leaders legitimacy—through an official rank—to contact metropolitan administrators.

Conseils were crucial, then, for their legal function and because family networks latched onto them as nodes of power. Council affiliation was usually one of several roles played by colonial residents who sought to raise their economic and political status, and it often became a stepping-stone for local elites who aspired to higher office in France and elsewhere. A study of council members, then, reveals entire networks of elites, ranging from lawyers to planters to merchants.

The legal regime that emerged over the course of the long eighteenth century claimed to constitute a single political community supported by a network of legal entrepôts spread around the globe and maintained by an increasingly homogenized framework of codified legislation. This "archipelago of justice" accounts for the ways France's ancien régime empire, like other empires, imposed connectedness and uniformity upon its subjects, a set of strategies that Jane Burbank and Frederick Cooper have called "repertoires of imperial power."[4] For France's ancien régime empire, some of the most important repertoires were components of the conseils supérieurs: the common legal vocabulary, the familiar set of courtroom *accoutrements*, the standardized panel of conseillers and greffiers.

For powerful Antillean and Mascarene families and metropolitan administrators, these commonalities created opportunities to build successful transoceanic and global careers. Likewise, members of the nonelites like Madame Blot and Pitre Paul participated in judicial forums in the Antilles, the Mascarenes, and Europe via the conseils and metropolitan courts and through interjudicial correspondence. Conseillers like Desgranges de Richeteau, discussed in chapter 1, could travel from a job in the Paris Parlement to the Île de France conseil without having to learn a new language or skill set. Legal knowledge acquired in France was so useful in colonial contexts that Martinican families like the Dessalles and the Moreaus made sure to have at least one member per generation who had trained in France.

The French subjects analyzed in this book negotiated legal issues in legal entrepôts in new zones of French sovereignty such as Île de France and Martinique. They also frequently continued to work out these same issues in metropolitan centers like the Paris Parlement. These subjects often managed these different forums at different stages in the same cases, drawing lines of connection across the traditional metropole-colony binary with their physical movement in and out of courtrooms across France's early modern empire. These movements were enmeshed by networks of correspondence among legal entrepôts in France and its colonies that supported the movement of court cases through channels of hearing, adjudication, and appeal.

Oceanic Routes Ahead

France's global constellation of law courts connected these spaces into a coherent whole, a pattern that counters the claims of historians who have argued that the Indian and Atlantic Oceans were separate "legal regions" or "regional regulatory spheres" beginning early in the eighteenth century.[5] Recognizing the contributions of Atlantic and Indian Ocean historians, we can find the beginning of an oceanic comparison by looking specifically at law courts (in this case, French conseils supérieurs) as discrete sites in and through which transoceanic migrants interacted.[6] Local cases from plantations and roads just out of eyesight made their way into the courtroom, or conseil magistrates went out to visit the sites of crimes. Likewise, by waiting in port to see which ships (and their passengers) make their way onto land and into the courtrooms—or watching to see what letters and passengers go out on the next voyage—we can delineate global patterns of movement. Court participants—whether innkeepers, itinerant shipworkers, or lawyers—made frequent use of these physical pathways. However, they needed—and often made special efforts to access—the particular legal pathways that they could access only via the conseil and its employees, opening up new routes among colonial and imperial centers of power. By standing at the threshold of the conseils supérieurs, we can observe the global and the local within the same frame.

Noting that specific, local zones of intense interaction have characterized the Indian Ocean region for much of its history, many scholars have sought to name and distinguish patterns primarily among urban trading areas and islands. Abdul Sheriff has identified a "compradorial system" whereby local intermediaries, often stationed in coastal cities such as those along the East African coast, helped foreigners conduct trade. Compradorial systems flourished in intermediate commercial zones between producing and consuming zones. Along the Swahili coast, for example, one cultural stream coming from the African interior (and bringing trade goods, such as ivory, timber, and slaves) met an opposite stream from the Indian Ocean (including Arab, South Asian, and eventually European traders).[7] For Sri Lanka, Sujit Sivasundaram has argued that "partitioning" and "islanding" formed an incomplete process by which the island became a laboratory (distinct from South Asia) for British state-making plans, simultaneously disconnecting Sri Lanka both in spatial and in political terms.[8]

The Mascarenes and the Antilles fit neither of these patterns, however. Though like compradorial systems, they succeeded as intermediary sites of exchange between the East African and Malagasy interiors and Asia and they operated as exclusive zones for French subjects who, like Rose, sought to anchor global family businesses or those who, like Sobobobié-Betty, sought to leverage non-French heritage as useful expertise in exchange for naturalization.[9] Though they became sites for colonial experimentation like British Ceylon, their spatial and political-legal formation did not rely upon "partitioning" from a larger mainland territory. Madagascar did not become a French colony until 1897, and vast distances remained among small colonial territories, even when accounting for the Antilles (though excepting Louisiana and Canada).

The simultaneous development of island colonies in contrasting oceanic contexts but similar insular economies and societies emerges thanks to the survival of so many materials from the Atlantic and Indian Ocean islands. Antillean conseils were much more careful about keeping good legal records, and they developed a more robust court system than those in the Mascarenes. The later development of the Mascarene conseils shows that they depended upon Antillean and metropolitan models. Their relative focus on local issues points to a heightened isolation from the Atlantic networks of legal correspondence, which kept the Antilles and the metropole much more consistently connected.

The individual and local actions of Martinican and Île de France residents were the most fundamental forces that built the urban, social, and legal layers of their conseil cultures. But those actions also occurred within an oceanic and global context in which an empire-wide ancien régime legal culture develped during the eighteenth century. Each conseil lay within a much larger judicial ecosystem that encompassed metropolitan France, borderland territories in Europe such as Alsace and Corsica, and other colonies such as Louisiana, Canada, and Pondichéry, so the conseil both shared a family resemblance to similar courts, such as conseils provincials and parlements, and participated in the constant relay of cases from small courts of first instance (such as the sièges royaux) to appellate courts that reached as high as the king's personal council.

Though both the Antilles and the Mascarenes had developed cash-crop colonial economies by the mid-eighteenth century, the bias of the Mascarenes toward regional and global commerce reflected the Indian Ocean's origins and continuing existence as a system built upon trade since at least the classical era.[10] As the Parisian astronomer Alexis Rochon implied when he called Île de France an entrepôt of commerce, the trading-station identity stuck to the French Mascarenes even after they became Antillean-style plantation colonies in the mid- to late eighteenth century. This difference between the Antilles and the Mascarenes points to important differences between the Atlantic and Indian Ocean worlds, which might be obscured by approaches to comparative history that might simply elide oceanic categories in favor of a global whole.[11]

Martinique's precocious commercial and judicial development in the Antilles, in the mid-seventeenth century, greatly influenced the later and extraordinary growth of Saint-Domingue as an economic engine of France's ancien régime empire in the eighteenth century and, by extension, paved the way for the emergence of a distinctive legal culture. The later creation of conseils in Saint-Domingue thus built upon *longue durée* patterns of imperial expansion and state building established by earlier, but often unacknowledged, models such as Martinique. Martinique's extraordinary track record of documentation and activism continued throughout the ancien régime in sites as scattered as the Antilles and the Mascarenes. Scholarship on the French Caribbean has highlighted the exceptional case of Saint-Domingue (leading to the rightfully emphasized Haitian Revolution), while neglecting islands like Martinique and Guadeloupe that continued to be important throughout the colonial period.[12]

Île de France likewise became an indispensable trading and legal entrepôt in the Indian Ocean. As French interest in Asian cotton textiles and spices grew, Île de France became a common waystation for traffic between France and Asian trading depots, such as Pondichéry. As European competition in South Asia intensified, military regiments stopped at Île de France to unload sick soldiers and restock food and muntions as they journeyed between European bases, such as Rochefort, and sites of confrontation in the Carnatic and along the Coromandel Coast.

Early visitors to France's Atlantic and Indian Ocean colonies often questioned whether these new territories were too chaotic in environment and inhabitants to be governed by a rationalized legal regime guaranteed by a divinely guided monarch. In the mid-seventeenth century, Guillaume Coppier, a servant from Lyon, wrote about his "appalling adventures" in the Caribbean.[13] He visited many Caribbean islands, including Martinique, Guadeloupe, Saint Eustatius (a major Dutch entrepôt), and Saint-Barthélemy.

Coppier emphasized the rapacity of colonial leaders, quoting the Latin dictum "Necessitas non habet legem," or "Necessity has no law."[14] Coppier recalled his life as an indentured servant as being permeated with constant hunger, thirst, and weakness. Scorning these basic needs as impedients to quick profit, colonial proprietors demanded perpetual toil from their indentured servants. A survivor mentality, not a political order, governed the colonies. Coppier reported on these conditions and argued that "without poverty the two rarest virtues of the century, which are mercy [*miséricorde*] and patience, would be banished from the world."[15] Necessity, then, was the primary motivator for the colonial social and political order in the initial decades of colonization. Coppier's cynical nonelite point of view would have been shared by most inhabitants of the Antilles and the Mascarenes throughout the long eighteenth century—especially by the majority enslaved populations that displaced indentured servants by the early 1700s. Slaves, we know, were treated much worse.

Yet, within a hundred years of Coppier's writing, necessity had, in fact, *proven* the need for law in all of France's domains. In the late seventeenth and eighteenth centuries, aspiring elites and their families latched onto positions in the conseils supérieurs to advance their careers and gain power in France and its colonies. Colonial defendants and litigants such as Pitre Paul and Magdeleine Françoise similarly sought to defend their rights and claims in the conseils, and they (and their enemies) used the conseils to access judicial forums at home in the colonies and by appeal to France. Though episodes like the Gaoulé and the Dumas affair revealed weaknesses within the conseils, they ultimately demonstrated the centrality of the conseils as legal entrepôts in which questions of local and imperial authority could be worked out. They also showed that the conseils were durably linked by personnel and correspondence to metropolitan legal resources like the king's councils, even in times of controversy. Over the course of the long eighteenth century, from the 1680s to the 1780s, France's ancien régime empire had been successfully united under one common, if still piecemeal, legal regime from its metropolitan frontiers to its outposts in the Atlantic and Indian Oceans, anchored by the conseils supérieurs.

Visitors to these outposts recognized that they were valuable commercial centers, but they could be so only by the creation and maintenance of the conseils supérieurs as legal entrepôts. Although Rochon called Île de France the "arsenal of our forces and the entrepôt of our commerce" at the end of the ancien régime, not at the beginning of the long eighteenth century like Coppier, he also recognized the strategic value of France's insular colonies for military and trading purposes.[16] As in metropolitan France, commercial transactions made in these colonies and crimes could only be dealt with as long as there were judicial forums in place to adjudicate cases through court hearings and to affirm the validity of laws and decisions in the conseil greffes.

This wider geopolitical and legal context was intrinsic rather than parallel to agricultural and commercial colonial enterprises. Court participants such as the *Pondichéry*'s captain and the seditionists La Grange and Bordenave in the Antilles and, equally, legal writers stationed in Paris such as Le Moyne des Essarts recognized the global net cast by the conseils. Le Moyne des Essarts could only describe this array from a distance, but the French imperial subjects who participated as litigants, witnesses, and magistrates constituted and sustained a coherent, though contested, global state framework that was centered on the conseils. Greffiers, such as Lousteau, maintained court registers, while magistrates promoted access to that legal knowledge. Ship captains, like Querangal from chapter 4, sought hearings in these entrepôts when duels happened aboard ship, while conseil participants, like Ribes from chapter 4, employed interjudicial correspondence to work their way back in to the conseils when they were kicked out. Court users, such as Madame Blot, appealed court cases from colonial to metropolitan entrepôts when their cases did not turn out the way they wanted. Together, these examples reveal the lives and judicial experiences of mobile subjects as they navigated France's early modern empire. As they articulated and contested understandings of legitimacy and order in the law courts known as conseils supérieurs, French subjects forged a dynamic global legal regime.

The conseils supérieurs became portals between and among France and its new territories during a transformative era from 1680 to 1780. French subjects, such as ship workers and colonial magistrates, articulated and contested understandings of legitimacy and order in the conseils, together building France's first global empire in the Atlantic and Indian Oceans. Imperial subjects like Pitre Paul sought new political and legal influence via law courts, but with strategies that reflected local and regional priorities, particularly regarding slavery, war, and trade. Over the course of the eighteenth century, the conseils supérieurs became a tool by which colonial elites (becoming in the process global themistocrats), and, increasingly, subservient court users such as slaves, free people of color, and maritime workers like Pitre Paul leveraged formal and informal legal power at local, regional, and imperial levels.

Anchored in government documents that are often read but rarely culturally contextualized, this book describes day-to-day actions of imperial/colonial participants. It also charts global imperial processes that connect to research in many disciplines, such as sociology and political science, in spaces in which access to power, resources, and autonomy were negotiated. Evidence from the conseils begins to substantiate the connections among Atlantic, Indian Ocean, and European histories by drawing, however preliminarily, a sketch of France's first global empire.

Glossary

amirauté An admiralty court, responsible for hearing all cases regarding matters at sea and along French coasts. These jurisdictions were sometimes separate from the conseils (though they were staffed by a similar mix of magistrates and military officers) and sometimes composed of the conseil or local jurisdiction magistrates, who could hear admiralty cases as well as civil and criminal cases. Unlike the conseils, admiralty cases (whether in France or the colonies) had recourse specifically to the admiral of France and a court of appeal in Paris known as the marble table (*table de marbre*).

armateur A ship owner and/or outfitter. *Armateur* can refer, too, to an investor in a ship's cargo, so the term tends to have a dual connotation of owner and operator.

arrêt A generic term for decree (as in legislation) or ruling (on a court case).

avocat A lawyer with specialized training and admission to higher courts, such as the conseils supérieurs or parlements. These lawyers were often members of metropolitan bars, especially the Parisian bar. Similar to an English barrister.

béké, alt. bequet Elite European-descended Antilleans. Then as now it referred to European elites, usually planters, who dominated Antillean society and economy. The term "béké" is still used to denote the descendants of these Antilleans, who continue to wield significant power.

cassation A ruling by a higher court quashing a lower court's decision (e.g., an arrêt) or legislation. In more general usage, it could refer to any rejected legal document.

conseil des dépêches The top royal council specifically charged with domestic matters. The royal council decided upon matters conveyed in correspondence (dépêches) from French territories by both provincial and colonial administrators, such as intendants. Council membership varied somewhat over time, but tended to be composed of the chancellor, the four secretaries of state, and the chief finance officer (contrôleur général).

conseil du roi The king's council, which generally consisted of ministers (e.g., of the Marine) and other top officials and nobles who advised the king formally and informally. Membership on the king's council could vary and encompass configurations of other councils (such as the conseil des dépêches).

conseiller A magistrate on the conseil supérieur. Initially drawn from the planter and military elite in the colonies, these magistrates were increasingly trained in metropolitan law schools and sometimes had careers in both colonial and metropolitan law courts.

conseil supérieur A French law court with jurisdiction over appealed, and for certain areas first instances of, criminal and civil cases. They were most often established in new French territories in Europe, the Americas, and the Indian Ocean region. In composition and privileges they were very similar to the parlements but held less prestige due to their younger age and the smaller territories and populations they oversaw.

entrepôt A trading station.

gaoulé Antillean term for "uprising," from a mixed etymology of French and possibly Arawak or African origin, that refers to various colonial uprisings by Caribs, slaves, maroons, and planters. When capitalized, refers specifically to a 1717 rebellion by planters in Martinique.

governor A military office organized by region in France and its overseas territories. A governor was the king's representative (and embodiment) in the colonies and was mostly responsible for provisioning, fortifications, and defense. Many governors saw themselves as guardians of justice, too, and fought with intendants for political power. They co-administered the colonies with the intendants and oversaw the conseils. This contrasts with the British Empire, where governor was a civilian position.

greffe Court registers, usually kept in the palais de justice.

greffier A clerk (or court registrar) with the responsibility of maintaining the greffes. They managed the day-to-day affairs of courts such as the conseils. A role akin to *escribano* in Spanish civil-law systems at the time.

habitant Literally an "inhabitant" of a particular place. In the Antilles and Mascarenes this term often specified planters, with the connotation of resident landlords. In some cases colonial habitants owned plantations but lived in metropolitan France as absentee landlords.

huissier A bailiff and/or town crier.

intendant An office, which reported directly to the king, created in the seventeenth century to counter the regional loyalties of governors. Intendants oversaw "justice, finance, and police." In the metropole, they tended to focus on financial matters, such as taxation, but in the colonies they were often associated with scientific projects like botanical experiments and irrigation systems designed to make colonial agriculture more profitable. As colonial administrators, they oversaw the conseils ("justice") alongside the governors and had varying levels of authority over local police forces.

interjudicial correspondence Correspondence among various administrators, judges, and other royal officials that worked alongside or instead of traditional judicial mechanisms like formal court cases.

juridiction A local court ruling in the first instance. These were usually composed of a small group of magistrates, which could be drawn from the conseils. Their cases could be appealed to the sénéchaussées and conseils. Also known as a siège local or siège royal.

letters patent (*lettres patentes*) Legally binding letters or orders granting rights or privileges to a person or corporation, usually by a monarch.

Marine The French Navy. In 1715 it became the ministry with oversight for all colonial affairs, including the conseils and associated areas, such as the intendance and the military.

metropole An imperial center and capital region. This generally refers to France as a whole but can denote Paris and its environs (often labeled the Île de France region), such the king and his government, who were based at Versailles and occasionally other palaces, such as Fontainebleau.

négociant A trader. This term implied a large-scale trader (especially involved in overseas commerce) as opposed to a small-scale retailer (or *marchand*), as noted by the fifth edition of the *Dictionnaire de l'Académie français* (1798).

notable A local-elite person, usually identifying a prominent citizen in a town or region. Informal (and sometimes official) associations *of notables* tended to complement and overlap with the legal personnel, especially magistrates (conseillers), who made up the conseils supérieurs.

palais de justice A courthouse, most often constructed at the center of regional and/or colonial capital.

parlement Parlements were law courts established throughout ancien régime France from the fourteenth century onward. Royal legislation was issued to the parlements, which registered laws to make them active. Parlements tended to concentrate regional power, often against royal power, and were dissolved during the French Revolution.

procureur général An attorney general, responsible for initiating cases (chiefly criminal) in the kingdom's interest. At least one procureur général served each jurisdiction, whether a local siège or a conseil supérieur.

procureur A legal official responsible for drafting basic legal documents like wills and contracts. When they worked for the conseils, procureurs often gathered initial court documentation like depositions, similar to the discovery process in contemporary common-law practice. Similar to an English solicitor.

remonstration Originally an appeal drafted by a law court (such as a conseil supérieur) to the king's judgment following an adverse decision or edict, this legal instrument became associated specifically with the parlements' practice of negotiating with the king over new legislation. In the eighteenth century, the parlements would remonstrate as a strategy to declare their disapproval of the king's authority more generally. *Remonstrances* enabled parlement members to advocate for more judicial autonomy and legislative power, a pattern that signaled cracks in the ancien régime and led directly to the judicial crises of the 1780s.

royaume The most common term for France and its overseas possessions during the ancien régime. Literally translated as "kingdom," this concept denoted a community of French subjects united under the sovereignty held in the person of the monarch and dispensed by his ministers, and so forth.

sénéchaussée A mid-level law court, between the sièges locaux and the conseils supérieurs. Cases from the sénéchaussées could be appealed to the conseils. Sometimes also known as a *bailliage*.

Notes

Introduction

1. Catalogued in the Archives nationales, section outre-mer, as Fonds ministériels, premier empire colonial, Secrétariat d'état à la marine—Personnel colonial ancien (série E, XVIIe–XVIIIe [seventeenth and eighteenth centuries]). Hereafter cited as ANOM COL E followed by the file number and the person's name. Here ANOM COL E 337, Pitre Paul. These are available online at http://anom .archivesnationales.culture.gouv.fr/. Court documents in Pitre Paul's personnel file do not always agree on whether his first name was Pitre or Paul. For clarity, I refer to him as Pitre Paul because that version appears most frequently. "Ancien régime" refers to France in the period before the French Revolution beginning in 1789, that is, before the fall and dissolution of the Bourbon monarchy. The case of Pitre Paul seems to have been initiated by a sailor, Pierre Lesenet, who recognized (or thought he recognized) him upon arriving in port in Île Bourbon as the husband of Julienne Datin (the supposed Saint-Mâlo wife), whom he had known in Saint-Mâlo, and then discovered that Pitre Paul had an Île Bourbon wife. He and other passengers on board the ship the *Sirenne* had made a declaration to the governor of Île Bourbon accusing Pitre Paul of polygamy. According to the testimony of the Île Bourbon wife, Marianne Fontaine, that was how she first heard about the possible other wives. As it turned out, Fontaine knew about the other women, but Pitre Paul had told her that they were only his concubines. 18 July 1725. Interrogatory, Île Bourbon conseil supérieur.
2. ANOM COL E 337, Pitre Paul.
3. Ibid.
4. Ibid.
5. Ibid.
6. For Louisiana, Saint-Domingue, and French Guiana, respectively, Dawdy, *Building the Devil's Empire*; Ghachem, *The Old Regime*; Spieler, *Empire and Underworld*.
7. Andrews, *Law, Magistracy, and Crime*, 269.
8. Beik, *Absolutism and Society*; Beik, "Social Collaboration"; Swann, *Politics and the Parlement of Paris*.

9. Conseils provincials adjudicated cases via small courts composed, usually, of a governor and a few magistrates. They were subordinated to conseils supérieurs in the same region (for example, Mahé to Pondichéry; Île de France to Île Bourbon, initially). Conseils supérieurs were regional appellate courts that could judge in the first instance or on appeal. The term "souverain" identified courts that ruled in final judgment, but this term faded in use because conseil judgments could be, and often were, appealed to metropolitan resorts, such as the conseil des dépêches.

10. This figure accounts for conseils provinciaux and conseils supérieurs together—the former were not courts of final judgment, but over time most of them were converted to the latter (that is, as sovereign courts). For an example of a conseil established within metropolitan France toward the end of this period, see Louis XV, and France, *Édit . . . portant création d'un Conseil supérieur à Nîmes . . .*, 1772. For a map of parlements and conseils in France as of the mid-eighteenth century, see "La France divisée en ses parlemens et conseils souverains," 1720–1770.

11. The endurance and reconfiguration of these courts beyond the ancien régime and into the nineteenth century iteration of French global imperial projects deserves detailed and separate treatment, which has yet to be undertaken.

12. The concept of a trading entrepôt is most developed in work on the Dutch West Indies: Klooster, *Illicit Riches*; Rupert, *Creolization and Contraband*. For the concept of entrepôt as applied to a port in a continental interior, see Cangany, *Frontier Seaport*. For an account of Paris as a hub of judicial activity that acknowledges its economic context, see Andrews, *Law, Magistracy, and Crime*.

13. This contrasts with Lauren Benton's preferred term, "enclave," which I see as having a defensive connotation that implies surrounding lawlessness. Benton, *A Search for Sovereignty*, 8, 10, passim. Two other approaches that emphasize overlapping jurisdictions are Tomlins, "The Legal Cartography of Colonization," and Gould, "Zones of Law."

14. Patoulet, "Profil et eslevation."

15. Studies of early modern correspondence networks have suggested new avenues for exploring similar international and transregional relationships, but this scholarship has so far emphasized elite relationships based on shared intellectual interests rather than the practical legal and financial matters that formed the substance of interjudicial correspondence. Lindsay O'Neill has utilized new tools in network analysis to analyze British correspondence networks, while digital correspondence projects such as *Mapping the Republic of Letters* have shed new light on the epistemological revolutions of this period. O'Neill, *The Opened Letter*.

16. In reviewing this concept, Benoît Garnot has proposed a refinement of this distinction along two lines, which he calls "parajustice" and "extrajustice." "Justice, infrajustice."

17. In colonial British North American historiography, scholars have sought to identify "model" colonies and develop genealogies of colonial development, a trend that I want to avoid by privileging *simultaneous* developments while acknowledging distinct trajectories over time. Candidates for the origin story of British America (and, by extension, the United States) have ranged from New England to Barbados. Key studies in this vein include Greene, *Pursuits of Happiness*; O'Shaughnessy, *An Empire Divided*; Kupperman, *The Jamestown Project*.

18. Important models for analysis across large spaces but within empires include Hatfield, *Atlantic Virginia*; Jennings, *Vichy in the Tropics*; Marshall, *The Making and Unmaking of Empires*; Banks, *Chasing Empire across the Sea*; Wilson, "Rethinking the Colonial State." For two influential transimperial studies in Atlantic, but not Indian Ocean contexts, see Pagden, *Lords of All the World*, and Elliott, *Empires of the Atlantic World*. For a global scale, see Burbank and Cooper, *Empires in World History*. A more recent wave of scholarship has sought to overcome imperial boundaries at a more local scale, emphasizing themes such as trade and go-betweens; see, for example, Koot, *Empire at the Periphery*.

19. Régent, *La France et ses esclaves*.

20. Benton, *A Search for Sovereignty*, 137. Headnote, ANOM COL A, Secrétariat d'état à la marine. Actes du pouvoir souverain (1628, 1663–1779). Materials from the Archives nationales d'outre-mer are cited as ANOM followed by the series and box number with relevant identifying information.

21. Greene and Morgan, eds., *Atlantic History*; Vaughan, *Creating the Creole Island*; Bose, *A Hundred Horizons*.

22. For microhistory as a method (here, in Atlantic contexts), see Putnam, "To Study the Fragments/Whole"; Ferreira, "Atlantic Microhistories." For an influential transimperial comparison of entrepôts, see McNeill, *Atlantic Empires of France and Spain*. The present book emphasizes the entanglements of Atlantic and Indian Ocean worlds, as the conseils supérieurs, notably, were not established in any Pacific locales. For Pacific connections to many of the patterns described in the book, see Mapp, "Silver, Science, and Routes to the West"; Igler, *Great Ocean*.

23. This approach thus follows what Trevor Burnard has characterized for early American historiography as an "emphasis . . . on the porous nature of early modern borders. It privileges dynamism and the mobility of goods, peoples and ideas within a geographic unit where the borders are very vague." Burnard, "Empire Matters?"

24. For Saint-Domingue in the eighteenth century, see Garrigus, *Before Haiti*, and Ghachem, *The Old Regime*.

25. For judicial negotiation and state building in the parlements, see Beik, *Absolutism and Society*; Stone, *The French Parlements*; Major, *From Renaissance Monarchy*; Hurt, *Louis XIV and the Parlements*. For the first twenty years of this debate, see Beik, "The Absolutism of Louis XIV." For social and judicial negotiation at the municipal and community levels, see Breen, *Law, City, and King*; Hardwick, *Family Business*. For a comparative look at similar processes in England during this era, see Hindle, *The State and Social Change*.

26. Hardwick, *Family Business*; Dawdy, *Building the Devil's Empire*; Ghachem, *The Old Regime*; Peabody, "There Are No Slaves in France"; Garrigus, *Before Haiti*.

27. Delaney, *Nomospheric Investigations*. For the origins of this approach to law and geography, see Blomley, "From 'What?' to 'So What?' "

28. Spieler, *Empire and Underworld*. Here I narrow Jane Burbank and Frederick Cooper's analysis of imperial repertoires in *Empires in World*, 8.

29. In the colonies, conseil personnel could also sit in the palais de justice as admiralty courts and lower courts of first instance (for example, the sièges and juridictions).

30. Braverman et al., *The Expanding Spaces of Law*, 1. Key works on legal geography include Ewick and Silbey, *The Common Place of Law*; Blomley et al., *The Legal Geographies Reader*; von Benda-Beckmann et al., *Spatializing Law*; Delaney, *Nomospheric Investigations*.

31. Sarat et al., *The Place of Law*. For spatial thinking in the eighteenth century, see Withers, *Placing the Enlightenment*, and Safier, "The Tenacious Travels."

32. Gerbeau sets up the illegal slave trade in Île Bourbon as a lesser-known foil to Atlantic slavery in his "L'Océan Indien n'est pas l'Atlantique"; see also Allen, "The Constant Demand of the French."

33. Vaughan, *Creating the Creole Island*.

34. For example, Frédéric Régent's survey of French slavery synthesizes both regions throughout: *La France et ses esclaves*. Francophone literary debates about creolization have recently begun to have a strong comparative component: see, for example, Bernabé et al., *Éloge de la créolité*; Lionnet, *Le su et l'incertain*.

35. Montesquieu served as a conseiller in the Bordeaux Parlement. Kingston, *Montesquieu and the Parlement of Bordeaux*; Ghachem, "Montesquieu in the Caribbean." For conseils as civil and criminal courts, see, for example, Dépôt des papiers publics des colonies (DPPC), 6 DPPC 2709, Île Bourbon, ruling of 8 May 1770 that Mascarene conseils will judge civil and criminal affairs.

36. Ferrière, vol. 1, 365.

37. Larger jurisdictions, such as the Paris and Bordeaux Parlements, heard criminal cases separately from civil ones, in a chamber known as the *tournelle*. The Bordeaux tournelle, a typical example, heard appeals of definitive sentences and interlocutory decisions (that is, before the final judgment). Kingston, *Montesquieu and the Parlement of Bordeaux*, 102.

38. The array of king's advisers who handled these appeals varied somewhat during the ancien régime (as did the name of the appellate body), but it usually included the Marine minister and other officials tasked with overseas affairs. For the Artois conseil, see Sueur, *Le conseil provincial d'Artois*. For the Alsace conseil, see Burckard, *Le conseil souverain d'Alsace*, and Livet and Wilsdorf, *Le conseil souverain d'Alsace*. Ghachem, "Montesquieu in the Caribbean," 203. Garrigus states that Petit worked for Léogane's conseil supérieur in the 1750s, as do my sources, implying that the council moved to Port-au-Prince sometime in the middle of the eighteenth century. Garrigus, *Before Haiti*, 42; Garrigus, "Le Patriotisme americain."

39. For example, Pritchard, *In Search of Empire*.

40. Blanc, *Officiers et commissaires du conseil souverain du Roussillon*.

41. Beik, *Absolutism and Society*; Stone, *The French Parlements*; Hurt, *Louis XIV and the Parlements*.

42. Entries for "Conseil supérieur de la Martinique," Diderot and d'Alembert, eds., *Encyclopédie*, vol. 4, 14. "Conseil d'Alsace," vol 4., 2. "Conseil de Roussillon," vol. 4, 16. *L'état de la France*, vol. 5, 284–85. Des Essarts, *Essai sur l'histoire générale*, vol. 3, 142–43.

43. For Colbert in a solely metropolitan context, see Soll, *The Information Master*.

44. Gerber, *Bastards*, 17. See also Maza, *Private Lives and Public Affairs*. For these themes, with a family-state component, see Hanley, *The Lit de Justice*, "The Pursuit of Legal Knowledge," and "The Jurisprudence of the Arrêts."

45. Breen, *Law, City, and King*.

46. Miranda Spieler has usefully surveyed the legal structure of France's overseas possessions: "The Legal Structure of Colonial Rule." Mousnier, *The Institutions of France*. Mousnier presents institutions as static structures, a pitfall overcome here by demonstrating how subjects moved across France's global empire.

47. A privilege used so intensively in Saint-Domingue that of the colony's two conseils, the more restive Port-au-Prince conseil was finally merged into the Le Cap conseil in 1787 in an act of royal prerogative that matched Maupeou's more famous condemnation of metropolitan *parlements*. Ghachem, *The Old Regime and the Haitian Revolution*, 160–62.

48. There were, at least in Martinique, Guadeloupe, and Saint-Domingue, industry organizations called *chambres d'agriculture* and *chambres de commerce*, but they were more associated with planters and primarily attended to economic matters, such as setting prices. They are as yet little known to historians, but they appear not to have been granted as nearly much judicial power as the conseils. Evidence has not yet been uncovered that references similar organizations in the Mascarenes, though they likely existed. Malick Ghachem notes in passing that a chambre d'agriculture was established in Saint-Domingue in 1787 to replace the conseils supérieurs after they were dissolved that year, but the chambres d'agriculture coexisted with the conseils in at least Martinique, Guadeloupe, and Saint-Domingue from the 1760s. Magistrates, such as Lhéritier de Brutelles in Saint-Domingue, sometimes served on both. In the mid-1760s in Martinique, a man named d'Anglebermes worked for both the chambre d'agriculture and the chambre de commerce. Conseiller Robert Philippe Claude Deshayes was a member of Guadeloupe's chambre d'agriculture around the same time. Raymond Bernardin was a member of the Port-au-Prince chambre d'agriculture around 1785. Ghachem, *The Old Regime and the Haitian Revolution*, 192. ANOM COL E 285, Lhéritie de Brutelles; E 396, d'Anglebermes; E 125, Robert Deshayes; E 27, Raymond Bernardin. For merchant courts as distinct jurisdictions in France, see Kessler, *A Revolution in Commerce*.

49. Compiled from ANOM COL series A (Actes du pouvoir souverain) and E (Personnel colonial ancien). One of the five courts in Île de France, the admiralty court, was actually constituted by the conseil magistrates. Even the new territory of Corsica had nine local jurisdictions (juridictions) under its conseil, as illustrated in a 1783 map, "L'isle de Corse divisée par juridictions extraite de plusieurs cartes nationales." Many of the Parisian courts, such as the Châtelet, were large and multifaceted organizations unto themselves. Andrews, *Law, Magistracy, and Crime*, 23.

50. Some of these court registers do appear in archival collections designated as greffes: Archives nationales, section d'outre-mer, Aix-en-Provence, France. Dépôt des papiers publics des colonies, Greffes (1674–1912). Hereafter ANOM DPPC Greffes.

51. See, for example, his personnel file, which includes the arrêt issued by the conseil in 1758. ANOM COL E 295, Macandale. For scholarship that relies upon conseil records, see, for example, Garrigus, "Vincent Ogé Jeune"; Ogle, "Policing Saint Domingue." For Macandal: Fick, *The Making of Haiti*, 59–75, and Garrigus, *"Macandal Is Saved!"*

52. Moreau de Saint-Méry, *Loix et constitutions*.

53. Burns, "Notaries, Truth, and Consequences," 355. For a similar argument in a postcolonial context, see Stoler, "Colonial Archives and the Arts of Governance."

54. Two models have informed this approach: Taylor, *Magistrates of the Sacred*, and Tweed, *Crossing and Dwelling*.

55. ANOM COL E.

56. For a detailed exploration of how these archives were constructed, see Houllemare, "La fabrique des archives coloniales."

57. One influential line of colonial research emphasizes imperial failure, while another dominant trend focuses on revolution. Dawdy, *Building the Devil's Empire*; Banks, *Chasing Empire across the Sea*; Pritchard, *In Search of Empire*; Marchand, *Ghost Empire*. See, for example, Dubois, *A Colony of Citizens*.

58. Two additional long-standing scholarly debates that center on variations of "creole" sit adjacent to this project but do not figure in its analysis or argument. These debates have further muddied the terminological waters, so it is necessary to begin again with new, and more precise, language for identities in the Antilles and the Mascarenes. First, scholars of slavery have long debated how, and to what extent, enslaved Africans acculturated to the New World—centering their concerns on concepts of "creolization" versus African cultural retention. Second, postcolonial debates about identity, especially among Francophone activists and literary scholars over *négritude* and *créolité*, have brought Antillean and Mascarene versions of creolization into view, but again without innovating more precise terminology. For the creolization debate in terms of the Middle Passage, see especially Mintz and Price, *The Birth of African-American Culture*; Thornton, *Africa and Africans in the Making of the Atlantic World*; Smallwood, *Saltwater Slavery*; Palmié, "Is There a Model in the Muddle?"; Sweet, "Mistaken Identities?" For "négritude" and "créolité," see especially Bernabé, Chamoiseau, and Confiant, *Éloge de la créolité*; Lionnet, *Le su et l'incertain*. For "creole" in Atlantic history as somewhat synonymous with "cosmopolitan," or perhaps "go-between," see Landers, *Atlantic Creoles in the Age of Revolutions*.

59. Warren, *Creole Medievalism*, xvii.

60. Sue Peabody and Jennifer Palmer, for example, have spotlighted the legal, economic, and cultural changes that slavery forced, both formally and informally, within France. Peabody, *"There Are No Slaves in France"* and *Madeleine's Children*; Palmer, *Intimate Bonds*.

61. For Louisiana as distinctive from, but also embedded within, an Atlantic world, see Vidal, ed., *Louisiana*.

62. Rochon, *Voyage à Madagascar*, vi.

Chapter 1. The Human Ecology of Justice

1. "Monsieur le General de Poincy, & Monsieur du Parquet, lors que leur santé le permettoit se trouvoient toutes les semaines à l'Audiance, le premier sous le grand Figuier à la Basse-terre de Saint Christophe, & le second à la Martinique sous son calbacier au Fort Saint Pierre, où ils accommodoient tous les differents, & ne renvoyoient jamais les Parties qu'ils ne fussent d'accord, & ne se fussent embrassée." Du Tertre, *Histoire générale*, vol. 2. (1667), 446. In the seventeenth century, a *different* could refer to a "debat, contestation, querelle." Entry for "different" in *Dictionnaire de l'Académie française*, 1st edition (1694).

2. See my remarks on "creole" in the Introduction, in the section "A Note on Terminology."

3. Conseils and local police strictly managed alcohol sales in the colonies (assessing extra taxes on tavern owners) because of the volatile behavior associated with sailors (and other low-status whites), free people of color, and slaves. Planters, especially, feared taverns as sites in which runaway slaves might concoct revolts. Dessalles, *Les annales du conseil*, part 1, vol. 1, 160–61.

4. A pattern that likely contributed to and correlated with seasonal market days, as has been documented for British North America. Isaac, *The Transformation of Virginia*, 88–93.

5. Unpaid conseil magistrates disliked this schedule, however, as it interrupted time during which they could be working on their more valuable plantations. They changed their scheduled meetings to every other month until 1700, when they resumed monthly meetings. Hayot, *Les officiers du conseil*, 33–34.

6. A 1724 royal ruling had changed the meeting time to last from six in the morning until 12:30 in the afternoon. In response to royal apprehension about large, unfinished caseloads, this schedule was revised to two sessions: one from seven in the morning until noon and a second from three to six in the afternoon. Lettre du roi, sur les séances du conseil souverain. 17 October 1725, Petit de Viévigne, ed., *Code de la Martinique*, 275–76.

7. Andrews, *Law, Magistracy, and Crime*, 64.

8. One exception was Île Bourbon following the transfer of the conseil from the town of Saint-Paul to Saint-Denis in 1739. The conseil met every Wednesday and Saturday until it cleared up a backlog of cases and finished the transition. ANOM 6 DPPC 2708, Île Bourbon Greffe. 1 June 1739, 93.

9. ANOM 6 DPPC 2708, Île Bourbon Greffe. 27 January 1731. Extrait des Régistres du greffe du conseil supérieur de l'isle Bourbon.

10. Scholars of North American slavery and, more recently, of Latin America, have explored these social fields. Isaac, *The Transformation of Virginia*; Gross,

Double Character; Olwell, *Masters, Slaves and Subjects*; Olwell, "Practical Justice." For a Latin American corollary, see Premo, "Before the Law."

11. Ghachem, *The Old Regime and the Haitian Revolution.*

12. Agnew, *Worlds Apart.* For French theater during this period, see Ravel, *The Contested Parterre,* and Clay, *Stagestruck.*

13. Here I follow Susan Silbey's insight that "many scholars find the concept of culture particularly useful when they want to focus on aspects of legal action that are not confined to official legal texts, roles, performances, or offices." Silbey helpfully explains the development of the term "legal culture" alongside similar terms, such as "legal ideology, legal consciousness, legality, and cultures of legality," in Silbey, "Legal Culture and Cultures of Legality," 471 and passim.

14. In the colonies (and similar to their counterparts in metropolitan France), intendants were royal administrators charged with managing matters related to justice, finance, and police.

15. Patoulet, "Profil et eslevation."

16. In 1722, Intendant Benard bought the house for twelve thousand livres to make it government property. Petitjean Roget, *Le Gaoulé,* 148.

17. Ibid., 147–48.

18. Silbey, "Legal Culture and Cultures of Legality."

19. ANOM COL E 218, Charles Haudoyer.

20. Though many cases were originated in lower courts, such as the sièges royaux and sénéchaussées, the conseils were by far the most dominant law courts in all of these sites, in terms both of caseloads and of prestige. Very little research has been done on the lower and admiralty courts for the ancien régime in general and especially for overseas colonies. For lower courts in France, see Hardwick, *Family Business*; Schneider, *The King's Bench*; Hayhoe, *Enlightened Feudalism.* For French colonial courts in the nineteenth century, see Savage, "Between Colonial Fact and French Law."

21. "Huissier," *Enyclopédie,* vol. 8, 340. "Audiencier," *Enyclopédie,* vol. 1, 867. *Audiencier* was a higher-status job than a regular bailiff, very similar to the higher status accorded to regular greffiers over the scribes (*commis greffiers*) who worked under them.

22. In Normandy, bailiffs could also be process servers, a task they likely performed in the colonies, too, though I have yet to find specific evidence of this. Schneider, *The King's Bench,* 281. In Louisiana, too, bailiffs acted as town criers and process servers. Dawdy, *Building the Devil's Empire,* 195.

23. ANOM COL E 382, Ursule.

24. Mauritius Archives, B 57, quoted in Toussaint, *Early Printing in the Mascarene Islands,* 83. I have not found reference to "crieurs publics" for any other colony. This gap may exist because bailiffs typically fulfilled these duties.

25. For an overview of criminal, especially extraordinary, punishment in France, see Friedland, *Seeing Justice*.

26. For example, Martineau, *Correspondance du conseil supérieur de Pondichéry . . . Tome V: 1755–1759*, 61.

27. ANOM COL B 37 F° 13 and 14, 9 January 1715.

28. ANOM COL E 332 bis, Pellet. For this case and public legal knowledge in the context of criminal justice, see Wood, "Murder on the Road."

29. Guët, *Les origines de l'île Bourbon*, 199. Poisoning preoccupied colonial magistrates during this period, especially because they often attributed it to enslaved Africans who held (supposedly) secret botanical, and (possibly) supernatural, knowledge alien to European pharmacopoeia that threatened the colonial sociolegal order. For the logic of poisoning cases in French colonial courts as evidenced in the nineteenth century, see Savage, "Between Colonial Fact and French Law."

30. Entry for "publicité" in *Dictionnaire de l'Académie française,* 4th edition (1762) and 5th edition (1798).

31. Louis XIV, and France. *Ordonnance de Louis XIV*, 2, 13.

32. Melton, *The Rise of the Public*, 160.

33. Toussaint, *Early Printing in the Mascarene Islands*, 83–84.

34. Ibid.

35. Ibid., 83.

36. Règlement général du conseil supérieur, pour la police intérieure de la colonie, 14 August 1762, in Bonnefoy, ed., *Arrêts administratifs*, 89.

37. Toussaint notes that many of these have not survived in the archives because they were poorly kept (presumably as official court registers were). Toussaint, *Early Printing in the Mascarene Islands,* 83–84.

38. For example, "Il résulte du défaut de publicité de celles de ces Loix qui seroient propres au pays, qu'elles n'y peuvent être regardées que comme raison écrite, dans les cas où les Loix publiées sont muettes, comme les Loix Romaines dans les Provinces de la France régies par leurs Coutumes." Avertissement, Petit de Viévigne, ed., *Code de la Martinique*, i.

39. Arrêt du Conseil Supérieur du 14 Avril 1780, referencing Arrêt du conseil supérieur du 9 Décembre 1779 fixant les droits à payer aux greffiers et autres officiers de la cour d'amirauté. Rouillard, ed., *A Collection of the Laws of Mauritius*, vol. 1, 180.

40. For example, Premo, "Before the Law"; Burns, *Into the Archive*; Ogborn, *Indian Ink*.

41. ANOM COL E 206, Giraudet. The heading for this file says that his commission included Grande Anse, Martinique, but this is an error. This commission

was registered with the Saint-Domingue intendance as well as with local courts for which Giraudet worked. By 1764, Giraudet was serving as a greffier in a different town, Jérémie, when he mysteriously resigned.

42. Mousnier, *The Institutions of France,* vol. 1, 746. For the development of lawyers as a political class in France during this period, see Bell, *Lawyers and Citizens.*

43. For more on Moreau de Saint-Méry, see Taffin, ed., *Moreau de Saint-Méry.* It is possible that some of those listed as "avocat au conseil" merely held the experience and privilege of avocat, rather than any function specific to the conseil, though many appear in case records, too. In general, for colonial records the term "avocat" identifies persons with experience and knowledge of French law more than a particular position.

44. Fewer studies have examined the political influence of the *gens de couleur* in the Mascarenes. For the social, economic, and legal opportunities and limitations faced by Mascarene gens de couleur; see Allen, "Marie Rozette and Her World," and Peabody, *Madeleine's Children.*

45. Petit de Viévigne, *Supplément au Code de la Martinique,* 74. Also cited in Des Essarts, *Essai sur l'histoire générale,* 140. Des Essarts implied that the same was true for Guadeloupe, though I have been unable to find supporting evidence.

46. ANOM FM F/3/211, Île de France, 533. 9 January 1781. Lawyers were briefly banned in the Mascarenes, from 1778 to 1781. Delaleu, *Code des Îles de France et de Bourbon,* 289.

47. "Ces Loix, ainsi que la Coutume de Paris, qui est la Loi municipale des Colonies Françoises, sont dans les mains de tout le monde; ainsi il seroit superflu d'en grossir cette compilation," Petit de Viévigne, ed., *Code de la Martinique,* i.

48. Pritchard, *In Search of Empire,* 249. Louisiana litigants often represented themselves in court as lawyers (avocats). A few related professions (*procureur général* and *procureur des biens vacants*) were banned. Dawdy, *Building the Devil's Empire,* 205.

49. Most likely the minister of the Marine at the time, the comte de Luzerne.

50. ANOM COL E 214, Julien François Guérin.

51. This pattern thus complicates—and extends—the timeline of a later literature that has emphasized the military's role in enabling drastic social mobility during the revolutionary era, epitomized by (but by no means limited to) such figures as Toussaint Louverture and Napoleon Bonaparte. King, *Blue Coat or Powdered Wig;* Blaufarb, *The French Army;* Dubois, *Avengers of the New World;* Bell, *The Idols of the Age of Revolution.*

52. For the seventeenth-century origins of this pattern, as demonstrated in the Antilles, see Wood, "The Martinican Model."

53. Pritchard, *In Search of Empire*, 253; Arrêt de réglement du 12 Juin 1778. *Ordonnant aux avocats et praticiens devant les tribunaux de l'Ile de France, de produire leurs diplômes dans le délai de quinze jours, sous peine d'être empêchés d'exercer leur profession.* Rouillard, ed., *A Collection of the Laws of Mauritius*, vol. 1, 166.

54. Hayot, *Les officiers du conseil*, 200–205. ANOM COL E, 281 Jean Périnelle-Dumay (and Louis-Antoine Périnelle-Dumay).

55. For more on the parlement debates in France during this era, especially within the Paris Parlement, where many colonial magistrates began their careers, see Swann, *Politics and the Parlement of Paris.*

56. This pattern became particularly noticeable upon the outbreak of the French Revolution, in which political clubs (most notably the Club Massiac) emerged in the colonies to represent planter interests under the paradoxical rhetoric of universal rights *and* advocacy for slavery. An influential exposition of the relationship between slavery and the Enlightenment is Sala-Molins, *Dark Side of the Light.*

57. Hayot, *Les officiers du conseil*, 106–7. He also appears to have worked alongside Jean Assier (a codifier of Martinican laws) to promote Antillean interests. ANOM COL E 91, Cornette de Saint-Cyr de Cély (and Jean Assier).

58. At least seventy-one personnel records mention avocats who were admitted to metropolitan parlements. Based on a search for "avocat au parlement" in the ANOM COL E database.

59. Another intriguing possibility that deserves more research is the correlation between many of these requests and the early 1770s. This pattern may simply exist because most personnel records are dated between roughly 1770 and 1780, but it may also signal rising political conflict within the metropole in the decades immediately preceding the French Revolution. The early 1770s saw an upheaval in the French parlements when in 1770 Chancellor Maupeou canceled the parlements, which were only reconstituted in 1774. This development seems to have sent many court employees scrambling for new positions during this later period, possibly accounting for the surge in conseil requests. For those who were aware of this longer trend of a conseil appointment as a route to advancement, the colonial conseils may have appeared to be lucrative and safe alternatives to metropolitan judicial uncertainty. For Maupeou, see Echeverria, *The Maupeou Revolution*; Swann, "Disgrace without Dishonour."

60. Pierre Dessalles and Moreau de Saint-Méry also fit into this tradition. Moreau's family differed from most, however, because they tended to support the governor and intendant (or in Moreau de Saint-Méry's case, the Marine minister, Sartine) despite widespread local suspicion of metropolitan authorities. Many

other Antillean elites viewed the Moreaus as disloyal, distrusting their close alignment with the metropole. Scholars of British North American colonies have noticed a similar pattern for this period, for example, Flavell, "The 'School for Modesty and Humility.' "

61. In April 1789, the Marine did allow Guérin to go to Île de France to take care of the estate of his uncle. Guérin's actions suggest that he sought a great inheritance from his uncle. ANOM COL E 214, Julien François Guérin.

62. While traders (négociants) in the Antilles constantly complained about the restrictions placed on them by the *Exclusif*, a set of laws against transimperial commerce, as well as the paucity of foodstuffs and other necessities, Mascarene subjects traded throughout the Indian Ocean littoral with less concern for trading restrictions. For the *Exclusif*, see Covo, "L'assemblée constituante."

63. ANOM COL E 214, Julien François Guérin.

64. ANOM COL E 124, Desgranges de Richeteau. Two personnel files exist for Desgranges de Richeteau, so I cite information based on which file holds the relevant evidence. The other file is ANOM COL E 124, Desgranges de richeteau [*sic*], Guillaume. The correspondence with the Ministry of the Marine was precipitated by the chronic illness of Desgranges's wife, who had stayed behind in Paris.

65. This assertion may not have been entirely truthful, as his ailing wife (named Blot) testified that Desgranges more or less abandoned her. In 1773, Desgranges's wife wrote to the Marine minister for financial aid. She noted that her husband had been living in Île de France for the previous seventeen years without giving her any help even though she suffered from ill health. She recounted receiving an affectionate letter from her husband in 1772, but he only provided her a small annuity. When she died in 1776, she left outstanding loans from the Marine for Desgranges to pay back. ANOM COL E 124, Desgranges de richeteau, Guillaume, 1773.

66. ANOM COL E 124, Desgranges de Richeteau.

67. Ibid. In 1760, he requested a job as a greffier but was apparently denied.

68. Anthoine died in 1774. He also has two personnel records: ANOM COL E 397, Anthoine de Bacourt, Jean François; and ANOM COL E 397, Anthoine de Bacourt, Jean François.

69. Thus, it is not surprising that most planter revolts took place in the 1710s through the 1750s in the Antilles. I have yet to find similar cases for the Indian Ocean. In the wake of the Seven Years' War, the emergence of wealthy free planters of color (especially in Saint-Domingue) created a second wave of colonial reformism among local elites that crested during the French and Haitian Revolutions. Garrigus, *Before Haiti*; Ghachem, *The Old Regime*.

70. Though this book ends in roughly 1780, this pattern did continue up to the outbreak of the French and Haitian Revolutions. In the volatile revolutionary period, the same savvy colonial elites who had managed to juggle arguments for local autonomy with promises of loyalty to the French monarchy were often the ones who emerged from revolution in the best shape. See, for example, the endurance of the Martinican Dessalles family, as noted in Wood, "The Martinican Model"; Schloss, *Sweet Liberty*. Martinique and Guadeloupe (and Île Bourbon) seem to have played this game the most adroitly, as all of these islands continued to be French colonial possessions (and plantation economies) beyond the Revolution and well into the nineteenth century. They also currently exist as French overseas departments.

71. ANOM COL E 313, François Millon; ANOM COL A 19 F° 317. Arrêt cassant l'arrêt du conseil supérieur de l'île Bourbon du 10 mai 1774 qui déclarait la prise de corps contre Milon, ancien procureur général du conseil (n° 61) (11 novembre 1775). ANOM COL E 23, Beaumont, Christophe de, archevêque de Paris. Son intervention dans une contestation survenue entre François Millon, procureur général du Roi au Conseil supérieur de l'île Bourbon, et le sieur Le Bossu, curé de la paroisse Sainte-Marie, au sujet du refus de ce dernier d'accepter Millon pour parrain d'un enfant (1769/1772).

72. ANOM COL E 230. Charles Toussaint Jocet. He later became a commissioner of vacant successions, a new office created for managing unclaimed estates. Bonnefoy, *Table générale*, 257. Wood, "Recovering the Debris."

73. Hayot, *Les officiers du conseil*, 52, 71.

74. Martinican trading families and conseil members often had Norman and later Bordelais heritage.

75. For more on this ongoing tradition and its associated rhetoric, see Wood, "The Martinican Model."

76. Major, *From Renaissance Monarchy to Absolute Monarchy*, 302, 354–55.

77. Some conseillers had specifically legal backgrounds, but this pattern emerged later in the eighteenth century.

78. Arrêt de règlement. 5 July 1782. *Ordonnant que les Lettres Patentes du Roi, du mois de Juillet 1776, seront exécutées d'après leur forme ct teneur, et nommant plusieurs notables comme assesseurs pour assister le Juge Royal dans le jugement des affaires criminelles.* This decree was effectively repealed in 1850 by Ordinance 50, which established trial by jury, per the British common-law model. Rouillard, ed., *A Collection of the Laws of Mauritius*, vol. 1, 190.

79. Kingston, *Montesquieu and the Parlement of Bordeaux*, 104.

80. ANOM COL E 66, Cazaux Du Breuil, Statement from Guadeloupe government to Marine, 5 April 1727.

81. For more on the distinction between "séance" and "voix déliberative," see my extended discussion in chapter 1.

82. For example, the conseillers d'honneur and four maîtres des requêtes were granted séance before the parlement chair (doyen) and voix déliberative in the *grand-chambre. L'état de la France*, vol. 5, 5.

83. Montesquieu served an unprecedented ten and a half years consecutively on the Bordeaux Parlement, but normally magistrates were nominated for short-term appointments. Kingston, *Montesquieu and the Parlement of Bordeaux*, 101–2.

84. This was standard across all French colonies. A man named Ingrand was nominated to the Pondichéry, India, conseil supérieur, for instance, by the Compagnie des Indes orientales in 1741, granting him the privileges of séance and voix déliberative. The nomination cited royal edicts from 1664, February 1685, September 1714, and May 1719 and was done in Paris and signed by four company directors. ANOM COL E 227, Ingrand.

85. In general, conseillers could request an open position and send the governor and the intendant their qualifications along with recommendations. In Saint-Domingue's southern conseil, however (at Léogane, Petit Goave, then finally Port-au-Prince), residents (habitants) of various quarters each nominated a total of nine representatives for conseil membership in January–February 1723. Moreau de Saint-Méry, *Loix et constitutions*, vol. 3, 37. I have yet to find evidence for this pattern of nomination elsewhere.

86. Petitjean Roget, *Le Gaoulé*, 147. This included the *Te Deum* ceremony discussed in more depth in chapter 3.

87. Sometimes regular conseillers are referred to as conseiller titulaire to emphasize the contrast with conseillers honoraires, who held the rank of magistrate but did not serve regularly on the conseil.

88. "Conseillers honoraires," *Enyclopédie*, vol. 4, 29–30. Louis XIII had created this position in 1635 for each *bailliage* and *siége présidial* (regional jurisdictions). The practice remained in place with few modifications up to the time of the *Encyclopédie*'s publication.

89. Ibid., 148, citing ANOM COL C 8, B 3, Vaucresson. 25 January 1713. Canadian conseillers were apparently paid, according to this source, though it does not specify how much.

90. Burckard does not reference the colonial conseils specifically, though he recognizes the other metropolitan conseils. Burckard, *Le conseil souverain*, 155–57. Andrews, *Law, Magistracy, and Crime*, 66, 102.

91. Chanvalon, *Voyage à la Martinique*, 30. Immediately preceding these lines, Chanvalon had emphasized Antillean military preparedeness: "It is in these Islands that one sees accomplished this wish of nature and politics, which

ensures that no man is useless in society. All the Americans form one estate [*état*]. Some are destined to be armed. They practice all year long. Despite this continual exercise, one would not know that they make disciplined troops. One must only wait for the day of combat, of ardor and of courage."

92. A note in different handwriting dated 1726 added, "Nothing has changed." "Liste des membres du conseil supérieur de la Martinique et des officiers des justices royales de son ressort." Martinique, 1716. ANOM COL C 8 A, 21 F° 327. http://anom.archivesnationales.culture.gouv.fr/ark:/61561/zn401plmqmw.

93. A classic analysis of arguments for autonomy among Saint-Dominguan white elites is Frostin, *Les révoltes blanches.* For an account that challenges Frostin's inattention to race, see Garrigus, "Le patriotisme americain."

94. ANOM COL E 119, Jean André de Ribes. 13 January 1768. Ribes to the duc de Praslin. This is the same Ribes discussed in detail in chapter 3.

95. ANOM COL E 134, Didier de Saint-Martin.

96. Petitjean Roget, *Le Gaoulé,* 145. See below for Du Tillet's case.

97. ANOM COL E 119, Jean André de Ribes.

98. Which is not to discount the labor of scribes, secretaries, and other clerks who produced the massive amount of paperwork required to keep France's ancien régime empire, especially its courts, running. For court scribes as essential functionaries in Spain's vast imperial criminal justice infrastructure at this time, through the case study of Mexico City, see Scardaville, "Justice by Paperwork."

99. ANOM COL E 167, Du Tillet. The conseil had instructed the commis greffier to make the majority (*moitié*) of *expéditions* (letters and other official documents) and other acts and one-third of the sales (*ventes*), all other rights were given to the greffier.

100. The affair was also noteworthy enough to local administrators that it appeared as well in the report of the conseil's attorney general, Ribes, to the minister of the Marine in 1768. ANOM COL E 119, Jean André de Ribes. 13 January 1768.

101. The text says "vingt douze livres." Ibid.

102. ANOM COL E 350, Ricatte. He requested instead to be placed at the *bureau du contentieux* in the Marine offices.

103. Letter 11, Port Louis, Bernardin de Saint-Pierre, *Journey to Mauritius,* 123.

104. ANOM COL E 318, Moustier. Letter from Guadeloupe intendant Peynier (or Peinier) to the Marine ministry. 14 January 1764.

105. ANOM COL E 274 bis, Lejean. The first admiralty court had met at Basse-terre; the second was based at Pointe-à-Pitre, to join a local court known as the Sainte-Anne juridiction.

106. ANOM COL E 135, Charles Ponce Vivant Dognon.

107. Much of the interjudicial correspondence that has been collected in the personnel records (ANOM série E) concerns requests for free passage to or from the colonies on royal ships, which the royal administration tried to limit to trips on official business. Some writers also asked the king to give them free passage due to dire circumstances (travel mishaps, poverty, and so on).

108. I have been unable to ascertain exactly how the role of *conseiller secret greffier* differed from the roles of other types of greffier. Vivaraix appears to be a spelling for Vivarais, the area around Viviers, Ardèche, on the Rhône River in France near Lyon.

109. ANOM COL E 244, François Auguste Ladreyt. The personnel file does not indicate whether Ladreyt received the job.

110. Doyle, *The Parlement of Bordeaux*, 13. ANOM COL E 101, Pierre Barbe Cullet de Pugieu. ANOM COL E 10, Jean Louis Aubert. Marine report dated 10 August 1786.

111. For similar processes during court days in eighteenth-century Virginia, see Isaac, *The Transformation of Virginia*, 88–93.

Chapter 2. Justice Between Plantation and Port

1. Hearing by the Martinique conseil supérieur, 16 May 1752, ANOM COL F^3 245 Martinique, 69–73.

2. ANOM COL E 127, François Desperron.

3. Ibid. Though torture appears frequently in criminal cases from the eighteenth century (including conseil cases), the frequency of torture in judicial cases decreased consistently during the early modern period in Europe. In France, judicial torture was officially abolished in 1788. By the mid-eighteenth century, debates raged in France and across Europe over the question of judicial torture, with Enlightenment figures like Voltaire and Beccaria famously weighing in against high-profile cases of torture. The classic study of this phenomenon is Foucault, *Discipline and Punish*. For a critique of Foucault that looks at criminal cases in the Parisian Châtelet and Parlement courts that finds much less torture was practiced than Foucault claimed, see Andrews, *Law, Magistracy, and Crime*. Changing cultural and legal attitudes in France contributed to the end of judicial torture by the late 1780s. By the late eighteenth century, however, even colonial legal commentators like Pierre Dessalles advocated for an end to judicial torture amid widespread calls for penal reform. Judicial torture was abolished in the Mascarenes in 1781. In Saint-Domingue, torture was abolished only after its conseils supérieurs dissolved in 1787, a fact that scholars such as

Charles Frostin have attributed directly to the appeals by free agitators of color like Julien Raimond to reduce abuses. Ruff, *Violence in Early Modern Europe*, 95; Silverman, *Tortured Subjects*; Dessalles, *Les annales du conseil*, part 1, vol. 1, 149; Rouillard, ed., *A Collection of the Laws of Mauritius*, vol. 1, 184. Arrêt de réglement, 11 August 1781; Frostin, *Les révoltes blanches*, 230.

4. ANOM COL E 127, François Desperron. Maillard-Dumesle is an alternate spelling that appears frequently for the intendant.

5. Entry for "publicité" in *Dictionnaire de l'Académie française*, 4th edition (1762) and 5th edition (1798), Accessed through ARTFL, *Dictionnaires d'autrefois*.

6. Henry, *Report on the Criminal Law at Demerara*, 40.

7. ANOM COL E 337, Pitre Paul. January 1727.

8. For sedition in the Mascarenes, see, for example, the complaint of Sieur Igou, curate of Port-Bourbon, concerning public insults to his character he claimed to have endured from "the Sieur de Saint-Martin, the woman Toutain and several soldiers and inhabitants [*habitants*]." Bonnefoy, ed., *Arrêts administratifs*, 41. 7 July 1730. For similar public verbal attacks in Louisiana, see Dawdy, "Scoundrels, Whores, and Gentlemen." For slander in early modern France, see Darnton, *The Devil in the Holy Water*. For the early modern links between reputation and credit, see especially Muldrew, *The Economy of Obligation*.

9. For example, Kettering, *Patrons, Brokers, and Clients*; Chapman, "Patronage as Family Economy"; Dubé, "Les biens publics"; Dubé, "Making a Career out of the Atlantic."

10. For example, Martineau, *Dupleix et l'Inde française*, 1920.

11. For example, Hodson and Rushforth, "Absolutely Atlantic"; Soll, *The Information Master*.

12. For example, Dessalles, *Histoire générale des Antilles*. The setup described for Martinique also seems to match the urban legal setting of the Saint-Domingue conseils. See, for instance, Moreau de Saint-Méry's detailed descriptions of Cap-Français and Port-au-Prince (with accompanying maps and illustrations) in his description of Saint-Domingue. Moreau de Saint-Méry, *Description topographique*.

13. Entry for "Conseil supérieur de la Martinique," Diderot and d'Alembert, eds., *Encyclopédie*, vol. 4, 14.

14. Moitt, *Women and Slavery in the French Antilles*.

15. Petitjean Roget, *Le Gaoulé*, 149.

16. Ibid., 147.

17. Hayot, *Les officiers du conseil*, 33–36, 41; Des Essarts, *Essai sur l'histoire générale*, 140.

18. Hayot, *Les officiers du conseil*, 33–34.

19. Petitjean Roget, *Le Gaoulé*, 149.

20. The military officers were the *commandant en second*, a major general (or an equivalent), a *commissaire de marine*, and the oldest commissaire de marine. Des Essarts, *Essai sur l'histoire générale*, 140.

21. ANOM COL E 66, Cazaux Du Breuil, Statement from Guadeloupe government to Marine, 5 April 1727. Compare this statement with a declaration from Cayenne, Guyane, in 1776 that described a similar conseil configuration and likewise allowed magistrates from other conseils (with a few caveats concerning bar admittance for lawyers, which could vary immensely depending upon time and place, as discussed throughout below). Des Essarts, *Essai sur l'histoire générale*, 144.

22. For the development of military fortifications in Martinique during this period, see Verrand, "Fortifications Militaires." A large literature on French metropolitan port cities also exists, notably Paul Butel's studies of Bordeaux. Scholarship on colonial towns has been slower to develop. None of this literature does much to account for the legal landscape of these places. Butel, *Vivre à Bordeaux*. The best work on colonial towns has been on the enslaved and free people of color who were more likely to live in urban areas than in rural plantation areas: Rogers, "Les libres de couleur," and Pérotin-Dumon, *La ville aux Îles*. A long-standing tradition of scholarship emphasizes connections between colonial port cities and the wider Atlantic. Fewer global studies integrate the Atlantic and Indian Oceans. Knight and Liss, eds., *Atlantic Port Cities*, and de la Fuente, *Havana and the Atlantic*. For colonial architecture in Saint-Domingue as its functional landscape and infrastructure, see Cauna, "Vestiges of the Built Landscape." Though he mentions plantations, roads, and military fortifications, Cauna does not discuss the urban government buildings that would have housed the headquarters of the colony's two conseils.

23. A 1726 instruction from the king to the conseils of Saint-Domingue forbade them to meet as a body in churches or other places besides their official chambers ("salle de réunions"). ANOM COL A 28 F° 132. 17 September 1726.

24. Hayot, *Les officiers du conseil*, 34. The governor-general presided over Martinique, Guadeloupe, and Saint-Domingue at this time.

25. Calle, *Relation du S. de la Calle*. For an illustration of this battle, see "[Plan de l'attaque Du Fort Royal par les Hollandais]."

26. Hayot, *Les officiers du conseil*, 33–34.

27. The leader of the conseil would "recueille les voix & prononce." "Conseil supérieur de la Martinique," *Encyclopédie*, vol. 4, 14.

28. Hayot, *Les officiers du conseil*, 33–34.

29. Letter 19, Réunion [Île Bourbon], 21 December 1770, Bernardin de Saint-Pierre, *Journey to Mauritius*, 181.

30. I have found better maps for Pondichéry than for the Mascarenes, even from early in the eighteenth century: for example, "Carte Generalle des Villes Fortes et Dependances de Pondichery . . . [1707]." This map has remarkable detail, including the gallows on the edge of town, outlying lands own by various religious orders, and several cemeteries marked out for Christians, lapsed Christians ("des Parias Chrétien"), and Indian Christians. A palais de justice was not labeled, however. Pondichéry's conseil had only been created in 1701, so it likely met in the governor's house.

31. Toussaint, *Early Printing in the Mascarene Islands*, 77.

32. In terms of a regional arrangement, then, Martinique and Pondichéry's conseils played similar roles as dominant courts in the Atlantic and the Indian Ocean, respectively. This lasted until 1789, when Île de France became the center of Indian Ocean governance.

33. The name was changed in 1793 during the French Revolution. For the edict, see ANOM FM F/6/2.

34. Like Guadeloupe with Martinique, Île Bourbon was administered concurrently with Île de France. Like Guadeloupe and Martinique, each island eventually had its own conseil. Unlike Martinique and Guadeloupe, however, the Mascarenes came under direct royal control only in 1767.

35. For a recent exception, see Peabody, *Madeleine's Children*.

36. Joucla, *Le conseil supérieur*. On administrative privileges, Joucla quotes Delabarre, nos. 16–17.

37. For example, Governor David. ANOM COL E 111.

38. Fields for military exercises (for example, the Champs de Mars) in French colonial towns were often constructed on the side of town away from the water, which appears to be a strategic decision to demarcate a space in which to amass troops in the event of an attack by sea. Presumably, this is how the Champ de Lorraine was used, though Bernardin de Saint-Pierre does not specify. Letter 19, Réunion [Île Bourbon], 21 December 1770, Bernardin de Saint-Pierre, *Journey to Mauritius*, 185.

39. ANOM 6 DPPC 2708 (Île Bourbon). 20 April 1732. Extrait des Régistres du greffe du conseil supérieur de l'isle Bourbon.

40. Toussaint, *Early Printing in the Mascarene Islands*, 7.

41. AN AB XIX 2271, dossier 1.

42. Emilien Petit's second-best-known work compares French, English, and Spanish colonial government as a direct response to the imperial rivalries that characterized Caribbean colonies, especially in the era surrounding the Seven Years' War. Caribbean islands, especially in the Lesser Antilles, switched own-

ership at a dizzying pace during the seventeenth and eighteenth centuries. Petit, *Dissertations sur le droit public.*

43. "Isle de Bovrbon; Isle de Diego Rodrigo."

44. Letter 19, Réunion [Île Bourbon], 21 December 1770, Bernardin de Saint-Pierre, *Journey to Mauritius*, 181.

45. The original conseil, known as a conseil provincial, was established to include a royal lieutenant (to take the place of Sieur Dioré if absent), a second conseiller (Sieur de Saint-Martin, also bookkeeper and general guard of the stores), and a third conseiller (Sieur Dugard d'Auterive, major), plus they could choose up to seven people to fill out the remainder. ANOM FM F/3/210 Île de France, 29. 31 May 1726.

46. Des Essarts, *Essai sur l'histoire générale,* vol. 3, 142–43. As a point of comparison, Pondichéry's conseil had been created in 1701, a decade earlier than those in the Mascarene islands, and included seven conseillers, the same number of prosecutors, one chief greffier, and two assesseurs in addition to the usual array of governor and intendant (plus a lieutenant general).

47. Mahé de La Bourdonnais, discussed later in this chapter.

48. In the same way that the fertile Lamentin plain was adjacent to Fort Royal in Martinique. A map by the prolific royal cartographer Jacques Nicolas Bellin from 1764 marks out property lines (almost certainly all plantations) on Île de France that reveal where planters had concentrated on the island. The 1760s were a period of strong agricultural growth in the Mascarenes, so this map most likely reflects new and emerging economic development on the island. Bellin, "Carte de l'Isle de France." 1764. For Île Bourbon at the same time, see Bellin and Choiseul. "Carte de l'Isle de Bourbon." 1763.

49. Bernardin de Saint-Pierre, *Journey to Mauritius*, 95.

50. Letter 6, Port Louis, 6 August 1768, Bernardin de Saint-Pierre, *Journey to Mauritius*, 95–96. Contrast such basic colonial infrastructure with elaborate nineteenth-century projects, such as those in British India. For the development of imperial landscapes in the nineteenth century, see Chopra, *A Joint Enterprise.*

51. Married people, by contrast, tended to stay at home on their plantations, Bernardin reported. Bernardin de Saint-Pierre, *Journey to Mauritius*, 123.

52. Leech emphasizes the influence of durable indigenous building techniques throughout the Americas and the Caribbean for overcoming this problem. Leech, "Impermanent Architecture." For Virginia, Leech cites Carson et al., "Impermanent Architecture in the Southern American Colonies." For vernacular architecture in Martinique in this period, including the plantation house from which the Gaoulé began, see Marry et al., *Martinique, maisons des îles.*

53. This seems have been a problem in Saint-Domingue as well. An arrêt from Cap-Français issued in 1722 required four bailiffs to stand guard outside conseil meetings as well as outside the door of the court's meeting space ("à la porte du Banc destiné pour le Conseil") on Sundays and holidays to prevent intrusions. If the bailiffs failed to meet these criteria, they could be fined (fifty livres per person per infraction) or fired (*cassé*). Moreau de Saint-Méry, *Loix et constitutions*, vol. 3, 1–2. 3 February 1722.

54. Sedition was a perennial court matter in the early modern era, prosecuted in terms of both speech and print. For the metropolitan dynamics of sedition, see Darnton, *The Devil in the Holy Water*, and Butterworth, *Poisoned Words*.

55. Entry for "sellette," *Dictionnaire de l'Académie française*, 4th edition (1762) and 5th edition (1798).

56. The exact wording for the signs: "seditieux et perturbateur du repos public." ANOM COL E 248, La Grange.

57. Ibid. Done in the conseil on 6 May 1718 and signed by Moreau.

58. Foucault, *Discipline and Punish*. Paradoxically, many of the same jurists who issued violent punishments for convicted criminals, especially those who were enslaved, in these colonies also advocated for ending judicial torture, a movement that was gaining traction in both the colonies and the metropole in the mid-eighteenth century at precisely the moment of the Damiens affair (both before and because of it). Judicial torture was abolished in France and its colonies in 1788, though it had been abolished by the Île de France conseil in 1781. Malick Ghachem covers this political and judicial debate in French colonial Saint-Domingue, particularly surrounding the law of slavery, more comprehensively in Ghachem, *The Old Regime and the Haitian Revolution*. A long-term assessment of these high-profile moments within many centuries of French history is provided by Friedland, *Seeing Justice Done*. Rouillard, ed., *A Collection of the Laws of Mauritius*, 184. Arrêt de règlement, 11 August 1781.

59. Attracting, of course, illicit as well as licit trade: see Banks, "Official Duplicity."

60. For the admixture of various professions (artisans, and so forth) and statuses (free, enslaved) as revealed through the configuration of Guadeloupean towns, see Pérotin-Dumon, *La ville aux Iles*.

61. ANOM COL E 41, André Chauton de Bordenave, arrêt rendu contre lui par le conseil supérieur de la Martinique, 1724.

62. Ibid.

63. The arrêt does not give the person's name and indicates only that he was a "substitut"—likely the substitute procureur. Ibid.

64. ANOM COL A, E, F/3.

65. Articles XXXI and XXXII of France, ed., *Le code noir*. 1685. Wood, "Murder on the Road."

66. Freedom suits regarding similar paperwork (or lack thereof) pervaded court dockets across slave societies. For such suits in Francophone contexts, see Scott and Hébrard, *Freedom Papers*; Peabody, *Madeleine's Children*. For a Latin American comparison, see Premo, "An Equity against the Law." For British colonial analogues, see Aljoe, "Going to Law."

67. Spanish *audiencias* (law courts very similar to the conseils supérieurs) were likewise required to take cases by people who claimed to be free but were currently enslaved, based on slave laws promulgated in 1680. Goveia, *The West Indian Slave Laws*, 13.

68. Rheims Rose is but one example in a wide and well-documented tradition of Malouin trading and political influence in this area sustained throughout the early modern era. See the discussion later in this chapter for more about this. ANOM COL E 359, Rheims Rose, Mémoire.

69. Conseillers (magistrates) were thus not always lawyers—in the Antilles they tended to come from the planter class and were occasionally (though less often than in the Mascarenes) merchants. By this time Rheims Rose had himself become a planter, owning three plantations by 1779. ANOM COL E 359, Rheims Rose, Letter to Sartine (minister of the Marine), 15 March 1779 and Letter to Bertrand (minister of the Marine), 14 October 91.

70. ANOM COL E 359, Rheims Rose, Mémoire.

71. For more on contraband in the Antilles, see Pérotin-Dumon, "Cabotage, Contraband, and Corsairs"; Banks, "Official Duplicity."

72. The nickname La Bigorne could refer to a two-horned creature ("bi-horned") and possibly a mythical animal from the folklore of Anjou and Normandy.

73. It's unclear from this documentation which Malagasy group was meant by the term "East Malagasy."

74. ANOM COL E 184, Filet, dit La Bigorne. Filet is sometimes spelled "Fillet." Part of the anger Poivre displayed undoubtedly stemmed from his belief that he had been specifically left out of the plan to support Filet because he disapproved of it, which tied into his wider dissatisfaction with the management of the colony overall and his ongoing feud with Dumas. For Poivre's ideas on colonial management, especially regarding agricultural resources, see Wood, "Political Science."

75. According to his succession. Eventually, the conseil issued a ruling to divide up his property in a succession that left thirty-six slaves that he personally owned (sold for 8,800 livres) and lesser sums to the company and to his family. ANOM COL E 184, Filet, dit La Bigorne.

76. For more on local politics in Madagascar during this era, see Ellis, "Tom and Toakafo"; Hooper, "Pirates and Kings."

77. For the phenomenon of female rulers in the Indian Ocean during this period, with attention to their European counterparts, see Amirell, "Female Rule." In Amirell's appendix of female rulers, Sobobobié-Betty is listed at number 134 as "Bety" of Sainte-Marie Island, Madagascar, ruling circa 1750–1754, citing Truhart, *Regents of Nations*, 1057.

78. It's unclear whether this was her phrasing, or the Île de France clerk's, as this was a common expression used in petitions—particularly by women—concerning financial misfortunes precipitated by events such as the death of a father or husband. Wood "Recovering the Debris of Fortunes."

79. ANOM COL E 371 bis, Sobobobié-Betty. Sobobobié-Betty herself likely descended from a mixture of Malagasy and European ancestors (a hybrid ethnicity known as *zana-malata*), as her brother Ratsimilaho was commonly assumed to be zana-malata. For more on her family, including Ratsimilaho, as negotiators with European (including British) traders and would-be colonizers, see Hooper, "Pirates and Kings"; Vaughan, *Creating the Creole Island,* 105–7.

80. ANOM COL E 184, Filet, dit La Bigorne.

81. ANOM COL E 371 bis, Sobobobié-Betty. Île de France conseil register extract, 5 June 1780.

82. Such requests for patronage, or protection, appear throughout the interjudicial correspondence I survey in this book and form perhaps the most notable aim of such correspondence. See also requests by François Michalet, Jean André de Ribes, and the Gaoulé participants.

83. Rochon, *Voyage à Madagascar.* For Madagascar during this period, see Campbell, *An Economic History of Imperial Madagascar*; Larson, *Ocean of Letters.*

84. For piracy and illegality in the Indian Ocean and beyond, see Hooper, "Pirates and Kings"; McDonald, *Pirates, Merchants, Settlers, and Slaves*; Lane, *Pillaging the Empire.*

85. For different (colonial and postcolonial) approaches to centers and peripheries, see Kaps and Komlosy, "Centers and Peripheries Revisited."

Chapter 3. Between "Île Deserte" and "Île de France"

1. "Il va arriver un grand malheur, les bequets vont faire un gaoulet comme les nègres." Letter from Cornette de Saint-Cyr, cited in Petitjean Roget, *Le Gaoulé,* 492. "Bequet" or "béké" then as now referred to the European elites, usually planters, who dominated Antillean society and economy.

2. Letter 5 [1768], Bernardin de Saint-Pierre, *Journey to Mauritius,* 92.

3. ANOM COL E 119, Jean André de Ribes, Letter to Praslin, 5 March 1768. One other personnel record exists for Ribes, which is only four pages long and summarizes the key issues (conseiller status, passage to and from France) that arise in the other, longer case file. ANOM COL E 350, Jean André de Ribes.

4. I capitalize the term "gaoulé" when referring to the events of 1717. When uncapitalized, I refer to the wider usage of the term both before and after 1717.

5. Petitjean Roget, *Le Gaoulé*, is the definitive study of this uprising. It relies upon a fairly encyclopedic reading of material from the Archives nationales d'outre-mer, especially série A (actes du pouvoir souverain) and série C (correspondance à l'arrivée). Petitjean Roget underplays, however, the impact of the banishment itself and the significance of the conseil as a venue for colonial and metropolitan tensions.

6. The fact that Guadeloupe appears to have lacked its own prison indicates a more long-standing dependence on Martinique for judicial and executive matters in practice, not just an acknowledgment of Martinique's designation as the regional government for the Lesser Antilles throughout most of the eighteenth century. In 1714, Martinique had become the regional headquarters for the islands of Guadeloupe, Saint Lucia, and Grenada, while Saint-Domingue had become a separate administrative region.

7. Petitjean Roget, *Le Gaoulé*, 253. As in the Gaoulé itself and the Ribes case discussed below, petitions were critical to local protests. The Guadeloupeans also drafted a petition "in the name of all the inhabitants of Guadeloupe" that reasserted their loyalty to the French Crown, pointing out that they had recently participated in the defense of the island during a recent war and were always ready to follow orders and laws that they received from France. For the previous three years, however, they had lacked sufficient supplies of beef, cloth, and other provisions from France, so they requested permission to seek sources elsewhere. They also wanted permission to do as they saw fit with the supplies and to pay enslaved Africans (that is, their owners) ten *sous* a day when they were working on the colony's infrastructure (*travaux du Roi*) and to be reimbursed if they died on the job. Imperial construction projects, managed by the governor and military engineers, were a continual source of conflict between administrators and planters, who resented having their slaves taken away to build roads, irrigation canals, and so on. Guillaume Dorange, a participant in the Gaoulé, had a notarized request deposited with the Martinique conseil greffe in February 1728 requesting exemption from the *corvée* (road tax) for him and his family, citing his military service for the French against Caribs and English as meriting the privilege. ANOM COL E 135, Guillaume Dorange.

8. Because they had the governor-general, they did not need La Varenne's presence at the conseil meeting.

9. Petitjean Roget, *Le Gaoulé*, 254–55.

10. Ibid., 259–60.

11. Ibid., 263.

12. Ibid., 265. ANOM COL E 236, Michel Labat. This latter fact indicates that local resentment was aimed primarily at the king's representative, the governor, as it would be in the Dumas affair in Île de France in 1768.

13. Petitjean Roget, *Le Gaoulé*, 265–66.

14. Ibid., 265, citing ANOM C 8 A 25, Dep. La Mothe, No. 14 fo. 72.

15. "Nous avons ordre de la Colonie de vous tuer si vous branlez, de vous casser la tête si vous faites résistance." Quoted in Petitjean Roget, *Le Gaoulé*, 266.

16. Ibid., 265, 297.

17. Ibid., *Le Gaoulé*, 297–99. The mob from Le Diamant (by the eighteenth at Lamentin) elected Jorna, a colonel (and longtime militia leader), as their leader, but he was rejected by the *petit blancs* (non-planter whites), who insisted upon Dubucq instead. ANOM COL E 231, Jorna.

18. In ancien régime sources, "habitant" sometimes refers simply to an inhabitant of a specified place but it could also designate a planter, which is the meaning in this instance.

19. ANOM COL E 24, Belair, Cathier, Dorange, Labat, et Bourgelas.

20. Michel Labat had recently married Marie Catherine Dorange, so the two men were related by marriage. Petitjean Roget, *Le Gaoulé*, 263. Mademoiselle Labat seems to have been Michel Labat's daughter, or perhaps another female relative, but the relationship is not specified in the document. Pas de Feuquières was an Antillean *notable* himself, with extensive ties to the conseil and planter community, which was also linked into an older order of Antillean families who had made careers in the military before becoming planters.

21. ANOM COL E 236, Michel Labat.

22. The king did this via his regent uncle, the duc d'Orléans.

23. ANOM COL E 24, Belair, Cathier, Dorange, Labat, et Bourgelas.

24. ANOM COL E 219, Hauterive, d.' 21 November 1717.

25. Martinican conseil members perfected this strategy over the eighteenth century by drafting legal codes: at once solving an administrative problem (inaccurate legal records) and advancing legal claims for autonomy for themselves. For example, Petit de Viévigne, ed., *Code de la Martinique*; Dessalles, *Les annales du conseil*.

26. Petitjean Roget, *Le Gaoulé*, 345.

27. Ibid., 189.

28. Hayot, *Les officiers du conseil*, 104. Clermont seems to have been part of an older demographic among the Antillean elite who participated in the Gaoulé: he was fifty-four when it happened. Clermont also had a controversial tenure on the conseil. He was forbidden to continue serving on the conseil in 1715, and his membership was revoked in 1716, after he had been accused of soliciting bribes (*épices*). The next year, he participated in the Gaoulé, but Feuquières (who supported the rebels' appeals) changed his opinion of Clermont, calling him a "great villain" (*grand scélérat*).

29. ANOM COL E 135, Guillaume Dorange.

30. ANOM COL E 24, Belair, Cathier, Dorange, Labat, et Bourgelas.

31. Petitjean Roget, *Le Gaoulé*, 515.

32. Joucla, *Le conseil superieur*, 17–18.

33. Petitjean Roget, *Le Gaoulé*, 492.

34. "Il va arriver un grand malheur, les bequets vont faire un gaoulet comme les nègres." Letter from Cornette de Saint-Cyr, cited in Petitjean Roget, *Le Gaoulé*, 492.

35. I have been unable to confirm this hypothesis with extant sources, though Philippe Fabry makes the connection between "guivi" and the Carib language in a footnote. *La relève de l'Escadre de Perse*, 48. A similar term ("quivis" or "kivi") appears in Mascarene contexts in 1674 as a "word of Malagasy [*malgache*] origin" to refer to people who had taken refuge in the mountainous center of Île Bourbon (the "hauts" of the island). Ordinance of J. de la Haye (1 December 1674). Referenced in Nicole, *Noirs, cafres et créoles*, 330.

36. The whole controversy appears to have been known at the time (or at least a little after) as the "Dumas affair," a designation that appears in ANOM COL E 153, Jean Daniel Dumas, unsigned ruling at Versailles, 5 October 1775.

37. Auguste Toussaint noted a similar shift in focus from India to the Mascarenes following the American Revolution. The loss of most French Indian possessions in the 1740s makes it more likely, however, that this shift had already occurred, except in entrepôts like Pondichéry. In contrast to Toussaint, I argue that the mid-1760s marked an earlier transitional period in which France focused on the Mascarenes, a necessary step for later plans to seem plausible. Auguste Toussaint, *Le route des iles*, 95.

38. Poivre, *Discours prononces par M. Poivre*. For the Pacific in this era, see Mapp, "Silver, Science, and Routes to the West"; Igler, *Great Ocean*.

39. In France, syndics also acted as community representatives who initiated and organized petitions. See, for example, the case of a Paris syndic helping to organize

a petition to banish Germain Barthélemy to the colonies, discussed in more detail in Wood, "Family or Foe?" ANOM COL E 203, Barthélemy Germain.

40. ANOM COL E 393, Edmé Charles Yardin.

41. The Yardin fortune was somewhat unstable, however. This mention of Yardin arises in a letter to the minister of the marine regarding Yardin's failure to keep up with the payments on this plantation, prompting the previous owner's widow to request royal support in forcing him to pay, initiating a conflict that lasted until at least 1774. Letter from widow of André Hyacinthe to De Boynes, minister of the Marine, December 1771. ANOM COL E 226 André Hyacinthe.

42. Some of his copies of notarized documents and report ledgers (*répertoires*) have survived: ANOM DPPC NOT MAUR REP 5; ANOM DPPC NOT MAUR 512.

43. Ordonnance du Roi, 1 August 1768. *Supprimant la Chambre Syndicale; et conférant aux Commandants de Quartier quelques unes des fonctions de la dite Chambre Syndicale*, n. (1): "Il n'y a plus de Commandants de Quartier, leurs fonctions sont pour la plupart du ressort des chefs de la police." Rouillard, ed., *A Collection of the Laws of Mauritius*, vol. 1, 24. Entry for "chambre syndicale" in Bonnefoy, *Table générale*, 80. Cf. ANOM COL A 18 F° 135, Ordonnance qui supprime la chambre syndicale créée aux îles de France et de Bourbon, en 1762 (n° 30B) (1 August 1768).

44. ANOM COL E 119, Jean André de Ribes, 13 January 1768. Letter to Praslin.

45. Ibid.

46. Ibid., Letter to Sartine, 7 May 1775.

47. Dumas was installed as commander of the Mascarenes in 1766 and served in that post until 26 November 1768. Colonial governors were granted direct control over many colonial residents, unlike legal employees such as Ribes. Dumas was sent to the Indian Ocean with twelve hundred men, of whom eight hundred were to stay in Île de France, while the rest were sent to Réunion. Twenty-four slaves (previously owned by the company) were also transferred to his possession upon his arrival. ANOM COL E 153, Jean Daniel Dumas.

48. ANOM COL E 119, Jean André de Ribes, 13 January 1768. Letter to Praslin.

49. The syndic assembly was, however, dissolved in 1768. Syndic responsibilities were then transferred first to the neighborhood (that is, militia) chiefs (*commandants du quartier*) and later to the police chiefs (*chefs de la police*).

50. ANOM COL E 119, Jean André de Ribes.

51. Du Tertre, *Histoire générale*, vol. 3, 67–68.

52. Ibid. Versions of this idea were common in early modern European empires. For comparisons with Spanish and British colonial empires, see Cañeque, *The King's Living Image*, and McConville, *The King's Three Faces*.

53. Du Tertre, *Histoire générale,* vol. 3, 67–68.

54. Otherwise known as the "Hymn of Saint Ambrose and Saint Augustine," with reference to its attributed authors.

55. Montagnier, "Le *Te Deum,*" 206–8.

56. I thank Aaron Alejandro Olivas for advice on this topic, including references to *Te Deums* sung in other parts of France.

57. Montagnier, "Le *Te Deum.*"

58. ANOM COL A 28 F° 7, 14 November [or 14 May] 1713. Date on manuscript is unclear.

59. ANOM COL A 26 F° 29v, 1 February 1749.

60. ANOM COL E 318, Moydieu. This evidence comes from the late 1770s, however, so it is uncertain whether Ribes was in contact with Moydieu in the 1760s.

61. Montagnier argues that the *Te Deum* was much more politically powerful than court music (as by Lully and Lalande) because it was required to be performed. This evidence for the colonies extends his argument beyond metropolitan France. Montagnier, "Le *Te Deum.*"

62. ANOM COL E 119, Jean André de Ribes, Letter to Praslin, 5 March 1768.

63. This problem persisted across the French Empire. Boucher makes an almost identical assessment for the Antilles in the seventeenth century, citing the first intendant, Patoulet, and Blénac as setting a precedent for this tension. Boucher, *France and the American Tropics,* 210.

64. ANOM COL E 379 bis, Tiver. For more on Tiver, see below.

65. ANOM COL E 352, Rivals de Perles.

66. For example, Ly-Tio-Fane, *The Triumph of Jean Nicolas Céré;* Grove, "Protecting the Climate of Paradise." Pier Larson and Richard Allen have decentered this point of view by focusing on the lives of Malagasy and enslaved Africans in the western Indian Ocean. See Larson, *Ocean of Letters,* and Allen, *Slaves, Freedmen, and Indentured Laborers,* for cultural and social approaches to this period.

67. Letter 5 [1768], Bernardin de Saint-Pierre, *Journey to Mauritius,* 92.

68. Editorial note, ibid., 241.

69. ANOM FM F/3/211, Île de France, 413. 9 July 1778.

70. Ibid., 415. The ruling specified that it was pending the approval of the king.

71. Ibid., 621.

72. ANOM COL E 119, Jean André de Ribes, Letter to Sartine, 7 May 1775.

73. See, for example, the report submitted by Rheims Rose from Île de France to the Marine in the 1780s, which complained that Spanish silver sent to the Mascarenes was almost immediately traded to Africa and Asia, creating a shortage. The monarchy sought a paper money solution, which merchants especially

hated. ANOM COL E 359, Rheims Rose. For examples of legislation regarding this problem that Rose was criticizing, see especially ANOM FM F/3/211, Code de l'Île de France, for example, the August 1779 edict outlining a new printing of paper money for the Mascarenes.

74. By contrast, Dumas appears to have lost the favor of the Marine and court society more thoroughly. In 1775, the Marine ruled that the Dumas affair be expedited before the court's departure from Versailles for Fontainebleau (reflecting the seasonal movement of the court). It specified to Dumas that it was "not possible to satisfy him on this regard," referring to his requests to the Marine. Instead, the Marine required Dumas to produce a certificate from the Île de France treasurer noting the exact date when he ceased to be paid for his appointment in the colony to determine the retroactive date to begin his "traitement" of six thousand livres. It also noted that he owed the military regiment associated with Île de France more than 16,578 livres and that he was indebted to the Compagnie des Indes orientales for more than 35,119 livres. ANOM COL E 153, Jean Daniel Dumas, unsigned ruling at Versailles, 5 October 1775.

75. ANOM COL E 119, Jean André de Ribes.

76. Entry for "Appointement," Diderot and d'Alembert, eds., *Encyclopédie*, vol. 1, 554; Bernardin de Saint-Pierre, *Journey to Mauritius*, 95.

77. Benton, *A Search for Sovereignty*, 110.

78. Peabody, *"There Are No Slaves in France."*

79. Bernardin de Saint-Pierre, *Journey to Mauritius*, 184.

80. Davidson, *Voltaire*, 9. For family sanctioning through *lettres de cachet* within France, see Farge and Foucault, *Disorderly Families*. For the logic of colonial banishment, see Wood, "Family or Foe?"

81. It was not officially ceded to France until 1697, seven decades after Martinique and Guadeloupe.

82. Frostin, *Les révoltes blanches*, 13. For more on the regional variation within Saint-Domingue in the eighteenth century, and the distinctiveness of the southern province, Garrigus, *Before Haiti*, especially chapter 1. Another revolt broke out in Louisiana in 1768 by French and German settlers who contested the cession of Louisiana to Spain following the Seven Years' War. This revolt was aimed at a foreign power, however, unlike the Saint-Domingue, Martinique, and Île de France conflicts, which illustrated tensions *within* the French Empire.

83. ANOM COL E 24, Belair, Cathier, Dorange, Labat, et Bourgelas.

84. For example, the general amnesty granted to the inhabitants of Tortuga and Saint-Domingue in 1671. ANOM COL B 3 F° 75, 10 October 1671.

Chapter 4. Entrepôts in a Changing Empire

1. "Le port de l'île de France est l'arsenal de nos forces et l'entrepôt de notre commerce." Rochon, *Voyage à Madagascar*, vi.

2. Chanvalon, *Voyage à la Martinique*, 30.

3. ANOM FM F/3/210, Île de France, 5 March 1729, 57–59. Though the *Aleyon* apparently did not arrive as expected, a small ship, the *Mars*, left Île de France on 24 November 1728 to get help from Île Bourbon.

4. For the cultural and political ramifications of such interactions in French India, see Agmon, *A Colonial Affair*.

5. For one analysis of how to think about islands within the wider Indian Ocean system, see Alpers, "Indian Ocean Africa." For the specific example of Sri Lanka, see Sivasundaram, *Islanded*.

6. Here defined as the era in which the Indian Ocean has been a space connected by the migrations of humans, especially since the rise of Islamic trading from the seventh century C.E.

7. Dull, *The French Navy*, 62–63.

8. ANOM COL E 298, Armand François de Maizière de Maisoncelle. He was born on 14 February 1724 in the village of Grave, near Epernay in Champagne, and died at Port Louis.

9. Haudrère, ed., Introduction to *Les Français dans l'océan indien au XVIIIe siècle*. ANOM COL E 359, Rheims Rose, Mémoire.

10. ANOM COL E 271, Jean Baptiste Nicolas Claude Lefebvre.

11. For an overview of Pondichéry and Chandernagor that compares differing English and French success along India's eastern coast, see Sinha, *The Politics of Trade*.

12. Sections 2–4 and passim, Letter to Messieurs du conseil supérieur à l'Isle de Bourbon from the directors of the Compagnie des Indes orientales, Paris, 5 September 1729, sent via the *Vierge de Grace* with a duplicate sent via the *Diane*. Bourbon Conseil Supérieur et al., *Correspondance du conseil supérieur de Bourbon et de la Compagnie des Indes*, vol. 1, 1724–1731, 83–85.

13. Ibid.

14. For the slave trade in the Indian Ocean during this period, see Allen, "The Constant Demand of the French"; Hooper and Eltis. "The Indian Ocean in Transatlantic Slavery."

15. Letter to Messieurs du conseil supérieur à l'Isle de Bourbon from the directors of the Compagnie des Indes orientales, Paris, 4 October 1732. Bourbon Conseil Supérieur et al., *Correspondance du conseil supérieur de Bourbon et de la Compagnie des Indes*, vol. 2, 1732–1736, 8–10. Most likely also along the Sofala Coast, though the term "Pays des Cafres" could designate much of southern Africa, as

shown by Figure 8, a circa-1730 reissue of Delisle's map from 1708, which was widely copied and circulated. Note especially the "Cafres Independans" and "Cafres alliez avec les Portuguais" along the Sofala Coast next to the "Luabo River" (now the Zambezi River). Delisle, "Carte du Congo et du pays des Cafres."

16. Letter to Messieurs du conseil aupérieur à l'Isle de Bourbon from the directors of the Compagnie des Indes orientales, Paris, 4 October 1732. Bourbon Conseil Supérieur et al., *Correspondance du conseil supérieur de Bourbon et de la Compagnie des Indes,* vol. 2, 1732–1736, 9.

17. Ibid., 10. Cf. A similar letter deployed several ships to Bourbon with instructions to acquire three hundred slaves at Madagascar and trade them at Cap-Français, Saint-Domingue. The letter gave an additional general charge to sell as many slaves as possible in Martinique and Saint-Domingue, with a preference for introducing Guinean and Senegalese slaves where possible in the areas where Malagasy (*Malgache*) slaves were not known. Letter to the conseil supérieur à l'Isle de Bourbon from the directors of the Compagnie des Indes orientales, Paris, 6 March 1734. Bourbon Conseil Supérieur et al., *Correspondance du conseil supérieur de Bourbon et de la Compagnie des Indes,* vol. 2, 1732–1736, 88. Letter to the conseil supérieur à l'Isle de Bourbon from the directors of the Compagnie des Indes orientales, Paris, 11 December 1734. Ibid., 229.

18. Letter to the directors of the Compagnie des Indes orientales from the conseil supérieur à l'Isle de Bourbon, 12 December 1733. Bourbon Conseil Supérieur et al., *Correspondance du conseil supérieur de Bourbon et de la Compagnie des Indes,* vol. 2 1732–1736, 88. The company agreed, noting that Martinique's coffee industry was more advanced: Letter to the conseil supérieur à l'Isle de Bourbon from the directors of the Compagnie des Indes orientales, Paris, 17 November 1732. Ibid., 88.

19. Banks, *Chasing Empire.* For the British South Asian equivalent in the next century, see Bayly, *Empire and Information.*

20. Compare Paul Butel's explanation of the seventeenth-century "sugar revolution" in the Antilles with Megan Vaughan's analysis of the slower growth of the Mascarene economies. Butel, *Histoire des Antilles,* 87–105 and passim; Vaughan, *Creating the Creole Island,* 20–32.

21. Mercier's career appears in a series of documentation intended to support his request for nobility, initiated in 1753 and granted in 1779. ANOM COL E 310, Antoine Mercier. ANOM COL A 17 F° 81, Lettres d'anoblissement en faveur d'Antoine Mercier, ancien avocat et doyen des notaires de la Guadeloupe (n° 15), 6 February 1779.

22. For successive iterations of this company, founded by Colbert in 1664, see Haudrère, *La compagnie française*; Ames, "Colbert's Indian Ocean Strategy."

23. ANOM FM F-3-206, Île Bourbon (1712–1768), 29 January 1750, 193–204; ANOM 6 DPPC 2708, Île Bourbon, 1731–1769; ANOM FM F-3-210, Île de France, 1556–1768.

24. Per Ruggiu, "India and the Reshaping."

25. ANOM 6 DPPC (Greffes) 2708, Île Bourbon, two Ordonnances du Roy, 1 August 1768: one concerning the establishment of militias on Île de France and Bourbon, the other relating to the officers of the new militias.

26. Delaleu begins 6 August 1766. *Code des Îles de France et de Bourbon*.

27. *Arrêts administratifs et règlements du Conseil provincial et du Conseil supérieur de l'Île de France*.

28. Villiers, *Marine royale*, 479–81. Citing Christian Schnakenbourg, Villiers elaborates that Basse-Terre and some other towns had been burned before 1759, eighty-four sugar mills (*sucreries*) had been destroyed out of a total of 331 in 1752, and five thousand slaves had been killed out of forty-one thousand. Schnakenbourg, "L'essor économique."

29. Dull, *The French Navy*, 62–63.

30. Many planters sought to outsource plantation management (including policing of slaves) altogether by becoming absentee landlords. But these planters, once ensconced in Paris, did not serve as colonial magistrates. Régent, *La France et ses esclaves*. For the politics of militia service and military support in France and its empire, see Garrigus, *Before Haiti*, 31.

31. How this played out is, of course, the subject of a lively debate among British imperial historians. For a provocative and influential argument that the military governors-general of Britain's early modern empire played a disproportionate role in establishing royal agendas through "garrison government," see Saunders Webb, "Army and Empire"; Johnson, "The Imperial Webb."

32. ANOM COL E, database. For a survey, see Hayot, *Les officiers du conseil*. Compare Hayot with Bernardin de Saint-Pierre's account of local militia and planter groups in Bernardin de Saint-Pierre, *Journey to Mauritius*.

33. This title required good standing in the military, high moral character, and a devout reputation in the Catholic Church. In 1750, for example, Jean Jolif du Colombier, a ship captain for at least one voyage to Southeast Asia on behalf of the Compagnie des Indes orientales, turned in an affidavit by Abbé Chalon from Lorient. ANOM COL E 145, Du Colombier, Jean Jolif. Archival headnote. ANOM Correspondance à l'arrivée d'Extrême-Orient (1658–1863), C 12, folios 25–40, « Journal d'un voyage fait à la Cochinchine pour la Compagnie des Indes » par Laurens, depuis son départ de France, le 23 octobre 1748,

jusqu'à son retour à l'île de France, le 10 avril 1750, suivi, folios 38 à 40, d'observations abrégées sur le commerce qu'on pourroit faire à la Cochinchine (1750).

34. For a more sustained analysis of this pattern in colonial Saint-Domingue, King, *Blue Coat or Powdered Wig*.

35. Ruggiu, "The Kingdom of France."

36. For example, Gabriel Debien evaluated the colonial plantation complex through evidence from individual plantations, while Robert Forster examined the commercial side of France's overseas empire through French merchant families. Debien, *Une plantation de Saint-Domingue*; Forster, *Merchants, Landlords, Magistrates: The Depont*.

37. The Hurault family endures as one of the wealthiest in Martinique, associated with the béké class that still dominates the Martinican economy and political culture.

38. Catherine Cacqueray de Valmeinière appeared as a witness in a 1685 marriage between Edmond Claude Hurault and Marie Dugas, for example. ANOM COL E 226. See ANOM COL E 382 bis for the Valmeinières in Saint-Christophe and military service.

39. ANOM COL E 357.

40. ANOM COL E 151. Files survive for various members of this family, covering most of the eighteenth century.

41. See the files for Rivals family members in ANOM COL E 352.

42. ANOM COL E 172, Blaise Estoupan de Saint Jean.

43. ANOM COL E 111, Pierre Félix David. Mémoire de service. David's career lasted from 1729 to 1791. This career summary possibly embellishes David's heroism, but the events themselves line up with other sources about the involvement of French forces from the Mascarenes in the defense of French interests in India. The end of this report attributes French losses to the British in 1756 (at the beginning of the Seven Years' War) to a lack of preparation despite superior forces, implying that attention to David's purportedly stellar example of defense preparation might have prevented these setbacks. The African dimensions of colonial and imperial history deserve more scholarly treatment, especially as they relate to colonial slave societies. For an overview of French and other European incursions into West Africa, see Brooks, *Eurafricans in Western Africa*. Most African slaves in the Mascarenes came from the region of Mozambique and Madagascar, with some South Asians. For slavery in the Indian Ocean, see Campbell, *The Structure of Slavery*; Carter, "Slavery and Unfree Labour in the Indian Ocean"; Allen, *European Slave Trading in the Indian Ocean*.

44. Sieur de la Calle, *Relation du S. de la Calle*. La Calle was himself a magistrate in Martinique's conseil. ANOM COL E 241, de La Calle.

45. This military victory was later commemorated yearly on the day of Saint Marguerite throughout the Antillean colonies, documented in a later Saint-Domingue conseil ruling. Moreau de Saint-Méry, *Loix et constitutions*, 354.

46. Apparently it took two trips to Pondichéry to get rid of the surplus. ANOM COL E 111, Pierre Félix David. This seems to have been a result of the stronger need of the Mascarenes to grow their own provisions, as they could not rely on nearby mainland wheat producers, though they often traded for wheat, rice, and beef on Madagascar. This is a stark contrast to the Antilles, which never (to my knowledge) grew their own wheat and were nearly always struggling with shortages rather than surpluses. The Antilles depended upon ready (albeit often illicit) supplies of grain from North America, which often provoked subsistence crises and local revolts. For more on provisioning crises as prompting political crises, see chapter 3's discussion of uprisings in Martinique and Île de France.

47. ANOM COL E 153, Jean Daniel Dumas. Marine reports, December 1764 and 3 October 1766.

48. Ibid., 20 February 1742 nomination papers as governor of Senegal and president of its conseil by the Compagnie des Indes orientales. ANOM COL E 111. This is the only reference to a conseil supérieur in Africa that I have found to date. The trading center at Gorée in Africa had a conseil de justice run by its governor, a more informal tribunal. ANOM COL E 31, Eustache Bignon, 1764, theft case. The Senegal conseil seems to have resembled the one at Pondichéry, managing a small territory on a busy trading coastline (rather than a settler colony like the Antilles or Mascarenes).

49. For both Guadeloupe and Martinique conseils, letters patent issued on 11 October 1664. ANOM COL B 3 F° 114 (Departing Correspondence). Cayenne, Guyane (in South America), was managed as part of the Îles du Vent government in Martinique from 1669 until the mid-eighteenth century. In practice, it communicated directly with the metropolitan government and acted autonomously. Archival note, ANOM COL, série C 8A, Correspondance à l'arrivée en provenance de la Martinique (1635/1815). See also Polderman, *La Guyane française*. Guyane depended upon Martinique to supply its plantations with slaves and manufactured goods as a key transshipment center receiving cargo voyages from West Africa and Europe, respectively. Like the rest of the South American mainland, including such territories as Spanish New Granada (now Venezuela), Guyane was very heavily involved in illicit trade with the Antilles to make up for trade deficits and lack of provisions. Louisiana's conseil was founded around

the same time, though the date is a bit uncertain (between 1716 and 1731) due to difficulties in having the letters patent followed correctly by company and other Louisianan officials. Saadani, "Le Gouvernement de la Louisiane Française."

50. Guadeloupe served as a regional forum, too, but primarily for residents of its tiny offshore dependencies: Les Saintes, Marie-Galante, and La Désirade.

51. After these years, the colonies listed in parentheses became independent administrative regions. Appealed cases sometimes traveled, however, from one conseil, such as Guadeloupe, to the metropole, where royal administrators often chose to send appealed cases to a different conseil, such as in Martinique, rather than ruling themselves. See, for example, the Blot case described in chapter 2.

52. ANOM COL A 2 F° 120. 24 September 1731. This document does not specify it, but most property disputes like this involved plantations.

53. As, for example, compiled in Lougnon, *Correspondance du conseil supérieur de Bourbon et de la Compagnie des Indes*; Martineau, *Correspondance du conseil supérieur de Pondichéry avec le conseil de Chandernagor*; Martineau, *Correspondance du conseil supérieur de Pondichéry et de la Compagnie*.

54. Letter 19, Réunion [Île Bourbon], 21 December 1770, Bernardin de Saint-Pierre, *Journey to Mauritius*, 180.

55. ANOM 6DPPC 2708, Extrait des Registres du greffe du conseil supérieur de l'Îsle de Bourbon. 5 November 1732.

56. For French companies in the Indian Ocean, Haudrère, *Les Compagnies*.

57. For example, as mentioned in passing without explaining or describing any court rulings. Pondichéry Conseil Supérieur et al., *Correspondance du Conseil* and Bourbon Conseil Supérieur et al., *Correspondance du Conseil*, 22.

58. ANOM COL E 77, Louis Georges de Chaux. Report from aboard the *Pondichéry*, moored at Pavillon in Île de France, 22 March 1777.

59. Ibid.

60. Ibid.

61. Ibid.

62. Later, the case was appealed to the metropole and in 1778 Salavy was granted a pardon in the form of *lettres de grâce* from the king. ANOM COL A 20 F° 219, 19 September 1778.

63. ANOM COL E 77, Louis Georges de Chaux. So did the wife: Chaux's wife was the daughter of an accountant (*caissier*) in Île Bourbon.

64. ANOM COL E 379 bis, Tiver. It is not clear from this evidence whether the proposal was approved or ever put into action.

65. ANOM 6 DPPC 1323, Guadeloupe. Ordonnance des Messieurs les Général et Intendant establishing many *bureaux des règles* for the security of letters; regis-

tered 11 November 1765. Petit de Viévigne, *Code de la Martinique*, 536. 4 March 1766.

66. 21 January 1774. Ordonnant aux capitaines de navire de donner avis au Chef des Postes, un mois avant leur départ, du lieu de leur destination. Rouillard, ed., *A Collection of the Laws of Mauritius*, vol. 1, 284. Such preparations sometimes paid off, as when duplicate and triplicate copies were sent to multiple locations and have survived in the archives. For example, Archives départementales du Gironde (Bordeaux), 7 B 1632; Lougnon, ed., *Correspondance du conseil supérieur de Bourbon et de la Compagnie des Indes*, vol. 1, 80, 88, 96.

67. Lougnon, ed., *Correspondance du conseil supérieur de Bourbon et de la Compagnie des Indes*, vol. 1, 33–34.

68. Here, the administrators were still company directors who oversaw Mascarene colonies. By the mid-eighteenth century, Île de France tended take over this function for ships traveling between the Cape of Good Hope and South and East Asia, eventually becoming a key site for provisioning military regiments, too, which exacerbated the food shortages discussed below. This development also prompted visitors like Alexis Rochon to encourage more investment in the island's own economy, key to reducing the island's ongoing dependence upon trade with Malagasy principalities. Rochon, *Voyage à Madagascar*, vi.

69. This appears to be the same *Sirenne* (but a different journey) on which Pitre Paul's accusers arrived in Île Bourbon, where they recognized him and submitted a complaint of polygamy. Letter from the Compagnie des Indes to Messieurs du conseil supérieur de l'Isle de Bourbon, Paris, 23 December 1730, in Lougnon, ed., *Correspondance du conseil supérieur de Bourbon et de la Compagnie des Indes*, vol. 1, 106.

70. Letter from the Compagnie des Indes to Messieurs du conseil supérieur de l'Isle de France, Paris, 31 December 1727, in ibid., 65–66.

71. A contrast to entrepôts, such as the Cape of Good Hope, that welcomed traders of many nationalities. Ward, " 'Tavern of the Seas?' "

72. Conseil membership varied dramatically in Saint-Domingue due to the combined factors of high mortality rates and personal politics. In 1770, a colonial official wrote a letter nominating a Monsieur Hachin to replace the recently deceased Baret de Ranty for the Port-au-Prince conseil, noting that there were now three open places as the conseil already reduced "en petit nombre." Hachin had to wait at least five years and repeatedly petition governors, intendants, and finally the minister of the Marine to obtain the position of conseiller, even though in the intervening years the position remained vacant. ANOM COL E 17, Baret de Ranty, and E 217, Pierre Jacques Hachin.

73. Petitjean Roget, *Le Gaoulé*, 245.

74. ANOM COL E 281, Le Sauvage, François. Le Sauvage did not return to Martinique until 1731, when he asked to be reinstated as a conseil member, citing family business and poor health as extenuating circumstances.

75. Letters dated 13 February 1767 and 4 May 1767. ANOM COL E 41, Borde, Claude Albert. The file does not state whether Borde carried out these duties. He lasted as a Martinican magistrate until approximately 1775, when he was granted a government pension. Hayot does not list him as a conseiller, however, so he seems to have filled this role—if at all—only temporarily. Moreau died on 3 May 1767, so Borde at least served as a substitute admiralty court judge. Hayot, *Les officiers du conseil*, 190–92 and passim.

76. ANOM COL E 134, Didier de Saint-Martin.

77. ANOM COL A 18 F° 16. 6 August 1766. ANOM COL A 18 F° 192. 1 December 1770. Chevreau served as commissaire for the Marine in Île de France in 1760 and from 1769 to 1777, when he became the *ordonnateur* (equivalent to intendant) in Pondichéry. Chevreau also served as conseiller in Pondichéry's conseil supérieur from 1760 to 1769. He returned to Île de France in 1781 as intendant general. ANOM, Notice biographique, http://anom.archivesnationales.culture.gouv.fr/eac/?id=FRDAFANOM_EACP000188. Accessed 25 January 2018.

78. At the time, Pierre Poivre. ANOM COL A 18 F° 199. 4 April 1771. ANOM, Notice biographique, http://anom.archivesnationales.culture.gouv.fr/eac/?id=FRDAFANOM_EACP000188. Accessed 25 January 2018. These sources are unclear, but Chevreau may have fallen ill or died himself. ANOM COL A 18 F° 199. 4 April 1771.

79. Hayot, *Les officiers du conseil*, 58–59.

80. ANOM COL A 25 F° 269v. August 1742. *Lettres patentes en forme d'édit sur les assesseurs des conseils supérieurs des colonies, qui seront nommés par les gouverneurs* (n° 196).

81. Arrêt de Règlement, 9 July 1778. *Ordonnant que les Lettres Patentes du Roi, du mois de Juillet 1776, seront exécutées d'après leur forme ct teneur, et nommant plusieurs notables comme assesseurs pour assister le Juge Royal dans le jugement des affaires criminelles.* Rouillard, ed., *A Collection of the Laws of Mauritius*, vol. 1, 168.

82. Toussaint, *La route des iles*, 95.

83. Part of this pattern occurred with the complicity of French conseils. In 1736, the Pondichéry conseil supérieur agreed to provide a local nawab with fifty thousand pagodas in silver currency in exchange for exclusive trading rights for Indian cloth. "Engagement of the Superior Council of Pondicherry to Supply Annually to Sitizore Khan 50,000 Pagodas of Silver Bullion, Pondicherry, 12 September 1736," cited in Ray, *The Merchant and the State*, vol. 2., 1016–17.

84. Letter 5 [1768], Bernardin de Saint-Pierre, *Journey to Mauritius*, 92. To make matters worse, the island community was in chaos because Governor Dumas and Intendant Poivre were fighting, dividing conseillers, military officers, and *notables* according to personal loyalties.

85. *Lettres de change*, essentially checks backed by private issuers, were the predominant means of transferring funds in ancien régime France and its empire. Île de France (now the independent nation of Mauritius) still plays a central role in Indian Ocean finance as one of the region's primary banking and shipping centers.

86. All of the French Antillean possessions were governed as the "Îles d'Amérique" until 1714, when they were split into the "Îles du Vent" of the Lesser Antilles and Saint-Domingue as the "Îles Sous-le-Vent."

87. Du Tertre, *Histoire générale*, vol. 2, 46–99, 46–48.

88. Ibid., 46–48.

89. Many of these requests can be found in the personnel records. For example, in 1786 Tournachon de Sceincé, a conseiller assesseur in Cayenne's conseil, argued that he deserved free passage because he had invested a hundred and twenty thousand livres in Guyane. ANOM COL E 380, Tournachon de Sceincé.

90. ANOM COL E 311, François Michalet. Michalet had worked around the Indian Ocean littoral before, as a commercial agent in Pondichéry for ten years. On a return trip to France, he met Monsieur de Bellecombe, the former governor of Pondichéry, who offered to place him as the secretary for Chevreau, promising him his protection and support. Michalet headed back toward Île de France, only to be captured by the English.

91. ANOM COL E 311, François Michalet.

92. For West African slaves, note, for example, the voyages of the *Diligent*. Harms, *The Diligent*; Moitt, *Women and Slavery*, 21; Hall, *Africans in Colonial Louisiana*.

93. Subsistence crises happened in France, too, during this period, though the cycles of famine that characterized the medieval period had become somewhat less frequent by the eighteenth century. As in the colonies, French subjects depended upon royal regulation of bread supplies and considered the king responsible for provisioning, so much so that failures in this area were considered (especially in the early part of the French Revolution) as cause for political protest. For provisioning systems in France designed to prevent subsistence crises, see Kaplan, *The Bakers of Paris and the Bread Question*.

94. For colonial nobility, see Ruggiu, "The Kingdom of France and Its Overseas Nobilities."

95. For provisioning crises in the Antilles, see Mandelblatt, "How Feeding Slaves Shaped the French Atlantic."

96. Allen, *Slaves, Freedmen, and Indentured Laborers*, 11.

97. Mark Hauser notes, "Water's relative scarcity and abundance in the Caribbean triggered craft industries to store it." "A Political Ecology of Water and Enslavement," 229.

98. Villiers, *Marine royale, corsaires et trafic*, 482.

99. Hayot, *Les officiers du conseil*, 52.

100. Thus participating in a simultaneous metropolitan choreography centered on the king's presence. With his movements, Ribes thus physically mapped the linkages between Mascarene and metropolitan court venues. For more on how and why the king's court moved around in the eighteenth century, see Lemarchand and Le Roy Ladurie, *Paris ou Versailles?*

101. Cases could take several years and involve heirs in France, plantation managers in the colonies, and assorted representatives, such as lawyers and business agents. For vacant successions in Île de France, see Wood, "Recovering the Debris of Fortunes."

102. On the residents of Port Louis, Île de France, Bernardin de Saint-Pierre observed: "Few people are married in this town. Those who are not rich blame their mediocre financial circumstances on not having married; the rest, they tell us, prefer to wait and establish themselves back in France. But the real reason for not marrying is the ease with which they find black mistresses." Bernardin de Saint-Pierre, *Journey to Mauritius*, Letter 11, Port Louis, 123.

103. ANOM COL E 240, Gabriel Labour.

104. Ibid. Upon selling Angelique and the rest of Labour's possessions, the colonial government collected 1,081 livres.

105. For Indian Ocean successions, see Wood, "Recovering the Debris of Fortunes." Of course, inheritance was not a problem unique to French Indian Ocean migrants, as Kerry Ward has shown for Madurese princes in Southeast Asia. Ward, "Blood Ties."

106. Rochon, *Voyage à Madagascar*, vi.

107. For a combined British Atlantic and Indian Ocean, see Marshall, *The Making and Unmaking of Empires*; Stern, "British Asia and British Atlantic"; Bowen et al., *Britain's Oceanic Empire*. For French slavery in its Atlantic and Indian Ocean iterations, see Régent, *La France et ses esclaves*; Allen, *European Slave Trading in the Indian Ocean*; Peabody, *Madeleine's Children*.

108. Compare, for example, the voluminous literature on the French and Indian War as the Atlantic/North American theater with the much sparser accounts

of the Third Carnatic War, its iteration in South Asia: Anderson, *Crucible of War*; Crouch, *Nobility Lost*. For Europe, see Szabo, *The Seven Years' War in Europe*. Daniel Baugh's global synthesis covers an admirable geographical range but devotes only one chapter to an Indian Ocean topic: the Coromandel Coast. Baugh, *The Global Seven Years' War*. Jonathan Dull also ranges globally in his account of the French naval dimensions of this conflict but emphasizes the Caribbean, with only a few references to simultaneous Indian Ocean events. Dull, *The French Navy*. One study of the British side that attempts to account for the global scale of the war through the lens of disease is Charters, *Disease, War, and the Imperial State*.

109. Magedera, "Arrested Development"; Ruggiu, "India and the Reshaping"; Margerison, "French Visions of Empire."

110. For example, colonial experiments such as Kourou, in French Guiana. Rothschild, "A Horrible Tragedy"; Hodson, " 'A Bondage So Harsh"; Spieler, *Empire and Underworld*.

111. Rochon, *Voyage à Madagascar*, vi.

Conclusion

1. For example, James Pritchard has argued: "Whether in Saint-Domingue in 1698, Louisiana in 1712 and 1717, or Île St. Jean in 1719, the state continued to employ private companies to achieve its ends overseas." Pritchard, *In Search of Empire*, 231. Another version of this argument appears in Banks, *Chasing Empire across the Sea*. A useful model for intercolonial analysis is Hatfield, *Atlantic Virginia*.

2. Édit du Roi, Portant établissement à Versailles, d'un Dépôt des Papiers publics des Colonies. June 1776, ANOM COL F^6 1.

3. And, of course, many non-French subjects, though they are not the focus of this book.

4. Burbank and Cooper, *Empires in World History*.

5. Benton, "Legal Spaces of Empire."

6. For surveys of major debates in each field, see Greene and Morgan, *Atlantic History*; Bose, *A Hundred Horizons*; Prange, "Scholars and the Sea"; Worden, "Writing the Global Indian Ocean."

7. "The Rise of a Compradorial State," in Sheriff, *Slaves, Spices, and Ivory*, 8–32. For the relationship between South Asian and East African merchants during this period, see Machado, *Ocean of Trade*; "The Portuguese on the Coast" in Pearson, *Port Cities and Intruders*, 129–54.

8. Sivasundaram, *Islanded*, 13–15.

9. Auguste Toussaint counted only six foreign arrivals at Île Bourbon and three at Île de France from 1727 to 1735, out of roughly 160 ships total—so only around 6 percent of visiting ships were foreign. Toussaint, *Le route des iles*, 96. This exclusive status does not mean that the islands were fully "French" in any social or cultural context—quite the contrary, according to Vaughan and Lionnet. Vaughan, *Creating the Creole Island*; Lionnet, *Le su et l'incertain*.

10. For Indian Ocean trading pre-Islam, see, for example, Carlson, "Exploring the Oldest Shipwreck in the Indian Ocean"; Verlinden, "The Indian Ocean."

11. Contrast, for example, a classic, field-defining work of Atlantic history such as Alfred Crosby's with an Indian Ocean equivalent, such as K. N. Chaudhuri's. Where Crosby explores ecological and (eventually) trading exchanges as a means to grapple with contact between formerly separated societies, Chaudhuri sees trading itself as the object of Indian Ocean history. Crosby, *The Columbian Exchange*; Chaudhuri, *Trade and Civilisation*.

12. For Saint-Domingue, see Garrigus and Ghachem, as well as Dubois, *Avengers of the New World*; Popkin, *You Are All Free*; Ferrer, *Freedom's Mirror*; Cheney, *Cul de Sac*. For Guadeloupe in this revolutionary frame, see Dubois, *A Colony of Citizens*. Other early sites, such as Canada and Alsace, deserve to be incorporated into this analytic. For Martinique's influence as a model, particularly on Saint-Domingue, see Wood, "The Martinican Model."

13. Coppier is the only known indentured servant to have written a memoir of his experiences, which he described as "terrible ventures." Coppier, *Histoire et voyage*, 4.

14. Ibid., 5.

15. Ibid., 6.

16. Rochon, *Voyage à Madagascar*, vi.

Bibliography

Figures

Bellin, Jacques Nicolas. *Carte de l'Isle de France*. (Figure 10 in the present book.) Bibliothèque nationale de France, département cartes et plans, GE DD-2987 (8430). Paris, 1764. http://gallica.bnf.fr/ark:/12148/btv1b85957779.

———. *Carte de l'Îsle de la Martinique dressée Par Mr. Bellin, Ingénieur du Roy de France et de la Marine communiqué au Public par les Héritiers de Homann*. (Figure 9 in the present book.) Nuremberg: Héritiers de Homann, 1762. John Carter Brown Library, Map Collection, Cabinet Es762 BeJ. https://jcb.lunaimaging.com/luna/servlet/s/a1mgfl.

———. *Carte réduite des parties connues du globe terrestre dressée au Dépost des Cartes et plans et journaux de la Marine pour le service des vaisseaux du Roy. . . .* (Figure 1 in the present book.) Paris: Depost des cartes, plans et journaux de la marine, 1755. Bibliothèque nationale de France, département cartes et plans, GE SH 18 PF 1 DIV 0 P 18. http://gallica.bnf.fr/ark:/12148/btv1b59705892.

Bosse, Abraham. *La Galerie du Palais de Justice*. (Figure 5 in the present book.) Ca. 1638. Etching. Metropolitan Museum of Art. https://commons.wikimedia. org/wiki/File:Abraham_Bosse,_The_Gallery_of_the_Palace_of_Justice,_ ca._1638.jpg.

Brunias, Agostino. *A Linen Market with a Linen-Stall and Vegetable Seller in the West Indies*. (Figure 3 in the present book.) Ca. 1780. Oil on canvas. B2009.12.3. Yale Center for British Art. Paul Mellon Collection. http://collections.britishart. yale.edu/vufind/Record/1669690.

De L'Isle, G. (Guillaume). "Carte du Congo et du pays des Cafres." (Figure 8 in the present book.) Amsterdam: Chez Jean Covens et Corneille Mortier, Geographes, ca. 1739. https://commons.wikimedia.org/wiki/File:1730_Covens_ and_Mortier_Map_of_Southern_Africa_-_Geographicus_-_AfricaS-covensmortier-1730.jpg.

"Édit du Roi, Portant établissement à Versailles, d'un Dépôt des Papiers publics des Colonies." June 1776, ANOM COL F⁶ 1. (Figure 11 in the present book.)

Milbert, Jacques Gérard. *Île-de-France, Vue du Grand Chemin des Pamplemousses*. (Figure 6 in the present book.) 1812. *Voyage pittoresque à l'Ile-de-France, au cap*

de Bonne-Espérance et à l'île de Ténériffe. British Library. https://commons.
wikimedia.org/wiki/File:MILBERT(1812)_p117_-_Île-de-France,_Vue_du_
Grand_Chemin_des_Pamplemousses.jpg.

*Pont construit à l'isle de Bourbon qu[a]rtiers St. Denis par Mr. Mahé de La Bourdon-
nais, chevaliers de lordre militaire de St. Louis, officier des Vaisseaux du Roy,
Gouverneur General des Isle de France et de Bourbon Présidant aux dit Conseils:
commencé le Ier juillet et finy le mois de septembre suivant*. (Figure 7 in the present book.) 1738. Bibliothèque nationale de France, département Cartes et plans,
GE SH 18 PF 218 DIV 8 P 4. https://gallica.bnf.fr/ark:/12148/btv1b531052501.

Tubières, Comte de Caylus, after Edmé Bouchardon, Anne Claude Philippe de.
The Sign Poster. (Figure 4 in the present book.) 1742. Etching with some
engraving. Études Prises dans le Bas Peuple où les Cris de Paris: Quatrième
Suite. Metropolitan Museum of Art. https://www.metmuseum.org/art/
collection/search/399123.

Archival Sources

FRANCE

Archives nationales, section d'outre-mer (ANOM),
Aix-en-Provence, France

Fonds ministériels, Premier Empire colonial, Secrétariat d'état à la marine (COL)
Série A—Actes du pouvoir souverain (1628, 1663–1779). Summaries of these
can be browsed at http://anom.archivesnationales.culture.gouv.fr
/ark:/61561/ka455hct.
Série B—Correspondance au départ avec les colonies (première partie)
(1654–1715) Indexed online at http://anom.archivesnationales.culture
.gouv.fr/ark:/61561/ki665dxxl.
Série C—Correspondance à l'arrivée
Correspondance à l'arrivée d'Extrême-Orient (Sous-série C¹, 1658–
1863)
Correspondance à l'arrivée en provenance de la Martinique (Sous-
série C⁸ᴬ, 1635/1815).
Série E—Personnel colonial ancien (Série E, XVIIe–XVIIIe [seventeenth and
eighteenth centuries]). Available online: http://anom.archivesnationales
.culture.gouv.fr/ark:/61561/up424ojc.
Série F—Documents Divers
Collection Moreau de Saint-Méry (Sous-série F³, 1492/1817)
Papiers Dauvergne (Sous-série F⁶, 1648/1870)

Dépôt des papiers publics des colonies (DPPC)

  Greffes (1674–1912)

  Notariat (1637–1912)

Dépôt des fortifications des colonies (1639–1948) (DFC). Viewable via ANOM's Base Ulysse

  "[Plan de l'attaque du Fort Royal par les Hollandais]." ANOM, Dépôt des fortifications des colonies, 13DFC8B. Martinique, 28 August 1674.

  Duparquier (fils). "Plan de la maison du Roy, occupée par le conseil et le commissaire ordonnateur. Au Cap [Français, Saint-Domingue]." ANOM 15DFC385A.

  Patoulet, Intendant des îles d'Amérique, Jean Baptiste. "Profil et eslevation du plan cy-dessoubs pour le palais [conseil supérieur] et prisons du fort Saint-Pierre de la Martinique." ANOM, Dépôt des fortifications des colonies, 13DFC33C. Saint-Pierre, Martinique, 1683.

Bibliothèque nationale de France, Paris, France

Département cartes et plans

"L'isle de Corse divisée par juridictions extraite de plusieurs cartes nationales." GE D-27355. Paris: Chez Lattré, 1783. http://gallica.bnf.fr/ark:/12148/btv1b530794576.

"La France divisée en ses parlemens et conseils souverains." 1720–1770. GE DD-2987 (680). http://gallica.bnf.fr/ark:/12148/btv1b8593092z.

Bellin, Jacques Nicolas, and Étienne-François de Choiseul. "Carte de l'Isle de Bourbon." 1763. GE SH 18 PF 218 DIV 2 P 18/2. http://gallica.bnf.fr/ark:/12148/btv1b53105243z.

Bellin, Jacques Nicolas. "Carte de l'Isle de France." GE DD-2987 (8430). Paris, 1764. http://gallica.bnf.fr/ark:/12148/btv1b85957779.

Delisle, Guillaume. "Carte du Congo et du pays des Cafres." CPL GE DD-2987 (8249). Paris: Chez l'auteur, 1708. https://gallica.bnf.fr/ark:/12148/btv1b7759544n.

Le Moyne, François-Pierre. "Carte réduite de l'océan-Oriental ou Mers des Indes." 17??. GE SH 18 PF 213 DIV 3 P 22/1. http://gallica.bnf.fr/ark:/12148/btv1b53105197f.

Bibliothèque Mazarine, Paris

Coppier, Guillaume. *Histoire et voyage des Indes occidentales, et de plusieurs autres regions maritimes, & esloignées. Divisé en deux livres.* Lyon: Pour Jean Huguetan, ruë Merciere, au Plat d'Estain, 1645. Marcel Chatillon Collection.

UNITED STATES

Beinecke Lesser Antilles Collection, Hamilton College, Clinton, New York

Rawlin, William. *The Laws of Barbados, Collected in One Volume*. London: Printed for William Rawlin, esq., 1699.

Huntington Library, Pasadena, California

Henry, J. *Report on the criminal law at Demerara, and in the ceded Dutch colonies: drawn up by the desire of the Right Hon. the Earl Bathurst, principal secretary of state for the Colonial department; with an appendix on the nature of the office of fiscal*. London: H. Butterworth, 1821.

John Carter Brown Library, Providence, Rhode Island

Poivre, Pierre. *Discours pronounces par M. Poivre, commissaire du Roi; l'un, à l'Assemblee générale des habitants de l'isle de France, lors de son arrivée dans la colonie; l'autre, à la premiere assemblée publique du Conseil supérieur, nouvellement établi dans l'isle*. Published in London, sold in Lyon: Chez J. De Ville, & L. Rosset, libraires, rue Mercière, 1769.

Rochon, Alexis. *Voyage à Madagascar et aux Indes orientales*. Paris: Chez Prault, Imprimeur du Roi, Quai des Augustins, à l'Immortalité, 1791.

Newberry Library, Chicago, Illinois

"Carte Generalle des Villes Fortes et Dependances de Pondichery, sur la coste de Coromandel avec les nouvelles acquisitions faite depuis M.DCC.VII. [1707]." Cartes Marines Manuscript Map Collection, Ayer MS Map 30, Sheet 24. Pondichéry, 1710. Edward E. Ayer Manuscript Map Collection.

"Isle de Bovrbon; Isle de Diego Rodrigo." Cartes Marines Manuscript Map Collection, Ayer MS Map 30, Sheet 16 [ca. 1670–ca.1692].

Sieur de la Calle, "Relation du S. de la Calle: sur ce qui s'est passé a l'attaque du Fort Royal de la Martinique par la flote de Ruiter," Edward E. Ayer Manuscript Collection, MS 480 [1674?].

William Andrews Clark Library, Los Angeles, California

Lacombe, Jean de, sieur de Querçy. *A compendium of the East; being an account of voyages to the Grand Indies made by the Sieur Jean de Lacombe, of Querçy, formerly Captain at arms in the service of the Company of the Indies of Holland.* Trans. and ed. Stephanie and Denis Clark, intro. Ashley Gibson. London: Golden Cockerel Press, [1681] 1937.

Printed Primary Sources

[Anonymous]. *La relève de l'Escadre de Perse: voyage du navire du roy le Breton, commandé par monsieur Duclos avec deux houcres nommées le Guillot et le Barbot, Mars 1671.* Unedited text published from the manuscript, edited and annotated by Philippe Fabry. Montreuil: Ginkgo, [1671] 2004.

Bernardin de Saint-Pierre, Jacques-Henri. *Journey to Mauritius.* Translated with an introduction and notes by Jason Wilson. Oxford: Signal Books, [1773] 2002.

Bonnefoy, ed. *Arrêts administratifs et règlements du Conseil provincial et du Conseil supérieur de l'Ile de France sous le régime de la Compagnie des Indes, contenant les actes de la colonisation de l'île Maurice, 1722 à 1767.* Lille: L. Lefort, 1859. http://gallica.bnf.fr/ark:/12148/bpt6k3731797.

Bonnefoy, T. *Table générale (alphabétique et analytique) pour servir aux recherches à faire au greffe de la Cour suprême de l'île Maurice, concernant les lois et autres dispositions règlementaires et administratives de cette colonie, qui sont enregistrees et déposées à ce greffe . . . (1722–1850).* Port-Louis, Île Maurice: L. Channell, 1853.

Delaleu, Jean-Baptiste-Étienne. *Code des Îles de France et de Bourbon.* 2nd ed. Port-Louis, Île Maurice: Tristan Mallac, 1826. http://gallica.bnf.fr/ark:/12148/bpt6k9602576r.

Denis, François. *Vue du Fort Royal de la Martinique prise de la première embrasure de la Batterie de la Prison du côté du petit escalier qui monte au fort, ca. 1750–1760.* Archives anglaises. https://commons.wikimedia.org/wiki/File:Vue_du_Fort__Royal_de_la_Martinique.jpg.

Des Essarts, Nicolas-Toussaint Le Moyne. *Essai sur l'Histoire général des Tribunaux des peuples, tant anciens que modernes,* Vol. 3. Paris: Chez l'Auteur, 1778.

Dessalles, Pierre-François-Régis. *Les Annales du Conseil Souverain de la Martinique,* 2 parts, 2 volumes, 1st ed. Bergerac: J. B. Puynesge, 1786, Reedited and reprinted by Bernard Vonglis. Paris: L'Harmattan, 1995.

Dictionnaire de l'Académie française. 1st edition (1694), 4th edition (1762), 5th edition (1798). Accessed through ARTFL, *Dictionnaires d'autrefois,* http://artfl-project.uchicago.edu/content/dictionnaires-dautrefois.

Diderot, Denis, and Jean le Rond d'Alembert, eds. *Encyclopédie, ou Dictionnaire raisonné des sciences, des arts et des métiers, par une Société de Gens de lettres.*

ARTFL Encyclopédie Project. Paris: Briasson, David, et al., 1751–1772. https://encyclopedie.uchicago.edu/.

Domat, Jean. *Les loix civiles dans leur ordre naturel.* Paris: P. Aubouin, P. Emery et C. Clouzier, 1697. http://gallica.bnf.fr/ark:/12148/bpt6k55297429.

Du Tertre, Jean-Baptiste. *Histoire générale des Antilles habitées par les François.* 3 vols. Paris: T. Jolly, 1667. http://gallica.bnf.fr/ark:/12148/bpt6k114021k.

Durand-Molard. *Code de La Martinique, Nouvelle édition.* 5 vols. Saint-Pierre, Martinique: Imprimerie de Jean-Baptiste Thounens, fils, Imprimeur du Gouvernement, 1807–1814. http://gallica.bnf.fr/ark:/12148/bpt6k5510394k.

France and Louis XIV. *Ordonnance de Louis XIV. Roy de France et de Navarre. Donnée à Saint Germain En Laye Au Mois d'aoust 1670. Pour Les Matières Criminelles.* Paris: Chez les associez choisis par ordre de Sa Majesté pour l'impression de ses nouvelles ordonnances, 1670. https://gallica.bnf.fr/ark: /12148/bpt6k9602565z/.

France, ed. *Le code noir ou Edit du roy, servant de reglement pour le gouvernement & l'administration de justice & la police des isles françoises de l'Amerique, & pour la discipline & le commerce des negres & esclaves dans ledit pays: Donné à Versailles au mois de mars 1685. Avec l'Edit du mois d'aoust 1685. portant établissement d'un conseil souverain & de quatre sieges royaux dans la coste de l'Isle de S. Domingue.* A Paris, au Palais: Chez Claude Girard, dans la Grand'Salle, vis-à-vis la Grand'Chambre, au nom de Jesus, 1735. https:// archive.org/details/lecodenoirouedioofran.

Guët, Isidore. *Les origines de l'ile Bourbon et de la colonisation française à Madagascar: d'après des documents inédits tirés des Archives coloniales du Ministère de la Marine et des colonies, etc. Nouv. éd. refondue et précédée d'une introd. de l'auteur.* Paris: C. Bayle, 1888. http://gallica.bnf.fr/ark:/12148 /bpt6k64737f.

Haudrère, Philippe, ed. *Les Français dans l'océan Indien au XVIIIe siècle: Un mémoire inédit de La Bourdonnais, 1733 et Journal du voyage fait aux Indes sous les ordres de M. Mahé de La Bourdonnais, 1746 par M. de Rostaing.* Paris: Les Indes Savantes, 2004.

L'État de la France: Tome Cinquième, De l'établissement des Parlemens, Cours Supérieurs & autres Jurisdictions du Royaume. Des Généralités, Intendances & Recettes Générales. Paris: Chez Ganeau, 1749.

Lougnon, Albert, ed. *Correspondance du conseil supérieur de Bourbon et de la Compagnie des Indes.* 5 vols. Paris: Leroux, 1933.

Louis XV, and France. *Édit . . . portant création d'un Conseil supérieur à Nîmes . . . Registré au Conseil supérieur de Nîmes le 7 octobre [1771] . . .* Paris: Imprimerie Royale, 1772. http://gallica.bnf.fr/ark:/12148/btv1b86147897.

Martineau, Alfred, ed. *Correspondance du conseil supérieur de Pondichéry avec le conseil de Chandernagor.* 3 vols. Pondichéry: Société de l'histoire de l'Inde, 1915.

———. *Correspondance du conseil supérieur de Pondichéry et de la Compagnie.* 6 vols. Pondichéry: Société de l'histoire de l'Inde Française, 1920. http://gallica.bnf.fr/ark:/12148/bpt6k61017309.

Milbert, Jacques Gérard. *Voyage pittoresque à l'Ile-de-France, au cap de Bonne-Espérance et à l'île de Ténériffe.* Paris: A. Nepveu, 1812. http://gallica.bnf.fr/ark:/12148/bpt6k105222m.

Moreau de Saint-Méry, M. L. E. (Médéric Louis Elie). *Description topographique et politique de la partie espagnole de l'isle Saint-Dominque.* Philadelphia, 1796.

———. *Loix et constitutions des colonies française de l'Amérique sous le vent.* 6 vols. Paris: Chez l'auteur, 1784–1790.

Petit, Émilien. *Dissertations sur le droit public des colonies françoises, espagnoles et angloises, d'après les lois des trois nations comparées entr'elles.* Geneva and Paris: Knapen et fils, 1778. http://gallica.bnf.fr/ark:/12148/bpt6k6112149x.

Petit de Viévigne, Jacques, ed. *Code de La Martinique.* Saint-Pierre, Martinique: P. Richard, 1767. http://gallica.bnf.fr/ark:/12148/bpt6k113036j.

———. *Supplément au Code de la Martinique.* Saint-Pierre, Martinique: P. Richard, 1772. http://gallica.bnf.fr/ark:/12148/bpt6k113037x.

Rouillard, John, ed. *A Collection of the Laws of Mauritius and Its Dependencies . . .* 9 vols. Vol. 1 (1722–1787). Mauritius: L. Channell, 1866–68. http://nrs.harvard.edu/urn-3:HUL.FIG:002836695.

Thibault de Chanvalon, Jean-Baptiste. *Voyage à la Martinique, contenant diverses observations sur la physique, l'histoire naturelle, l'agriculture, les mœurs et les usages de cette isle, faites en 1751 & dans les années suivantes.* Paris: C.-J.-B. Bauche, 1763. http://gallica.bnf.fr/ark:/12148/bpt6k102016b.

Secondary Sources

Agnew, Jean-Christophe. *Worlds Apart: The Market and the Theater in Anglo-American Thought, 1550–1750.* Cambridge: Cambridge University Press, 1986.

Aljoe, Nicole N. " 'Going to Law': Legal Discourse and Testimony in Early West Indian Slave Narratives." *Early American Literature* 46, no. 2 (3 July 2011): 351–81.

Allen, Richard B. "The Constant Demand of the French: The Mascarene Slave Trade and the Worlds of the Indian Ocean and Atlantic during the Eighteenth and Nineteenth Centuries." *Journal of African History* 49, no. 1 (2008): 43–72.

———. *European Slave Trading in the Indian Ocean, 1500–1850.* Athens: Ohio University Press, 2014.

———. "Marie Rozette and Her World: Class, Ethnicity, Gender, and Race in Late Eighteenth- and Early Nineteenth-Century Mauritius." *Journal of Social History* 45, no. 2 (1 December 2011): 345–65.

———. *Slaves, Freedmen, and Indentured Laborers in Colonial Mauritius.* Cambridge: Cambridge University Press, 1999.

Alpers, Edward A. "Indian Ocean Africa: The Island Factor." *Emergences: Journal for the Study of Media and Composite Cultures* 10 no. 2 (2000): 373–86.

Ames, Glenn Joseph. "Colbert's Indian Ocean Strategy of 1664–1674: A Reappraisal." *French Historical Studies* 16, no. 3 (1990): 536–59.

Amirell, Stefan. "Female Rule in the Indian Ocean World (1300–1900)." *Journal of World History* 26, no. 3 (September 2015): 443–89.

Amrith, Sunil S. *Crossing the Bay of Bengal: The Furies of Nature and the Fortunes of Migrants.* Cambridge, MA: Harvard University Press, 2013.

Anderson, Fred. *Crucible of War: The Seven Years' War and the Fate of Empire in British North America, 1754–1766.* 1st ed. New York: Alfred A. Knopf, 2000.

Andrews, Richard Mowery. *Law, Magistracy, and Crime in Old Regime Paris, 1735–1789.* Cambridge: Cambridge University Press, 1994.

Banks, Kenneth J. *Chasing Empire across the Sea: Communications and the State in the French Atlantic, 1713–1763.* Montreal: McGill-Queen's University Press, 2006.

———. "Official Duplicity: The Illicit Slave Trade of Martinique, 1713–1763." In *The Atlantic Economy during the Seventeenth and Eighteenth Centuries: Organization, Operation, Practice, and Personnel,* ed. Peter A. Coclanis, 229–51. Columbia: University of South Carolina Press, 2005).

Baugh, Daniel A. *The Global Seven Years' War, 1754–1763: Britain and France in a Great Power Contest.* New York: Longman, 2011.

Bayly, C. A. *Empire and Information: Intelligence Gathering and Social Communication in India, 1780–1870.* New York: Cambridge University Press, 1996.

Beik, William. *Absolutism and Society in Seventeenth-Century France: State Power and Provincial Aristocracy in Languedoc.* New York: Cambridge University Press, 1985.

———. "The Absolutism of Louis XIV as Social Collaboration." *Past and Present* 188 (2005): 195–224.

Bell, David. *The Idols of the Age of Revolution: Charisma and Power in the Atlantic World, 1750–1830.* In progress.

Benda-Beckmann, Franz von, Keebet von Benda-Beckmann, and Anne M. O. Griffiths, eds. *Spatializing Law: An Anthropological Geography of Law in Society.* Burlington, VT: Ashgate, 2009.

Benton, Lauren A. "Legal Spaces of Empire: Piracy and the Origins of Ocean Regionalism." *Comparative Studies in Society and History* 47, no. 4 (2005): 700–724.

———. *A Search for Sovereignty: Law and Geography in European Empires, 1400–1900.* Cambridge: Cambridge University Press, 2010.

Benton, Lauren A., and Richard J. Ross, eds. *Legal Pluralism and Empires, 1500–1850.* New York: New York University Press, 2013.

Bernabé, Jean, Patrick Chamoiseau, and Raphaël Confiant. *Éloge de la créolité/In praise of Creoleness.* Paris: Gallimard, 1997.

Bilder, Mary Sarah. *The Transatlantic Constitution: Colonial Legal Culture and the Empire.* Cambridge, MA: Harvard University Press, 2004.

Blanc, François-Pierre. *Officiers et commissaires du conseil souverain du Roussillon, 1660–1790: Fonction publique judiciaire et dynamique socio-juridique.* Baixas: Balzac-Le Griot, 2016.

Blomley, Nicholas K. "From 'What?' to 'So What?': Law and Geography in Retrospect." In *Law and Geography,* edited by Jane Holder and Carolyn Harrison, 17–33. Oxford: Oxford University Press, 2003.

Blomley, Nicholas K., David Delaney, and Richard T. Ford, eds. *The Legal Geographies Reader: Law, Power, and Space.* Oxford: Blackwell, 2001.

Bose, Sugata. *A Hundred Horizons: The Indian Ocean in the Age of Global Empire.* Cambridge, MA: Harvard University Press, 2006.

Boucher, Philip P. *France and the American Tropics to 1700: Tropics of Discontent?* Baltimore: Johns Hopkins University Press, 2008.

Boulle, Pierre H. *Race et esclavage dans la France de l'Ancien Régime.* Paris: Perrin, 2007.

Bowen, H. V., Elizabeth Mancke, and John G. Reid, eds. *Britain's Oceanic Empire: Atlantic and Indian Ocean Worlds, c. 1550–1850.* New York: Cambridge University Press, 2012.

Braverman, Irus, Nicholas K. Blomley, David Delaney, and Alexandre Kedar, eds. *The Expanding Spaces of Law: A Timely Legal Geography.* Stanford: Stanford University Press, 2014.

Breen, Michael P. *Law, City, and King: Legal Culture, Municipal Politics, and State Formation in Early Modern Dijon.* Rochester, NY: University of Rochester Press, 2007.

Brooks, C. W. *Law, Politics and Society in Early Modern England.* Cambridge: Cambridge University Press, 2008.

Brooks, George E. *Eurafricans in Western Africa: Commerce, Social Status, Gender, and Religious Observance from the Sixteenth to the Eighteenth Century.* Athens: Ohio University Press, 2003.

Burbank, Jane, and Frederick Cooper. *Empires in World History: Power and the Politics of Difference*. Princeton: Princeton University Press, 2010.

Burckard, François. *Le conseil souverain d'Alsace au XVIIIe siècle, représentant du roi et défenseur de la province*. Strasburg: Société savante d'Alsace, 1995.

Burkholder, Mark A., and D. S. Chandler. *From Impotence to Authority: The Spanish Crown and the American Audiencias, 1687–1808*. Columbia: University of Missouri Press, 1977.

Burnard, Trevor. "Empire Matters? The Historiography of Imperialism in Early America, 1492–1830." *History of European Ideas* 33, no. 1 (March 2007): 87–107.

Burns, Kathryn. "Notaries, Truth and Consequences." *American Historical Review* 110, no. 2 (April 2005): 350–79.

Burns, Kathryn. *Into the Archive: Writing and Power in Colonial Peru*. Durham: Duke University Press, 2010.

Butel, Paul. *Histoire des Antilles françaises: XVIIe–XXe siècle*. Paris: Perrin, 2002.

———. *Vivre à Bordeaux sous l'Ancien Régime*. Paris: Perrin, 1999.

Butterworth, Emily. *Poisoned Words: Slander and Satire in Early Modern France*. Leeds: Legenda, 2006.

Campbell, Gwyn. *An Economic History of Imperial Madagascar, 1750–1895: The Rise and Fall of an Island Empire*. Cambridge: Cambridge University Press, 2005.

———. *The Structure of Slavery in Indian Ocean Africa and Asia*. Portland, OR: Frank Cass, 2004.

Cañeque, Alejandro. *The King's Living Image: The Culture and Politics of Viceregal Power in Colonial Mexico*. New York: Routledge, 2004.

Cangany, Catherine. *Frontier Seaport: Detroit's Transformation into an Atlantic Entrepôt*. Chicago: University of Chicago Press, 2014

Carlson, Deborah. "Exploring the Oldest Shipwreck in the Indian Ocean." *INA Quarterly* 40, no. 1 (Spring 2013): 9–14.

Carson, Cary, Norman F. Barka, William M. Kelso, Garry Wheeler Stone, and Dell Upton. "Impermanent Architecture in the Southern American Colonies." *Winterthur Portfolio* 16 (Summer/Autumn 1981): 135–96.

Carter, Marina. "Slavery and Unfree Labour in the Indian Ocean." *History Compass* 4, no. 5 (September 2006): 800–813.

Cauna, Jacques de. "Vestiges of the Built Landscape of Pre-Revolutionary Saint-Domingue." In *The World of the Haitian Revolution*, edited by David Patrick Geggus and Norman Fiering, 21–48. Bloomington: Indiana University Press, 2009.

Chapman, Sara. "Patronage as Family Economy: The Role of Women in the Patron-Client Network of the Phélypeaux De Pontchartrain Family, 1670–1715." *French Historical Studies* 24, no. 1 (2001): 11–35.

Charters, Erica. *Disease, War, and the Imperial State: The Welfare of the British Armed Forces during the Seven Years' War*. Chicago: University of Chicago Press, 2014.

Chaudhuri, K. N. *Trade and Civilisation in the Indian Ocean: An Economic History from the Rise of Islam to 1750*. Cambridge: Cambridge University Press, 1985.

Cheney, Paul Burton. *Cul de Sac: Patrimony, Capitalism, and Slavery in French Saint-Domingue*. Chicago: University of Chicago Press, 2017.

Chopra, Preeti. *A Joint Enterprise: Indian Elites and the Making of British Bombay*. Minneapolis: University of Minnesota Press, 2011.

Clay, Lauren R. *Stagestruck: The Business of Theater in Eighteenth-Century France and Its Colonies*. Ithaca, NY: Cornell University Press, 2013.

Covo, Manuel. "L'assemblée constituante face à l'Exclusif colonial (1789–1791)." In *Les colonies, la Révolution française, la loi*, edited by Jean-François Niort, Frédéric Régent, and Pierre Serna, 69–89. Rennes: Presses Universitaires de Rennes, 2014.

Crosby, Alfred W. *The Columbian Exchange: Biological and Cultural Consequences of 1492*. 30th anniversary ed. Westport, CT: Praeger, 2003.

Crouch, Christian Ayne. *Nobility Lost: French and Canadian Martial Cultures, Indians, and the End of New France*. Ithaca, NY: Cornell University Press, 2014.

Darnton, Robert. *The Devil in the Holy Water or the Art of Slander from Louis XIV to Napoleon*. Philadelphia: University of Pennsylvania Press, 2010.

Davidson, Ian. *Voltaire: A Life*. 1st ed. New York: Pegasus Books, 2010.

Dawdy, Shannon Lee. *Building the Devil's Empire: French Colonial New Orleans*. Chicago: University of Chicago Press, 2008.

———. "Scoundrels, Whores, and Gentlemen: Defamation and Society in French Colonial Louisiana." In *Coastal Encounters: The Transformation of the Gulf South in the Eighteenth Century*, edited by Richmond F. Brown, 132–50. Lincoln: University of Nebraska Press, 2007.

Debien, Gabriel. *Une plantation de Saint-Domingue: La sucrerie Galbaud du Fort (1690–1802)*. Cairo: Les Presses de l'Institut français d'archéologie orientale du Caire, 1941.

Delaney, David. *The Spatial, the Legal and the Pragmatics of World-Making: Nomospheric Investigations*. New York: Routledge, 2010.

Dorigny, Marcel, ed. *The Abolitions of Slavery: From L. F. Sonthonax to Victor Schoelcher, 1793, 1794, 1848*. New York: UNESCO/Berghahn Books, 2003.

Doyle, William. *The Parlement of Bordeaux and the End of the Old Regime, 1771–1790*. London: E. Benn, 1974.

Dubé, Alexandre. "Les biens publics: Culture politique de la Louisiane française, 1730–1770." Ph.D diss., McGill University, 2009.

———. "Making a Career out of the Atlantic: Louisiana's Plume." In *Louisiana: Crossroads of the Atlantic World*, edited by Cécile Vidal, 44–67. Philadelphia: University of Pennsylvania Press, 2013.

Dubois, Laurent. *Avengers of the New World: The Story of the Haitian Revolution.* Cambridge, MA: Belknap Press of Harvard University Press, 2004.

———. *A Colony of Citizens: Revolution and Slave Emancipation in the French Caribbean, 1787–1804.* Chapel Hill: University of North Carolina Press, 2004.

Dull, Jonathan R. *The French Navy and the Seven Years' War*. Lincoln: University of Nebraska Press, 2005.

Echeverria, Durand. *The Maupeou Revolution: A Study in the History of Libertarianism, France, 1770–1774.* Baton Rouge: Louisiana State University Press, 1985.

Elliott, John H. *Empires of the Atlantic World: Britain and Spain in America, 1492–1830.* New Haven: Yale University Press, 2007.

Ewick, Patricia, and Susan S. Silbey. *The Common Place of Law: Stories from Everyday Life*. Chicago: University of Chicago Press, 1998.

Farge, Arlette, and Michel Foucault. *Disorderly Families: Infamous Letters from the Bastille Archives*. Edited by Nancy Luxon. Translated by Thomas Scott-Railton. Minneapolis: University of Minnesota Press, 2016.

Ferrer, Ada. *Freedom's Mirror: Cuba and Haiti in the Age of Revolution*. New York: Cambridge University Press, 2014.

Fick, Carolyn E. *The Making of Haiti: The Saint Domingue Revolution from Below*. Knoxville: University of Tennessee Press, 1990.

Findlen, Paula, and Dan Edelstein, eds. *Mapping the Republic of Letters*. Stanford University, 2013. http://republicofletters.stanford.edu/index.html.

Flavell, Julie M. "The 'School for Modesty and Humility': Colonial American Youth in London and Their Parents, 1755–1775." *Historical Journal* 42, no. 2 (1 June 1999): 377–403.

Forster, Robert. *Merchants, Landlords, Magistrates: The Depont Family in Eighteenth-Century France*. Baltimore: Johns Hopkins University Press, 1980.

Foucault, Michel. *Discipline and Punish: The Birth of the Prison*. 1st American ed. New York: Pantheon Books, 1977.

Fraas, Mitch. "Making Claims: Indian Litigants and the Expansion of the English Legal World in the Eighteenth Century." *Journal of Colonialism and Colonial History* 15, no. 1 (2014). https://muse.jhu.edu/ (accessed 22 May 2019).

Friedland, Paul. *Seeing Justice Done: The Age of Spectacular Punishment in France*. Oxford: Oxford University Press, 2012.

Frostin, Charles. *Les révoltes blanches à Saint-Domingue aux XVIIe et XVIIIe siè-cles*. Preface by Olivier Pétré-Grenouilleau. Rennes: Presses Universitaires de Rennes, [1975] 2008.

Fuente, Alejandro de la. *Havana and the Atlantic in the Sixteenth Century*. Chapel Hill: University of North Carolina Press, 2008.

Games, Alison. *Migration and the Origins of the English Atlantic World*. Cambridge, MA: Harvard University Press, 1999.

Garnot, Benoît. "Justice, infrajustice, parajustice et extra justice dans la France d'Ancien Régime," *Crime, Histoire & Sociétés/Crime, History & Societies* 4, no. 1, Varia (1 January 2000): 103–20.

Garrigus, John D. *Before Haiti: Race and Citizenship in French Saint-Domingue*. New York: Palgrave Macmillan, 2006.

———. ' "Le Patriotisme americain': Emilien Petit and the Dilemma of French-Caribbean Identity before and after the Seven Years' War." *Proceedings of the Annual Meeting of the Western Society for French History* 30 (2002): 18–29.

———. *"Macandal Is Saved!": Disease, Conspiracy, and the Coming of the Haitian Revolution*. In progress.

———. "Vincent Ogé Jeune (1757–91): Social Class and Free Colored Mobilization on the Eve of the Haitian Revolution." *Americas* 68, no. 1 (2011): 33–62.

Gerbeau, Hubert. "L'Océan Indien n'est pas l'Atlantique: La traite illegale à Bourbon au XIXe siècle." *Revue outre-mers, Revue d'histoire* 89 (2002): 79–108.

Gerber, Matthew. *Bastards: Politics, Family, and Law in Early Modern France*. New York: Oxford University Press, 2012.

Ghachem, Malick W. *The Old Regime and the Haitian Revolution*. New York: Cambridge University Press, 2012.

Gould, Eliga H. "Zones of Law, Zones of Violence: The Legal Geography of the British Atlantic, circa 1772." *William and Mary Quarterly* 60, no. 3 (July 2003): 471–510.

Goveia, Elsa V. *The West Indian Slave Laws of the 18th Century*. Barbados: Caribbean Universities Press, 1970.

Greene, Jack P. *Pursuits of Happiness: The Social Development of Early Modern British Colonies and the Formation of American Culture*. Chapel Hill: University of North Carolina Press, 1988.

Greene, Jack P., and Philip D. Morgan, eds. *Atlantic History: A Critical Appraisal*. New York: Oxford University Press, 2009.

Gross, Ariela Julie. *Double Character: Slavery and Mastery in the Antebellum Southern Courtroom*. Princeton: Princeton University Press, 2000.

Grove, Richard H. "Protecting the Climate of Paradise: Pierre Poivre and the Conservation of Mauritius under the Ancien Régime." In *Green Imperialism:*

Colonial Expansion, Tropical Island Edens, and the Orgins of Environmentalism, 1600–1860*, 168–263. New York: Cambridge University Press, 1996.

Hanley, Sarah. ' "The Jurisprudence of the Arrêts': Marital Union, Civil Society and State Formation in France, 1550–1650." *Law and History Review* 21, no. 1 (Spring 2003): 1–40.

———. *The Lit de Justice of the Kings of France: Constitutional Ideology in Legend, Ritual, and Discourse.* Princeton: Princeton University Press, 1983.

———. "The Pursuit of Legal Knowledge and the Genesis of Civil Society in Early Modern France." In *Historians and Ideologues: Essays in Honor of Donald R. Kelley*, edited by Anthony Grafton and J. H. M Salmon, 71–86. Rochester, NY: University of Rochester Press, 2001.

Hardwick, Julie. *Family Business: Litigation and the Political Economies of Daily Life in Early Modern France.* Oxford: Oxford University Press, 2009.

Hatfield, April Lee. *Atlantic Virginia: Intercolonial Relations in the Seventeenth Century.* Philadelphia: University of Pennsylvania Press, 2004.

Haudrère, Philippe. *La Compagnie française des Indes au XVIIIe siècle.* 2nd ed., rev. and corrected. Paris: Indes savantes, 2005.

———. *Les compagnies des Indes orientales: Trois siècles de rencontre entre Orientaux et Occidentaux (1600–1858).* Paris: Éditions Desjonquères, 2006.

Hauser, Mark William. "A Political Ecology of Water and Enslavement: Water Ways in Eighteenth-Century Caribbean Plantations." *Current Anthropology* 58, no. 2 (3 March 2017): 227–56.

Hayhoe, Jeremy. *Enlightened Feudalism: Seigneurial Justice and Village Society in Eighteenth-Century Northern Burgundy.* Rochester, NY: University of Rochester Press, 2008.

Hayot, Émile. *Les officiers du conseil souverain de la Martinique et leurs successeurs les conseillers de la cour d'appel: Notices biographiques et généalogiques.* Fort-de-France: Annales des Antilles, 1965.

Hindle, Steve. *The State and Social Change in Early Modern England, c. 1550–1640.* Basingstoke: Macmillan, 2000.

Hodson, Christopher. ' "A Bondage So Harsh': Acadian Labor in the French Caribbean, 1763–1766." *Early American Studies: An Interdisciplinary Journal* 5, no. 1 (2007): 95–131.

Hodson, Christopher, and Brett Rushforth. "Absolutely Atlantic: Colonialism and the Early Modern French State in Recent Historiography." *History Compass* 8, no. 1 (1 January 2010): 101–17.

Hooper, Jane. "Pirates and Kings: Power on the Shores of Early Modern Madagascar and the Indian Ocean." *Journal of World History* 22, no. 2 (1 June 2011): 215–42.

Hooper, Jane, and David Eltis. "The Indian Ocean in Transatlantic Slavery." *Slavery and Abolition* 34, no. 3 (2013): 353–75.

Houllemare, Marie. "La fabrique des archives coloniales et la naissance d'une conscience impériale (France, XVIIIe siècle)/Colonial Archives and the Making of an Imperial Consciousness (France, 18th c.)." *Revue d'histoire moderne et contemporaine* 2, nos. 61–62 (8 September 2014): 7–31.

Hurt, John. *Louis XIV and the Parlements: The Assertion of Royal Authority.* Manchester: Manchester University Press, 2002.

Igler, David. *Great Ocean: Pacific Worlds from Captain Cook to the Gold Rush.* New York: Oxford University Press, 2017.

Isaac, Rhys. *The Transformation of Virginia, 1740–1790.* Chapel Hill: Published for the Omohundro Institute of Early American History and Culture, Williamsburg, Virginia, by the University of North Carolina Press, [1982] 1999.

Jennings, Eric T. *Vichy in the Tropics: Pétain's National Revolution in Madagascar, Guadeloupe, and Indochina, 1940–1944.* Stanford: Stanford University Press, 2001.

Johnson, Richard R. "The Imperial Webb: The Thesis of Garrison Government in Early America Considered." *William and Mary Quarterly* 43, no. 3 (1986): 408–30.

Joucla, Henri. *Le conseil supérieur des colonies et ses antécédents, avec de nombreux documents inédits et notamment des procès-verbaux du comité colonial de l'Assemblée constituante.* Paris: Éditions du monde moderne, 1927.

Kagan, Richard L., *Lawsuits and Litigants in Castile, 1500–1700.* Chapel Hill: University of North Carolina Press, 1981.

Kaplan, Steven Laurence. *The Bakers of Paris and the Bread Question, 1700–1775.* Durham: Duke University Press, 1996.

Kaps, Klemens, and Andrea Komlosy. "Centers and Peripheries Revisited: Polycentric Connections or Entangled Hierarchies?" *Review (Fernand Braudel Center)* 36, nos. 3–4 (2013): 237–64.

Kessler, Amalia D. *A Revolution in Commerce: The Parisian Merchant Court and the Rise of Commercial Society in Eighteenth-Century France.* New Haven: Yale University Press, 2007.

Kettering, Sharon. *Patrons, Brokers, and Clients in Seventeenth-Century France.* New York: Oxford University Press, 1986.

Kingston, Rebecca. *Montesquieu and the Parlement of Bordeaux.* Geneva: Librairie Droz, 1996.

Klooster, Wim. *Illicit Riches: Dutch Trade in the Caribbean, 1648–1795.* Leiden: KITLV Press, 1998.

Knight, Franklin W., and Peggy K. Liss, eds., *Atlantic Port Cities: Economy, Culture, and Society in the Atlantic World, 1650–1850*. Knoxville: University of Tennessee Press, 1991.

Koot, Christian J. *Empire at the Periphery: British Colonists, Anglo-Dutch Trade, and the Development of the British Atlantic, 1621–1713*. New York: New York University Press, 2011.

Kupperman, Karen Ordahl. *The Jamestown Project*. Cambridge, MA: Belknap Press of Harvard University Press, 2007.

Landers, Jane G. *Atlantic Creoles in the Age of Revolutions*. Cambridge, MA: Harvard University Press, 2010.

Larson, Pier M. *Ocean of Letters: Language and Creolization in an Indian Ocean Diaspora*. Cambridge: Cambridge University Press, 2009.

Leech, Roger H. "Impermanent Architecture in the English Colonies of the Eastern Caribbean: New Contexts for Innovation in the Early Modern Atlantic World." *Perspectives in Vernacular Architecture* 10 (2005): 153–67.

Lemarchand, Laurent, and Emmanuel Le Roy Ladurie. *Paris ou Versailles? La monarchie absolue entre deux capitales, 1715–1723*. [Paris]: Éd. du Comité des travaux historiques et scientifiques, 2014.

Lionnet, Françoise. *Le su et l'incertain: Cosmopolitiques créoles de l'océan indien/ The Known and the uncertain: Creole cosmopolitics of the Indian Ocean*. Trou d'Eau Douce, Ile Maurice: Atélier d'écriture, 2012.

Livet, Georges, and Nicole Wilsdorf. *Le conseil souverain d'Alsace au XVIIe siècle: Origines, création, activité judiciare et politique, installation à Colmar (1698): Les traités de Westphalie et les lieux de mémoire*. Strasburg: Société Savante d'Alsace, 1997.

Lynch, John. "The Institutional Framework of Colonial Spanish America." *Journal of Latin American Studies* 24 (January 1992): 69–81.

———. *Spanish Colonial Administration, 1782–1810: The Intendant System in the Viceroyalty of the Río de la Plata*. New York: Greenwood Press, 1969.

Ly-Tio-Fane, Madeleine. *The Triumph of Jean Nicolas Céré and His Isle Bourbon Collaborators*. Paris: Mouton, 1970.

Machado, Pedro. *Ocean of Trade: South Asian Merchants, Africa and the Indian Ocean, c. 1750–1850*. Cambridge: Cambridge University Press, 2014.

Magedera, Ian H. "Arrested Development: The Shape of 'French India' after the Treaties of Paris of 1763 and 1814." *Interventions* 12, no. 3 (1 November 2010): 331–43.

Major, J. Russell. *From Renaissance Monarchy to Absolute Monarchy: French Kings, Nobles, and Estates*. Baltimore: Johns Hopkins University Press, 1994.

Mandelblatt, Bertie. "How Feeding Slaves Shaped the French Atlantic: Mercantilism and the Crisis of Food Provisioning in the Franco-Caribbean during the

Seventeenth and Eighteenth Centuries." In *The Political Economy of Empire in the Early Modern World*, edited by Sophus A. Reinert and Pernille Røge, 192–220. Basingstoke: Palgrave Macmillan, 2013.

Mapp, Paul. "Silver, Science, and Routes to the West." *Common-Place*, special issue, *Pacific Routes*, 5, no. 2 (January 2005). http://common-place.org/book/silver-science-and-routes-to-the-west/.

Marchand, Philip. *Ghost Empire: How the French Almost Conquered North America*. Westport, CT: Praeger, 2007.

Margerison, Kenneth. "French Visions of Empire: Contesting British Power in India after the Seven Years' War." *English Historical Review* 130, no. 544 (1 June 2015): 583–612.

Marry, Brigitte, Roland Suvélor, and Jean-Luc de Laguarigue. *Martinique, maisons des îles*. Paris: Arthaud, 2001.

Marshall, P. J. *The Making and Unmaking of Empires: Britain, India, and America c. 1750–1783*. Oxford: Oxford University Press, 2005.

Martineau, Alfred. *Dupleix et l'Inde française*. Paris: E. Champion, 1920.

Maza, Sarah C. *Private Lives and Public Affairs: The Causes Célèbres of Prerevolutionary France*. Berkeley: University of California Press, 1993.

McConville, Brendan. *The King's Three Faces: The Rise and Fall of Royal America, 1688–1776*. Chapel Hill: Published for the Omohundro Institute of Early American History and Culture, Williamsburg, Virginia, by the University of North Carolina Press, 2006.

McNeill, John Robert. *Atlantic Empires of France and Spain: Louisbourg and Havana, 1700–1763*. Chapel Hill: University of North Carolina Press, 1985.

Mintz, Sidney Wilfred, and Richard Price. *The Birth of African-American Culture: An Anthropological Perspective*. Boston: Beacon Press, 1992.

Moitt, Bernard. *Women and Slavery in the French Antilles, 1635–1848*. Bloomington: Indiana University Press, 2001.

Mole, Gregory T. "Mahé and the Politics of Empire: Trade, Conquest, and Revolution on the Malabar Coast." *La Révolution française: Cahiers de l'Institut d'histoire de la Révolution française*, no. 8 (23 June 2015). http://journals.openedition.org/lrf/1294 (accessed 22 May 2019).

Montagnier, Jean-Paul C. "Le *Te Deum* en France à l'époque baroque: Un emblème royal." *Revue de musicologie* 84, no. 2 (January 1998): 199–233.

Mousnier, Roland. *The Institutions of France under the Absolute Monarchy, 1598–1789*. 2 vols. Translated by Brian Pearce. Chicago: University of Chicago Press, 1979.

Muldrew, Craig. *The Economy of Obligation: The Culture of Credit and Social Relations in Early Modern England*. New York: St. Martin's Press, 1998.

Nicole, Rose-May. *Noirs, Cafres et Créoles: Étude de la représentation du non blanc réunionnais—Documents et littératures réunionnais (1710–1980)*. Paris: Harmattan, 1996.

Ogborn, Miles. *Indian Ink: Script and Print in the Making of the English East India Company*. Chicago: University of Chicago Press, 2007.

Ogle, Gene Edwin. "Policing Saint Domingue: Race, Violence, and Honor in an Old Regime Colony." Ph. diss., University of Pennsylvania, 2003.

Olwell, Robert. " 'Practical Justice': The Justice of the Peace, the Slave Court and Local Authority in Mid-Eighteenth-Century South Carolina." In *Money, Trade, and Power: The Evolution of Colonial South Carolina's Plantation Society*, edited by Jack P. Greene, Rosemary Brana-Shute, and Randy J. Sparks, 256–77. Columbia: University of South Carolina Press, 2001.

———. *Masters, Slaves and Subjects: The Culture of Power in the South Carolina Low Country, 1740–1790*. Ithaca, NY: Cornell University Press, 1998.

O'Neill, Lindsay. *The Opened Letter: Networking in the Early Modern British World*. Philadelphia: University of Pennsylvania Press, 2015.

O'Shaughnessy, Andrew Jackson. *An Empire Divided: The American Revolution and the British Caribbean*. Philadelphia: University of Pennsylvania Press, 2000.

Owensby, Brian Philip. *Empire of Law and Indian Justice in Colonial Mexico*. Stanford: Stanford University Press, 2008.

Pagden, Anthony. *Lords of All the World: Ideologies of Empire in Spain, Britain and France C.1500-C.1800*. New Haven: Yale University Press, 1995.

Palmer, Jennifer L. *Intimate Bonds: Family and Slavery in the French Atlantic*. Philadelphia: University of Pennsylvania Press, 2016.

Palmié, Stephan. "Is there a Model in the Muddle? 'Creolization' in African American History and Anthropology." In *Creolization: History, Ethnography, Theory*, edited by Charles Stewart, 178–200. Walnut Creek, CA: Left Coast Press, 2007.

Peabody, Sue. *"There Are No Slaves in France": The Political Culture of Race and Slavery in the Ancien Régime*. New York: Oxford University Press, 1996.

———. *Madeleine's Children: Family, Freedom, Secrets and Lies in France's Indian Ocean Colonies, 1750–1850*. New York: Oxford University Press, 2017.

Pearson, M. N. *Port Cities and Intruders: The Swahili Coast, India, and Portugal in the Early Modern Era*. Baltimore: Johns Hopkins University Press, 1998.

Pérotin-Dumon, Anne. "Cabotage, Contraband, and Corsairs: The Port Cities of Guadeloupe and Their Inhabitants, 1650–1800." In *Atlantic Port Cities: Economy, Culture, and Society in the Atlantic World, 1650–1850*, edited by Franklin W. Knight and Peggy K. Liss, 58–86. Knoxville: University of Tennessee Press, 1991.

———. *La ville aux Îles, la ville dans l'île: Basse-Terre et Pointe-à-Pitre Guadeloupe, 1650–1820*. Paris: Karthala, 2000.

Petitjean Roget, Jacques. *Le Gaoulé: La révolte de la Martinique en 1717*. Fort de France: Société d'histoire de la Martinique, 1966.

Piat, Denis. *Mauritius on the Spice Route, 1598–1810*. Singapore: Editions Didier Millet, 2010.

Polderman, Marie. *La Guyane française, 1676–1763: Mise en place et évolution de la société coloniale, tensions et métissages*. Petit-Bourg: Ibis Rouge, 2004.

Popkin, Jeremy D. *You Are All Free: The Haitian Revolution and the Abolition of Slavery*. Cambridge: Cambridge University Press, 2010.

Prange, Sebastian R. "Scholars and the Sea: A Historiography of the Indian Ocean." *History Compass* 6.5 (2008): 1382–1393.

Premo, Bianca "An Equity Against the Law: Slave Rights and Creole Jurisprudence in Spanish America." *Slavery & Abolition* 32, no. 4 (December 2011): 495–517.

———. "Before the Law: Women's Petitions in the Eighteenth-Century Spanish Empire." *Comparative Studies in Society and History* 53, no. 2 (2011): 261–89.

———. *Children of the Father King: Youth, Authority, & Legal Minority in Colonial Lima*. Chapel Hill: University of North Carolina Press, 2005.

Pritchard, James S. *In Search of Empire: The French in the Americas, 1670–1730*. Cambridge: Cambridge University Press, 2004.

Ravel, Jeffrey S. *The Contested Parterre: Public Theater and French Political Culture, 1680–1791*. Ithaca, NY: Cornell University Press, 1999.

Ray, Aniruddha. *The Merchant and the State: The French in India, 1666–1739*. 2 vols. New Delhi: Munshiram Manoharlal, 2004.

Régent, Frédéric. *La France et ses esclaves: De la colonisation aux abolitions (1620–1848)*. Paris: Grasset, 2007.

Rogers, Dominique. "Les libres de couleur dans les capitales de Saint-Domingue: Fortune, mentalités et intégration à la fin de l'Ancien Régime (1776–1778)." Thèse de doctorat, Université Bordeaux III, 1999.

Rothschild, Emma. "A Horrible Tragedy in the French Atlantic." *Past and Present* 192, no. 1 (1 August 2006): 67–108.

Ruff, Julius. *Violence in Early Modern Europe, 1500–1800*. Cambridge: Cambridge University Press, 2001.

Ruggiu, François-Joseph. "India and the Reshaping of the French Colonial Policy (1759–1789)." *Itinerario* 35, no. 2 (August 2011): 25–43.

———. "The Kingdom of France and Its Overseas Nobilities." *French History* 25, no. 3 (2011): 298–315.

Rupert, Linda M. *Creolization and Contraband: Curaçao in the Early Modern Atlantic World.* Athens: University of Georgia Press, 2012.

Saada, Emmanuelle. "Nation and Empire in the French Context." In *Sociology and Empire: The Imperial Entanglements of a Discipline,* edited by George Steinmetz, 321–39. Politics, History, and Culture series. Durham: Duke University Press, 2013.

Saadani, Khalil. "Le gouvernement de la Louisiane française, 1731–43: Essai d'histoire comparative." *French Colonial History* 4 (2003): 117–32.

Safier, Neil. "The Tenacious Travels of the Torrid Zone and the Global Dimensions of Geographical Knowledge in the Eighteenth Century." *Journal of Early Modern History* 18, nos. 1–2 (11 February 2014): 141–72.

Sala-Molins, Louis. *Dark Side of the Light: Slavery and the French Enlightenment.* Minneapolis: University of Minnesota Press, 2006.

Sarat, Austin, Lawrence Douglas, and Martha Merrill Umphrey, eds. *The Place of Law.* Amherst Series in Law, Jurisprudence, and Social Thought. Ann Arbor: University of Michigan Press, 2003.

Savage, John. "Between Colonial Fact and French Law: Slave Poisoners and the Provostial Court in Restoration-Era Martinique." *French Historical Studies* 29, no. 4 (Fall 2006): 565–94.

Scardaville, Michael C. "Justice by Paperwork: A Day in the Life of a Court Scribe in Bourbon Mexico City." *Journal of Social History* 36, no. 4 (Summer 2003): 979–1007.

Schnakenbourg, Christian. "L'essor économique de la Guadeloupe sous l'administration britannique." *Bulletin de la Société d'histoire de la Guadeloupe* nos. 15–16 (1971): 3–40.

Schneider, Zoë A. *The King's Bench: Bailiwick Magistrates and Local Governance in Normandy, 1670–1740.* Rochester, NY: University of Rochester Press, 2008.

Scott, Rebecca J., and Jean M. Hébrard. *Freedom Papers: An Atlantic Odyssey in the Age of Emancipation.* Cambridge, MA: Harvard University Press, 2012

Sheriff, Abdul. *Slaves, Spices, and Ivory in Zanzibar: Integration of an East African Commercial Empire into the World Economy, 1770–1873.* London: J. Currey, 1987.

Silbey, Susan S. "Legal Culture and Cultures of Legality." In *Handbook of Cultural Sociology,* edited by John R. Hall, Laura Grindstaff, and Ming-cheng Miriam Lo, 470–79. London: Routledge, 2010.

Silverman, Lisa. *Tortured Subjects: Pain, Truth, and the Body in Early Modern France.* Chicago: University of Chicago Press, 2001.

Sinha, Arvind. *The Politics of Trade, Anglo-French Commerce on the Coromandel Coast, 1763–1793.* New Delhi: Manohar, 2002.

Sivasundaram, Sujit. *Islanded: Britain, Sri Lanka, and the Bounds of an Indian Ocean Colony.* Chicago: University of Chicago Press, 2013.

Smallwood, Stephanie E. *Saltwater Slavery: A Middle Passage from Africa to American Diaspora.* Cambridge, MA: Harvard University Press, 2007.

Soll, Jacob. *The Information Master: Jean-Baptiste Colbert's Secret State Intelligence System.* Ann Arbor: University of Michigan Press, 2009.

Spieler, Miranda Frances. *Empire and Underworld: Captivity in French Guiana.* Cambridge, MA: Harvard University Press, 2012.

———. "The Legal Structure of Colonial Rule during the French Revolution." *William and Mary Quarterly* 66, no. 2 (April 2009): 365–408.

Stern, Philip J. "British Asia and British Atlantic: Comparisons and Connections." *William and Mary Quarterly*, third series, 63, no. 4 (1 October 2006): 693–712.

Stoler, Ann Laura. "Colonial Archives and the Arts of Governance." *Archival Science* 2, nos. 1–2 (March 2002): 87–109.

Stone, Bailey. *The French Parlements and the Crisis of the Old Regime.* Chapel Hill: University of North Carolina Press, 1986.

Sueur, Philippe. *Le conseil provincial d'Artois (1640–1790): Une cour provinciale à la recherche de sa souveraineté.* Arras: Commission départementale des monuments historiques du Pas-de-Calais, 1978.

Swann, Julian. "Disgrace without Dishonour: The Internal Exile of French Magistrates in the Eighteenth Century." *Past and Present* 195, no. 1 (1 May 2007): 87–126.

———. *Politics and the Parlement of Paris under Louis XV, 1754–1774.* New York: Cambridge University Press, 1995.

Sweet, James H. "Mistaken Identities? Olaudah Equiano, Domingos Álvares, and the Methodological Challenges of Studying the African Diaspora." *American Historical Review* 114, no. 2 (1 April 2009): 279–306.

Szabo, Franz A. J. *The Seven Years War in Europe, 1756–1763.* 1st ed. Modern Wars in Perspective series. New York: Pearson/Longman, 2008.

Taffin, Dominique, ed. *Moreau de Saint-Méry: Ou les ambiguïties d'un créole des Lumières.* Actes du colloque organisé par les Archives départementales de la Martinique et la Société des Amis des archives et de la Recherche sur le Patrimoine culturel des Antilles. Fort-de-France: Société des Amis des archives et de la recherche sur le patrimoine culturel des Antilles, 2006.

Taylor, William B. *Magistrates of the Sacred: Priests and Parishioners in Eighteenth-Century Mexico.* Stanford: Stanford University Press, 1996.

Thomas, Marcel. "Le conseil supérieur de Pondichéry: 1702–1820: Essai sur les institutions judiciaires de l'Inde française." Law thèse, Paris, 1953.

Thornton, John K. *Africa and Africans in the Making of the Atlantic World, 1400–1800.* 2nd ed. Studies in Comparative World History. New York: Cambridge University Press, 1998.

Tomlins, Christopher L. "The Legal Cartography of Colonization, the Legal Polyphony of Settlement: English Intrusions on the American Mainland in the Seventeenth Century." *Law and Social Inquiry* 26, no. 2 (April 2001): 315–72.

Tomlins, Christopher L., and Bruce H. Mann, eds., *The Many Legalities of Early America.* Chapel Hill: Published for the Omohundro Institute of Early American History and Culture, Williamsburg, Virginia, by the University of North Carolina Press, 2001.

Toussaint, Auguste. *Early Printing in the Mascarene Islands, 1767–1810.* Paris: G. Durassié, 1951.

———. *La route des îles: Contribution a l'histoire maritime des Mascareignes.* Paris: S.E.V.P.E.N., 1967.

Trivellato, Francesca. *The Familiarity of Strangers: The Sephardic Diaspora, Livorno, and Cross-Cultural Trade in the Early Modern Period.* New Haven: Yale University Press, 2009.

Truhart, Peter. *Regents of Nations: Systematic Chronology of States and Their Political Representatives in Past and Present: A Biographical Reference Book.* Part 2: *America and Africa.* Munich: K. G. Saur, 2002.

Tweed, Thomas A. *Crossing and Dwelling: A Theory of Religion.* Cambridge, MA: Harvard University Press, 2006.

Vaughan, Megan. *Creating the Creole Island: Slavery in Eighteenth-Century Mauritius.* Durham: Duke University Press, 2005.

Verlinden, Charles. "The Indian Ocean: The Ancient Period and the Middle Ages." In *The Indian Ocean: Explorations in History, Commerce and Politics,* edited by Satish Chandra, 27–53. New Delhi: Sage, 1987.

Verrand, Laurence. "Fortifications Militaires de Martinique, 1635–1845." *Journal of Caribbean Archaeology,* Special Publication no. 1 (2004): 11–28.

Vidal, Cécile, ed. "L'Atlantique français." *Outre-Mers* 96, nos. 362–63 (2009): 7–139.

———. *Louisiana: Crossroads of the Atlantic World.* Philadelphia: University of Pennsylvania Press, 2013.

Villiers, Patrick. *Marine royale, corsaires et trafic dans l'Atlantique de Louis XIV à Louis XVI.* Dunkerque: Société dunkerquoise d'histoire et d'archéologie, 1991.

Vink, Markus P. M. "Indian Ocean Studies and the 'New Thalassology.'" *Journal of Global History* 2, no. 1 (2007): 41–62.

Wanquet, Claude. *La France et la première abolition de l'esclavage, 1794–1802: Le cas des colonies orientales, Île de France (Maurice) et La Réunion.* Paris: Karthala, 1998.

Ward, Kerry. "Blood Ties: Exile, Family, and Inheritance across the Indian Ocean in the Early Nineteenth Century." *Journal of Social History* 45, no. 2 (2011): 436–52.

———. *Networks of Empire: Forced Migration in the Dutch East India Company.* Cambridge: Cambridge University Press, 2008.

———. " 'Tavern of the Seas?' The Cape of Good Hope as an Oceanic Crossroads during the Seventeenth and Eighteenth Centuries." In *Seascapes: Maritime Histories, Littoral Cultures, and Transoceanic Exchanges*, edited by Jerry H. Bentley, Renate Bridenthal, and Karen Wigen, 137–52. Honolulu: University of Hawaii Press, 2007.

Warner, Michael. *The Letters of the Republic: Publication and the Public Sphere in Eighteenth-Century America*. Cambridge, MA: Harvard University Press, 1990.

Warren, Michelle R. *Creole Medievalism: Colonial France and Joseph Bédier's Middle Ages*. Minneapolis: University of Minnesota Press, 2011.

Webb, Stephen Saunders. "Army and Empire: English Garrison Government in Britain and America, 1569 to 1763." *William and Mary Quarterly* 34, no. 1 (1977): 1–31.

Wilson, Kathleen. "Rethinking the Colonial State: Family, Gender, and Governmentality in Eighteenth-Century British Frontiers." *The American Historical Review* 116, no. 5 (December 2011): 1294–1322.

Withers, Charles W. J. *Placing the Enlightenment: Thinking Geographically about the Age of Reason*. Chicago: University of Chicago Press, 2007.

Wood, Laurie M. "Family or Foe? The Politics of Juvenile Exile in France and Its Indies." In progress.

———. "The Martinican Model: Colonial Magistrates and the Seventeenth-Century Origins of a Global Judicial Elite." In *The Torrid Zone: Colonization and Cultural Interaction in the Seventeenth Century Caribbean*, edited by Louis H. Roper, 149–61. The Carolina Lowcountry and the Atlantic World series. Columbia: University of South Carolina Press, 2018.

———. "Murder on the Road: Surveillance, Slavery and Space in the Antilles." Under review.

———. "Political Science: Making Legal and Scientific Knowledge in the Indian Ocean, ca. 1769." In progress.

———. "Recovering the Debris of Fortunes between France and Its Colonies in the 18th Century." *Journal of Social History* 51, no. 4 (June 2018): 808–36.

Worden, Nigel. "Writing the Global Indian Ocean." *Journal of Global History* 12, no. 1 (March 2017): 145–54.

Page numbers accompanied by *f*, *t,* or "n" indicate a figure, table, or note, respectively.

admiralty courts (*amirautés*), 12, 13*f*, 15, 25, 57, 104, 152, 156, 183, 190n29, 192n49, 195n20, 202n105, 224n75

affair, Dumas, 48, 94–96, 100, 108–30, 146–47, 161–64, 179

Africa: coastal trading, 176; imperial careers in, 144–45; southern, 87*f*. *See also individual places by name*

Aix-en-Provence, xxi*t*, 16

Alsace, xx*t*, 3, 12–14, 51, 177

ancien régime empire: alienation via punishment, 62; compared with revolutionary era, 32, 157, 188n11; conflicts spanning, 119; development over time, 17–18, 178–79; global dimensions, 6–9; imagery of, 171–74; lawyers existing throughout, 37–42; legal functions and composition, 12–17; military dimensions of, 143–45; paperwork created by, 202n98; relative weakness and resilience, 95; slavery in, 10; subjects' understanding of, 129, 151, 164; transmission of legal knowledge across, 24

Antilles: comparison with Mascarenes, 8–9, 11, 17, 176–79; connections to Mascarenes, 154–55; development of legal culture, 45–46, 132–34, 139–42; economic and legal demand, 59–60, 95–96; lawyers compared with Mascarenes, 36–8; legal circuits, 72–84, 171, 175; location, 18; metropolitan

views, 41; militarization, 142–43; risks, 128–30, 161–64; themistocracy, 7

archives: conseil, 15–17; lost sources, 196n37; Marine, 9, 172; for revolutionary era, 32; for Seven Years' War era, 168

armateurs (ship owners/outfitters), 85, 183

arson, 60–61

Artois, xx*t*, 12

assemblies, local, 33, 47, 92, 94–96, 99–105, 110, 116, 126–28, 161–65, 174, 214n49. See also *mercuriales, notables, syndics*

assesseurs (substitute/advisory conseillers), 43, 47, 65, 69–70, 157, 207n46

Assier, Jean, 135, 198n57

attorney general (*procureur général*), 25, 30, 35, 38–39, 44, 46, 54, 64–65, 70, 73, 93, 99, 103, 110, 111, 116, 121, 127, 144, 151, 156, 159, 165, 173, 185

attorneys. *See* lawyers

avocats. See lawyers

bailiffs (*huissiers*), 20, 24–25, 29–35, 58, 132, 165, 184, 195n21–22, 195n24; arresting people, 74–75; penalties for allowing intrusions, 208n53

Baleine du Laurens (family), 135, 144

banishment, 21, 62, 73, 94, 96, 100, 102, 107, 118, 123–26, 128, 163–64, 174. *See also* affair, Dumas; Gaoulé bar (qualification to practice law), 35–38, 43–44, 59, 183, 205n21

Barbados, 18

barristers. *See* lawyers

Batavia, 170

Bayonne (port in France), 159

beef (as commodity), 87–88, 101, 211n7, 221n46

Bellin, Jacques Nicolas, 2–3, 4–5*f*1, 98*f*9, 109*f*10, 207n48

Bernardin de Saint-Pierre, Jacques-Henri, 16, 56, 67, 71, 93, 109, 118–19, 124, 126

Bonaparte, Napoleon, 197n51

Bordeaux, 2, 12, 40, 48, 50, 140, 152, 159, 170–71, 205n22. *See also* Guyenne (Bordeaux); Parlement

Bougainville, Louis Antoine de, 108, 126, 147

Britain, 2, 108, 140

cabarets (taverns), 24–25, 27–28, 33–34, 194n3

cabotage (short-distance maritime transit), 65, 79

Canada, 2, 52, 111, 134, 141, 147, 177

Cape of Good Hope, 2, 117, 135, 137, 145, 149, 159, 160, 223n68

Caribbean: architecture, 71–72; demand for slaves, 155; European settlement, 105; legal culture, 134–35; local elite networks, 16, 42, 135–36; military administration, 46, 64–65; region, 18–19, 135; travel writing, 178

Carnatic region (of South Asia), 18, 133, 140, 178, 227n108

Carnatic Wars, 133

cash crops, 17, 21–22, 24, 42, 59, 72–73, 91, 132–34, 143, 146, 149, 156, 161. *See also* coffee; indigo; rice; sugar

Castries, marquis de (minister of the Marine), 57, 85

Catholicism, 88, 219n33

Cayenne (port in Guyane). *See* Guyane (French Guiana)

Central America, 18

Chandernagor (port in South Asia), 91, 133, 136, 140, 149–50, 167. *See also* *conseil supérieur*, Chandernagor

Chanvalon, Jean-Baptiste Thibault de, 18, 51–53, 131

Chaux, Louis Georges (killed at sea in a duel), 151–53

Chennai, 133

children: of elites, 47; of free people of color, 78–82, 173; illegitimate, 1–2

China, 2, 85, 131, 136, 150, 168

Choiseul, duc de (minister of the Marine), 140

churches: ban on conseil meetings in, 205n23; configuration, 50; rituals and public ceremonies, 93, 99, 111–14, 173

civil-law system (as compared with common-law system), 91

clerks (of courts). *See* bailiffs; *greffiers*; scribes

cloth textiles, 140, 178, 211n7, 224n83

Code Noir, 25, 37, 78, 135, 141

coffee: cultivation of, 132, 137–8, 161, 218n18; economy, 41–42, 68, 138, 149; shipping of, 85, 168

Colbert, Jean-Baptiste, 12, 14, 63, 171

common-law system (as compared with civil-law system), 91

Compagnie des Indes orientales (East India Company), 133–35, 140–41, 144–45, 147, 149

Compiègne (royal court at), 120, 164

compradorial system, 176

conseil des dépêches, 80, 183, 188n9

conseil provincial, xx*t*, 3, 12, 68, 80, 135, 177, 188n9

conseil provincial, Artois, xx*t*

conseil provincial, Mahé, xx*t*, 188n9

conseil souverain, xx*t*, 188n9; request for
employment in, 58

conseil souverain, Alsace, xx*t*, 3, 12–14, 51,
177

conseil souverain, Corsica, xx*t*, 13, 177;
jurisdictions under, 192n49

conseil souverain, Roussillon, xx*t*, 3, 13

conseil supérieur, Chandernagor, xx*t*,
149–50, 167

conseil supérieur, Grenada, xx*t*

conseil supérieur, Guadeloupe, xx*t*, 48–49,
57, 65, 82–3, 147–48, 192n48, 206n34,
211n6, 221n49, 222n51

conseil supérieur, Guyane, xx*t*, 147,
205n21, 221n49

conseil supérieur, Île Bourbon, xx*t*, 2;
careers also in Atlantic, 46; commercial
expertise, 53–54; comparison with
Martinique counterpart, 68; development 69–71, 134–36; origin and
function, 68–71; regional hub, 70–71,
148–50, 188n9; schedule, 24, 194n8;
urban and rural layout, 70–71. *See also*
Paul, Pitre

conseil supérieur, Île de France, xx*t*, 68–71;
development, 69–71, 134–36; edicts
sent from Antilles, 112, 114; structure
and function, 70–71. *See also* Querangal

conseil supérieur, Île Royale (Louisbourg),
xx*t*

conseil supérieur, Louisiana, xx*t*, 15,
221–22n49

conseil supérieur, Madagascar, xx*t*

conseil supérieur, Martinique, xx*t*; court
system, 14–15; edicts also sent to
Mascarenes, 112, 114; family dominance, 46–47, 143–44; as largest and
busiest, 63–67; lawyers admitted, 36;
manumission case, 78–84; origin, 13,
147; physical structure, 26–27; public
hearings, 22–23; regional hub, 147,
211n6; schedule, 24; sedition cases,

72–78. *See also* Fort Royal (Martinique); Martinique

conseil supérieur, Nîmes, xx*t*

conseil supérieur, Pondichéry, xx*t*, 15, 31,
68, 135–36, 140–41, 149–50, 167, 188n9,
201n84, 206n32, 207n46, 221n48,
224n77, 224n83

conseil supérieur, Québec (alt. Canada or
New France), xx*t*, 3, 13

conseil supérieur, Saint-Domingue
(Cap-Français), xx*t*, 191n38, 191n47,
204n12

conseil supérieur, Saint-Domingue
(Port-au-Prince): origin at Petit Goave
and later Léogane, xx*t*, 191n38, 191n47,
201n85, 204n12, 223n72

conseil supérieur, Senegal, xx*t*, 221n48

conseillers (magistrates), 45–80, 184;
background, 38–40, 105, 209n69;
claims, 101–2; deliberative rights, 116,
122, 148, 157, 201n87; illness and
retirement, 121, 156–57; Montesquieu
as, 190n35; political alignments, 119,
126–27; royal rituals, 112; transimperial
networks, 114. *See also specific
conseillers by name*

conseillers honoraires (honorary magistrates), 50–51, 201n87, 201n88

conseils supérieurs, xx*t*, 13*f*; comparison
with parlements, 3, 6–7, 9, 12–14, 152,
177, 184, 185; conflicts with governors,
41, 43, 47–48, 86, 94, 96–100, 102–5, 107,
108–9, 111–13, 127, 173, 198n60; conflicts
with intendants, 41, 43, 47–48, 86, 94,
96–100, 102–3, 198n60; on Continent, 6,
12–14; counter to royal authority, 47–48;
facilitating feedback loops, 92; function
and development, 12–15, 17–18, 22–26,
61–62; personnel patterns, 58–59;
physical layout, 26–29; privileges, 49,
67; sources, 15–17. *See also individual
conseils and professions by name*

Coppier, Guillaume (indentured servant in
    Caribbean), 178–80
Cordon de Saint-Michel (royal honor), 85
Cornette de Cely, Philippe, 41, 43
Cornette de Saint-Cyr, 93, 105, 106, 146
Coromandel Coast, 18, 142, 178
correspondence. *See* interjudicial
    correspondence; mail
cotton, 146, 178
court fees (*épices*), 34, 51–52, 55, 166–67
court meetings (*audiences*), 53, 63, 74–78
courthouse (*palais de justice*), 185; control
    of space surrounding, 28, 50, 114; lack
    of, 206n30; rhythms of movement
    surrounding, 59, 61, 72–73; rituals
    within, 74–77; site for different kinds of
    courts and documents, 66, 184,
    190n29; structure, 10–11, 27–28;
    uniformity, 26
creole (French *créole*), 18–20
creolization, 11, 193n58
criminal jurisprudence. *See* arson;
    banishment; duels; murder; sedition;
    torture
Criminal Ordinance of 1670, 32
Cross of Saint Louis (military honor), 85,
    134
currency. *See* money
Custom of Paris, 25–26, 32, 141

Datin, Julienne (purported wife of Pitre
    Paul), 3, 187n1
daughters, 48, 53, 58, 81, 83, 88, 120, 122
David, Pierre Félix, 54, 145–47, 220n43
decrees. *See* legislation
deliberative voice (*voix délibérative*), 34,
    49, 51, 64, 121, 201n84
Des Essarts, Nicolas-Toussaint Le Moyne
    (legal history compiler), 13, 180
Dessalles, Pierre (Martinique conseiller),
    15, 41, 63, 107, 128, 135, 139, 175,
    198n60, 200n70, 203n3

Didier de Saint-Martin, 53
Dominica, 78–81, 162
Du Tertre, Jean-Baptiste, 16, 22, 64, 158
Du Tillet, Claude-Samout, 54–55
duels, 25, 50, 150–51, 173, 180
Dumas, Jean Daniel, 93–96, 100, 108,
    111–30, 144, 146–47, 160–64, 173. *See
    also* affair, Dumas
Dupleix (governor of French South Asia),
    63, 146, 158
Dutch colonies: criminal law in, 61;
    French illicit trading with, 94, 168;
    military conflict with French, 66,
    145–46; prizes, 2; settlement of Île de
    France, 71, 133; trading entrepôts, 178,
    188n12
Dutch colonization: competition with
    French, 66, 145–46; illicit trading with
    other Europeans, 94; settlements, 71,
    133, 168, 178

edicts. *See* legislation
Encyclopédie, 13, 29, 64
engineering, 71, 109, 126, 145–46, 211n7
England. *See* Britain
Enlightenment, the, 15, 34, 198n56, 203n3
Estoupan de Saint-Jean, Blaise, 144
Europe: as category, 15; French territorial
    expansion within, 6, 12–13, 177;
    identity, 19, 106; markets in, 73; military
    bases in, 18; "public" as concept, 32;
    state building and revolution, 17; trade
    routes from, 138; wars in, 170

family businesses, 46–47, 89–90, 176–77
Filet, Louis (adventurer), 84, 86–91, 171
fire, 60, 165; ritual fire, 112
Florida, 18
Fontaine, Marianne (wife of Pitre Paul),
    1, 3
Fontainebleau (royal court at), 120, 160,
    164, 185, 216n74

Fort Royal (Martinique), xxt; as capital,
    64–66; compared with other towns, 71,
    207n48; layout of town, 27–29, 97, 145,
    147; public rituals in, 72–77, 99, 102, 113
fortifications, 13f, 65–69, 71, 97, 105, 116,
    142, 146; sources, 16
Fouquet, Nicolas, 63
free people of color (*gens de couleur libres*):
    in colonial towns, 22, 205n22; as
    conseil court users, 78–84, 171, 181;
    contestation of status, 78–84, 204,
    209n67; as court audiences, 74, 77;
    estates of, 30; military service, 143; as
    planters, 36, 199n69; policing of,
    194n3; punishment of, 76
free soil principle, 124
freedom suits, 209n66
French monarchy: colonial administration,
    140–41; colonial aims, 101, 103, 126, 150;
    development, 14, 46, 86, 125; end of,
    200n70; as legal forum, 116; money
    issued by, 121, 215n73; resistance
    toward, 126; symbolism, 100, 113,
    172–73. See also *Te Deum*
French Revolution, 157, 163, 185, 187n1,
    198n56, 198n59, 199n69, 200n70
fugitive slaves, 79–82

Gaoulé (1717 uprising), 48, 93–108;
    comparison with Dumas affair, 123–30;
    origin and meaning of term, 106–7. *See
    also* Saint-Domingue: planter revolts
global themistocracy, 6–7, 41; access to, 95;
    change over time, 139, 181; expertise,
    4; families in, 104, 163; power in
    conseils, 18
Gorée, xxt, 221n48
governors, 13f, 184; background, 53–54,
    134; campaigns, 87, 91, 158; conflicts
    with conseils, 41, 43, 47–48, 86, 94,
    96–100, 102–5, 107, 108–9, 111–13, 127,
    173, 198n60; conflicts with intendants,

86, 93, 116–19, 128, 225n84; conflicts
    with local assemblies, 110; contrast
    with British counterparts, 64; crisis
    management, 125, 161–62; fortification
    efforts, 65–66, 145–46; jurisprudence,
    61, 150–51; in Paris, 49; petitions to,
    153–54; reports of death, 31, 156; role,
    7, 55, 145–47, 66–67, 70–71, 146–47,
    150, 165; selection, 69; selection of
    conseil members, 44, 50, 156–57; travel
    authorization, 124. *See also* affair,
    Dumas; banishment; governors-gen-
    eral; *and specific governors by name*
governors-general, 64–68, 97, 102, 105, 134,
    144–45, 147, 157–58; comparison with
    British counterparts, 219n31
Great Britain. *See* Britain
greffes (court registers), 184; as archival
    collections, 15, 192n50; content, 33, 67,
    76–78, 89, 102, 122, 140, 211n7; form,
    54, 78; location, 27, 32, 62, 66, 76–77
greffiers (clerks), 184; compensation of, 54;
    number typically employed, 65, 69–70,
    207n46; promotion on conseils, 56, 111,
    121; requests for employment as, 37, 42,
    55–57; work done by, 30, 35, 55, 76, 97,
    134, 180, 195n21, 202n99, 203n108
Grenada, 46, 52, 57, 147
Guadeloupe, 8, 11, 22, 42–33, 46, 48–49,
    56–57, 65, 67–69, 72, 79, 82–83, 97, 125,
    139, 141, 147–48, 153–54, 158, 161–62,
    164, 178, 192n48, 197n45, 200n70,
    206n34, 211n6–7, 222n50–51
guivi (Carib term for white uprising),
    106–7
Guyane (French Guiana), 10, 18, 225n89.
    See also *conseil supérieur*, Guyane
Guyenne (Bordeaux), xxit, 48

habitants, 184. *See also* planters
Haiti. *See* Saint-Domingue
Haitian Revolution, 6, 17, 144, 178, 200n70

huissiers. See bailiffs
Hurault (family), 46, 143, 220n37–38

Île Bourbon: agricultural production, 69,
   141, 162; comparison with other insular
   colonies, 8–9; current status, 11, 68;
   development 69–71, 135–36; economic
   dependence upon Martinique, 91, 137,
   154–55, 160–61, 218n17; lack of lodging,
   67; military units, 134, 148–49; prizes,
   2; regional identity, 19, 141, 169;
   runaway slaves (maroons), 106–7;
   strategic significance, 8–9, 21, 148–49,
   162, 138; trade and shipping, 85,
   136–38, 140, 228n9; travel, 124, 132
Île de France: comparison with other
   insular colonies, 8–9; court system,
   14–15; food crises, 161–62; harbors, 71;
   personnel patterns, 16; regional
   identity, 169; strategic significance,
   8–9, 138; trade and shipping, 85,
   139–40, 228n9; travel, 124; urban and
   rural layout, 70–71
India: French military in, 146, 167, 213n37,
   220n43; personnel assigned to, 144–45.
   See also specific places in
indigo, 146
intendants, 13*f;* agricultural projects, 38,
   109; appointing conseil members, 50,
   56–57, 84, 134, 157, 201n85, 223n72;
   building projects, 26–27, 64–65;
   conflicts with conseil members, 41, 43,
   47–48, 86, 94, 96–100, 102–3, 198n60;
   conflicts with governors, 86, 93, 116–9,
   128, 225n84; conflicts with local
   assemblies, 110; conseil authority,
   65–69, 75, 149–50, 156, 165, 183–84;
   jurisprudence, 61, 150–51; legislative
   power, 104; royal representation, 7,
   108, 112. *See also* affair, Dumas;
   Gaoulé; *and individual intendants
   by name*

interjudicial correspondence, 7–8, 11, 20,
   38, 175, 179, 180, 185; compared with
   other letter networks, 95, 133, 170–71,
   188n15; as complement to court
   proceedings, 27–28, 127, 129, 149; in
   Dumas affair, 93–95, 115, 120, 122–24;
   in Gaoulé, 92–94, 103; Indian Ocean
   dependence upon, 136–38, 140, 149,
   164, 167, 177; protest and, 126, 129;
   requests for free passage, leave,
   protection among, 155, 203n107,
   210n82; traveling via mail, 153–54, 161.
   See also mail

Jamaica, 18, 141
Jason (ship), 131–32, 149, 169
Java, 149, 170
Juda (West African slave trading port), 136
judges. See *conseillers*

La Varenne, Antoine d'Arcy de, 96–105,
   108, 124, 127, 159, 164
Labour, Gabriel (vacant succession case),
   165–66
Lacombe, Jean de, sieur de Querçy,
   170–73
lawyers (*avocats*), 183; admission to other
   courts, 205n21; admission to parlements, 198n58; colonial motivations,
   26, 42–45; distinction from conseillers,
   209n69; experience, 25, 35–40, 197n43;
   knowledge transmitted by, 24; politics
   of, 7, 10, 41–42; prevalence, 30, 40–41;
   self-representation as, 197n48. *See also
   specific law courts, lawyers by name*
Le Havre (port in France), 171
Le Mercier de la Rivière, Pierre-Paul
   (intendant), 41
legal entrepôts: access to, 95, 153;
   Antillean versus Mascarene, 20;
   colonial versus metropolitan, 5–6;
   commonalities among, 58–59; conflict

within, 94–95; distances between as
challenge, 158, 160; role in connecting
trading entrepôts, 157, 169, 178; as sites
for negotiation, 3, 6–8, 36–38, 175,
179; sought by non-French subjects,
88; whole formed by global network,
26, 170, 173–74. *See also specific
conseils*

legal geography, 10

legality, 10, 20, 28; in relation to legal
culture, 195n13

legislation: codification of, 174; by conseils,
12, 14, 50, 74, 139; about cultivation,
162; establishing conseils and their
officers, 65, 157, 201n84; increase in,
32; kinds of, 183, 185–86; about money,
97, 100, 216n73; about postal system,
154; about record keeping, 172–73;
regulating lawyers, 38–39, 51; royal, 32,
96, 104, 112–13, 100, 127; about *Te
Deum* ceremony, 114. *See also* Code
Noir

letters. *See* interjudicial correspondence;
mail

litigation, 37, 78, 138, 148–49

Lorient (port in France), 109, 118, 134, 144,
149, 150, 160

Louis IX (king of France), 22

Louis XIV (king of France), 12, 38

Louis XV (king of France), 125, 135, 158

Louis XVI (king of France), 158

Louisiana, 91, 161, 177; Code Noir in, 135;
creole culture, 19; litigants in 197n48;
magistrates and lawyers in, 10, 37;
planter revolt in, 216n82. See also
conseil supérieur, Louisiana

Lousteau, Jean, 55, 180

Louverture, Toussaint, 197n51

lower courts (called *juridictions* or *sièges*),
13f, 15, 29, 56, 60, 185, 190n29, 192n49,
202n105

Lyon, 10, 57, 69, 178

Macandal, 15

Madagascar: location, 68, 159, 167, 169,
176; natural resources, 108; piracy in, 2;
provisioning source, 156, 161, 221n46;
slave trade and local politics, 85–91,
131–32, 136–37, 155–56, 218n17, 220n43

Magdeleine Françoise (free woman of
color pursued as fugitive slave), 78–84,
171, 173, 179

magistrates. See *conseillers*

Mahé de la Bourdonnais, Bertrand-François, 145, 156, 161

mail, 85, 117, 153–54, 161. *See also*
interjudicial correspondence

Maizière de Maisoncelle, Armand
François de, 133

Malagasy (people), 84; French diplomacy
and trading with, 50, 86, 88–90, 176,
223n68; intermarriage with Europeans,
210n79; slaves, 19, 86, 155, 166, 218n17

Marine, Ministry of the: administrative
resources, 37; archives, 16–17, 42;
correspondence, 8, 31, 38, 43, 93–94,
123, 140, 164; credentialing, 35;
distance from colonies, 115–17;
employment, 40, 50, 54, 121–22;
military dimensions of colonization,
142–47; officials, 64; organization, 8–9,
13f, 15, 48, 135; relationship with
conseils, 52–53, 83–85, 101–5; strategic
decisions, 46, 133–34

markets (local), 20, 22–25, 23f, 28

marriage, 1–3, 19, 44, 47, 58, 113, 143,
212n20, 220n38. *See also* polygamy

Martinique: agricultural production, 162;
Caribs (indigenous people), 106;
comparison with other insular
colonies, 8–9, 67–68; current status, 11,
68; Dutch attacks, 145–46; economic
support of Guyane, 221n49; economic
support of Île Bourbon, 91, 137, 154–55,
160–61, 218n17; food crisis, 97, 101,

Martinique: (*continued*)
161–62; fugitive slaves, 79, 81; illicit trading, 79, 81, 97–98; migration to, 46, 143; personnel patterns, 16; plantocracy, 42; regional hub, 141, 147, 160–61; strategic significance, 8–9, 162, 178; urban and rural layout, 73, 207n48. See also *conseil supérieur*, Martinique

Mascarenes: comparison with Antilles, 8–9, 11, 17, 176–79; connections to Antilles, 154–55; development of legal culture, 45–46, 132–34, 139–42; economic and legal demand, 59–60, 95–96; lawyers compared with Antilles, 36–38, 42–43; legal circuits, 67–72, 84–91, 149, 171, 175; location, 18; metropolitan views, 41; migration to, 56, 108–9; militarization, 142–43; risks, 128–30, 161–64; strategic importance, 167–69; themistocracy, 7, 53

Maupeou coup (1771), 40–41

Mauritius. See *conseil supérieur*, Île de France; Île de France; Mascarenes

merchants. See *négociants*

Mercier, Antoine (Guadeloupe administrator), 139

mercuriales, 116

Michalet, François (stranded administrator), 159–60

militarization (of colonies), 142–47

militias, 13*f*, 33, 45, 48, 50, 64, 97, 99–101, 104, 109–11, 119, 124, 127, 140, 142–43, 146, 214n49

money: 84, 97–98, 126, 166, 224; court costs compared with typical wages, 51, 166; exclusive trading rights purchased, 224n83; letters of exchange, 121–22, 158; paper money, 93, 110, 118, 121, 158, 215n73, 216n73

monsoon, xviii (map), 145, 149, 160

Montesquieu, Charles-Louis de Secondat, baron de, 12, 201n83

Moreau de Saint-Méry, Médéric Louis Élie: family, 41, 156, 198n60; legal archive created by, 15, 175; regional influence, 36, 46, 128

Moreau, Jean Médéric, 41, 156, 175, 198n60

Mozambique, 85, 136, 155, 168, 220n43

Mozambique Channel, 159

murder, 10, 25, 28, 31, 50, 150, 173

Nantes (port in France), 140, 171

Navy. *See* Marine, Ministry of the

négociants, 36, 48, 54, 84, 157, 174, 185, 199n62

nobility, 49, 101, 107, 143, 161, 183

nomosphere, 10, 35

notables, 45–48, 94–96, 104, 111, 119, 127–28, 163–65, 185

notaries: inventorying estates, 30, 166; performing work of greffiers and other officials, 35, 55, 110

Old Regime. See ancien régime empire

ordinances. *See* legislation

overseers (of plantations), 23, 81, 83

Paris: as better site for archives, 171; laborers and lawyers in, 51; as legal access point, 2, 11, 15, 49, 120, 152, 159, 160, 163–64; origin of colonial officials, 38–39, 55–56, 119; perspective on overseas colonies, 41, 74, 180

parishes: church services, 93, 112, 114, 173; priests, 3

Parlement, Béarn (Pau), xxi*t*

Parlement, Bourgogne (Dijon), xxi*t*

Parlement, Bretagne (Rennes), xxi*t*, 1, 51, 62

Parlement, Dauphiné (Grenoble), xxi*t*, 114

Parlement, Dombes (Trévoux), xxi*t*

Parlement, Flanders (Lille), xxi*t*

Parlement, Franche-Comté (Besançon), xxi*t*

Parlement, Guyenne (Bordeaux), xxi*t*, 40, 48, 50, 190n35, 191n37, 201n83

Parlement, Languedoc (Toulouse), xxi*t*

Parlement, Lorraine (Nancy), xxi*t*, 58

Parlement, Normandy (Rouen), xxi*t*

Parlement, Paris (Île de France), 35, 40, 49, 53; lawyers admitted to, 7, 39, 43–46, 58, 59, 124, 156, 175; lawyers who sought overseas employment, 40–41

Parlement, Provence (Aix-en-Provence), xxi*t*

Parlement, Trois-Évêchés (Metz), xxi*t*

parlements (law courts): bar, 35; comparison with conseils, 3, 6–7, 9, 12–14, 152, 177, 184, 185; counter to royal authority, 47–48; Maupeou Coup, 40–41; organization, xxi*t*; prerequisite for conseil service, 47; privileges, 49, 67; purchase of seats, 143; remonstration, 185–86

Patoulet, Jean-Baptiste (intendant), 27, 66, 134

Paul, Pitre, 1–3, 6, 9, 62, 135, 149, 173, 175, 179, 180–81

Périnelle-Dumay, Jean (Paris, then Martinique lawyer), 39, 59

Peru, 134

Petit de Viévigne, Jacques, 63, 135

piracy: in Caribbean, 2; legality, 91; in western Indian Ocean, 2, 135, 159

plantations: arson, 60–61; bought by officials, 40, 42–43, 47–48, 58–59, 91, 110, 142–43, 146, 194n5, 209n69; circulation to/from, 20, 23, 30, 59, 98–100, 111, 124, 131; debt on, 214n41; demand for slaves, 83, 86, 221n49; development and location, 69, 79, 84–85, 126, 132, 162, 177 207n48; disputes, 222n52; value, 121, 166. *See also* overseers; planters

planters (*habitants*): absentee, 49, 74, 198n56, 219n30; abuse by, 24;

circulation, 23–24, 111; in court, 77, 92; legal protections, 101; legal training, 41; as litigants, 25, 64, 148; local organization, 96, 104, 110, 192n48; management, 162, 211n7; as officials, 33, 38, 48, 53–54, 142–43, 147, 157, 174; origin, 98, 105, 209n69, 210n1, 212n20; power, 26, 36, 42, 59, 100, 121–24, 139–40, 183–84, 194n3; revolts, 97, 104, 113, 126–28, 163, 199n69; wealth, 25

Poivre, Pierre, 15, 18, 38, 43, 55, 69, 86, 88–90, 108–9, 112–13, 118–19, 125, 127, 134, 156, 163–64, 173, 209n74

police, 13*f*; experience by other administrators, 44; intendant management of, 150, 184; overlap with bailiffs, 29–31; overlap with militias and syndics, 33, 50, 100, 111, 124, 214n49; surveillance of boundaries and neighborhoods, 69, 111

political power: Atlantic, 128; debates about in conseils, 21, 43, 59, 95, 109; exerted by administrators, 63, 111; local, 111, 139; metropolitan, 164; theorization of, 12

polygamy, 1–3

port cities, 40, 59, 140, 148, 153, 205n22. *See also individual ports by name*

Port Louis (port in Île de France), xx*t*; arson case near, 60–61; demographics, 226n102; layout of, 69, 71, 116, 176; town criers in, 32–33

priests, 3

printed broadsides, 28–33, 35, 61

prisons: colonies lacking, 211n6; holding unconvicted people, 159; interrogations and punishments in, 72, 75–76, 81, 97; layout, 26–27, 61–62, 66; open to recidivists, 1, 3, 62; of planters, 101

privilege: of conseillers, 49–51, 121–22, 201n84; of conseils, 14, 69, 184, 191n47; of greffiers, 57; of lawyers, 197n43; letters patent granting, 185 prizes (ships taken as), 2, 97, 159; court adjudication of, 12

procureurs, 30, 166, 185

property: boundaries, 69, 207n48; claims to, 89; criterion for conseil appointment, 45; disputes, 148; in estates, 166–67, 209n75; laws governing, 32–33, 141

provisioning (of food, supplies), 11, 89–91, 94–95, 101, 107, 128, 132, 138, 141, 154–57, 159, 161–63, 211n7, 221n46, 221n49, 223n68, 225n93

public outcry, 32

publicity: as component of punishment, 73, 77; of court proceedings, 74; legal understanding of, 32, 34, 61

Québec, xx*t*, 3, 13, 170

Querangal (ship captain during duel), 150–52, 173, 180

Réunion, La. *See* Île Bourbon

revolts: by enslaved people, 15, 45, 106–7, 142, 161; about food, by planters, 104–5, 126, 163–64, 199n69, 216n82; in France, 107; by indigenous people, 106–7; by local elites, 95, 102, 128, 162. *See also* affair, Dumas; Gaoulé

Ribes, Jean André de: banishment and Dumas affair, 21, 93–95, 108–23, 125, 173–74, 180; career, 54; compared with other officials, 124, 159–60, 163–65; desire for more personnel, 30–31; legal arguments, 41, 52–53. *See also* affair, Dumas

rice, 88, 131–32, 221n46

Ricouart, Louis Balthazar de, 96–108, 124, 127, 130, 159, 164

Rivals de Saint-Antoine, Raymond, 115, 118, 144

roads: circulation of information via, 30, 65; constructed by enslaved people,

211n7; crimes committed on, 75, 175; Marine construction of, 162; processions on, 113; proximity and circulation of people to courthouses, 25–27, 29, 32, 59, 62; taxes and maintenance (*corvées*), 110; urban planning, 71

Rochefort (port in France), 18, 178

Rochon, Alexis, 131, 167–69, 177, 179, 223n68

Rodrigues (island), 18, 120. *See also* Mascarenes

Rose, Rheims (Mascarene merchant), 46, 53–54, 63, 84–86, 89–91, 149, 157–58, 168, 176

rumor (*bruit*), 2, 31–34

sailors: in court, 1–3, 21, 28, 187n1; in imperial records, 16; navigation by, 160; in port towns, 67, 167, 173; possessions, 25; rituals at sea, 159

Saint-Barthélemy, 178

Saint-Christophe, xx*t*, 46, 105, 143

Saint-Denis (port in Île Bourbon), xx*t*, 67, 69, 70, 70*f*, 194n8

Saint-Domingue: court settings, 3, 13, 24, 31, 204n12; planter revolts, 126; regional hub, 135, 147–48, 192n48, 211n6; requests for employment, 40, 46; slave trade to, 218n17; *Te Deum* in, 114; torture abolished, 203n3; wealth, 74, 139, 178. *See also conseils and ports by name*

Saint Eustatius, 6, 178

Saint Helena, 159

Saint Kitts. *See* Saint-Christophe

Saint Lucia, 15, 30, 79, 98, 101, 147, 158, 211n6

Saint-Mâlo (port in France), 2–3, 41, 69, 84, 134, 149, 157, 187n1

Saint-Pierre (port in Martinique), xx*t*, 60, 64–66, 73, 79–80 scribes, 195n21, 202n98

sedition, 20, 62, 72–74, 180, 204n8, 208n54

sénéchaussées (mid-level courts), 13*f*, 15, 29, 56–57, 185–86, 195n20

Senegal, 54, 58, 136, 144–45, 147, 218n17, 221n48. *See also* conseil supérieur, Senegal

Seven Years' War, 17–18, 46; in Antilles, 56, 133, 141; connections between North America and Indian Ocean, 125–26, 147; conseil politics during and after, 139, 168, 206n42; in Indian Ocean, 140. *See also* Treaty of Paris

ship owners/outfitters (*armateurs*). See *armateurs*

Sirenne (ship), 149, 154, 187n1, 223n69

slave trade, African, 19, 84, 135–37, 144, 149, 155, 160–61, 168, 171, 176

slavery: colonial legal distinctiveness, 10–11, 181; connections between Atlantic and Indian Ocean, 168; economy and defense of, 161; legal sources about, 15. *See also* slave trade, African

slaves (enslaved people): colonial slave societies, 8, 10, 142–44; as court users, 92, 123–24, 181; English attacks on, 141; in estate inventories, 166; population in Antilles, 19, 106, 142; population in Mascarenes, 85–91, 137, 142; provisioning crises, 161–62; revolts by, 106; runaway (maroons), 110; work done by, 132–33, 179. *See also* slave trade, African

Sofala Coast, 136–37, 217–18n15

solicitors. See *procureurs*

South Asia. *See specific places in*

Spain, 3, 159

Sri Lanka (formerly Ceylon), 38, 176

state building, 9, 12–13, 17, 178

sugar: development, 134; efforts to protect, 17, 138–41; exports of, 22, 97, 138, 153;

investments in, 40, 166; production, 21, 126, 161; regional concentration, 42, 68. *See also* cash crops

Surate, xx*t*

syndics: for companies, 53; political conflict, 119, 127–28; responsibilities, 33, 109–11, 213n39, 214n49

taverns. *See* cabarets

taxation: collection, 156; colonial, 47, 110, 142, 194n3; exemptions, 23, 51, 161, 211n7; farming, 40; head tax (*capitation*), 50; metropolitan, 184

Te Deum, 112–15, 118, 127, 173; sung on ships, 158–59

torture (judicial), 60–61, 72, 203n3, 208n58

town criers, 28–29, 32–33, 35–61, 184. *See also* bailiffs

traders. See *négociants*

travel, global: by individuals, 1–3, 16, 145, 170–71; between legal sites, 8, 20, 103, 117–20, 124, 138, 148, 151; money transfers, 121–22, 158; risks, 159, 162, 167; routes, 2, 11, 85, 155

travel, local: to and from conseils, 30, 65, 73, 97–99

travel, regional: 78–79, 88, 149, 153

Treaty of Paris (1763), 108, 141

trees: for construction, 154; justice dispensed under, 22; lack of, 93, 118

Valmeinière (family), 143

Versailles: absentee planters nearby, 74; distance from colonies, 107–78, 116, 129, 145; edicts issued from, 173; imperial administration based at (and power of), 6, 8, 13*f*, 16, 27, 29, 46, 48, 58, 83, 86, 105, 123, 148, 153–54, 156, 162–63; repository for records, 145, 172–73, 173*f*, 185; royal court at, 58, 115, 164, 216n74; symbolic power, 116–18, 173*f*

war: catalyst for conseil debates and
reforms, 17–18, 45–46, 126, 139–41,
168–69, 181, 199n69; commemoration
of, 114; local skirmishes, 87–89, 106–7;
personnel assignments, 56, 125–26, 147,
170; theaters of, 142–43, 157; vulnerability of, 81, 86, 133, 155, 211n7, 220n43.
See also Seven Years' War

witnesses: of court proceedings, 28–29,
72, 77–78; enslaved people as, 78;
testimony registered in court, 1–2, 16,
25, 31–32, 61–62, 91, 98

Zambezi River, 136